Dear Bill,

thank you for your participation in
and contributions to
"Leading from the Heart!"

mark maei + Lorizucchi

Best Wishes

Roger Bobsoly

Eric K

ORANGE, CA • SUMMER 2008

Voices of Servant-Leadership

Servant-leadership is now part of the vocabulary of enlightened leadership. Bob Greenleaf, along with other notables such as McGregor, Drucker, and Follett, have created a new thought-world of leadership that contains such virtues as growth, responsibility, and love.

—Warren Bennis, Distinguished Professor, Marshall School of Business, University of Southern California; author of *On Leadership*

I truly believe that servant-leadership has never been more applicable to the world of leadership than it is today.

—Ken Blanchard, author, *The Heart of Leadership*

We are each indebted to Greenleaf for bringing spirit and values into the workplace. His ideas will have enduring value for every generation of leaders.

—Peter Block, author, *Stewardship*

Anyone can be a servant-leader. Any one of us can take initiative; it doesn't require that we be appointed a leader; but it does require that we operate from moral authority. The spirit of servant-leadership is the spirit of moral authority. . . . I congratulate the Greenleaf Center for its invaluable service to society, and for carrying the torch of servant-leadership over the years.

—Stephen R. Covey, author, *The Seven Habits of Highly Effective People*

The servant-leader is servant first. Becoming a servant-leader begins with the natural feeling that one wants to serve, to serve first.

—Robert K. Greenleaf, author, *The Servant as Leader*

With its deeper resonances in our spiritual traditions, Greenleaf reminds us that the essence of leadership is service, and therefore the welfare of people. Anchored in this way, we can distinguish the tools of influence, persuasion, and power from the orienting values defining leadership to which these tools are applied.

—Ronald Heifetz, author, *Leadership Without Easy Answers*

The most difficult step, Greenleaf has written, that any developing servant-leader must take, is to begin the personal journey toward wholeness and self-discovery.

—Joseph Jaworski, author, *Synchronicity*

After thirty years Robert K. Greenleaf's work has struck a resonant chord in the minds and hearts of scholars and practitioners alike. His message lives through others, the true legacy of a servant-leader.

—Jim Kouzes, coauthor, *The Leadership Challenge*

Robert Greenleaf takes us beyond cynicism and cheap tricks and simplified techniques into the heart of the matter, into the spiritual lives of those who lead.

—Parker Palmer, author, *The Courage to Teach*

Servant-leadership is more than a concept. As far as I'm concerned, it is a fact. I would simply define it by saying that any great leader, by which I also mean an ethical leader of any group, will see herself or himself primarily as a servant of that group and will act accordingly.

—M. Scott Peck, author, *The Road Less Traveled*

No one in the past thirty years has had a more profound impact on thinking about leadership than Robert Greenleaf. If we sought an objective measure of the quality of leadership available to society, there would be none better than the number of people reading and studying his writings.

—Peter M. Senge, author, *The Fifth Discipline*

Servant-leadership offers hope and wisdom for a new era in human development, and for the creation of better, more caring institutions.

—Larry C. Spears, President and CEO, The Greenleaf Center for Servant-Leadership; editor and contributing author, *Insights on Leadership*

I believe that Greenleaf knew so much when he said the criterion of successful servant-leadership is that those we serve are healthier and wiser and freer and more autonomous, and perhaps they even loved our leadership so much that they also want to serve others.

—Margaret Wheatley, author, *Leadership and the New Science*

Despite all the buzz about modern leadership techniques, no one knows better than Greenleaf what really matters.

—*Working Woman Magazine*

Practicing Servant-Leadership

Servant-leadership is being practiced today by many individuals and organizations. For more information about servant-leadership and The Greenleaf Center, contact

The Greenleaf Center for Servant-Leadership
921 East 86th Street, Suite 200
Indianapolis IN 46240
Phone: 317-259-1241; Fax: 317-259-0560
Web site: www.greenleaf.org

Books Created and Edited by Larry C. Spears

Practicing Servant-Leadership: Succeeding Through Trust, Bravery, and Forgiveness (with Michele Lawrence), 2004

The Servant-Leader Within: A Transformative Path (with Hamilton Beazley and Julie Beggs), 2003

Servant-Leadership: A Journey into the Nature of Legitimate Power and Greatness (25th Anniversary Edition), 2002

Focus on Leadership: Servant-Leadership for the 21st Century (with Michele Lawrence), 2002

The Power of Servant-Leadership, 1998

Insights on Leadership: Service, Stewardship, Spirit and Servant-Leadership, 1998

On Becoming a Servant-Leader (with Don M. Frick), 1996

Seeker and Servant (with Anne T. Fraker), 1996

Reflections on Leadership: How Robert K. Greenleaf's Theory of Servant-Leadership Influenced Today's Top Management Thinkers, 1995

As Contributing Author

Cutting Edge: Leadership 2000, edited by Barbara Kellerman and Larraine Matusak, 2000

Stone Soup for the World, edited by Marianne Larned, 1998

Leadership in a New Era, edited by John Renesch, 1994

Practicing Servant-Leadership

Succeeding Through Trust, Bravery, and Forgiveness

Editors
Larry C. Spears
Michele Lawrence

Foreword by
Warren Bennis

JOSSEY-BASS
A Wiley Imprint
www.josseybass.com

Published by Jossey-Bass
A Wiley Imprint
989 Market Street, San Francisco, CA 94103-1741   www.josseybass.com

Jossey-Bass books and products are available through most bookstores. To contact Jossey-Bass directly call our Customer Care Department within the U.S. at 800-956-7739, outside the U.S. at 317-572-3986, or fax 317-572-4002.

Jossey-Bass also publishes its books in a variety of electronic formats. Some content that appears in print may not be available in electronic books.

Readers should be aware that Internet Websites listed in this work may have changed or disappeared between when this work was written and when it is read.

Credits are on page 292.

Library of Congress Cataloging-in-Publication Data

Practicing servant-leadership : succeeding through trust, bravery, and forgiveness
  / editors, Larry C. Spears, Michele Lawrence ; foreword by Warren Bennis.
    p. cm.
  Includes bibliographical references and index.
  ISBN 0-7879-7455-2 (alk. paper)
  1. Leadership. 2. Associations, institutions, etc. 3. Organizational effectiveness.
  4. Management.   I. Spears, Larry C., date. II. Lawrence, Michele.
  HM1261.P7 2004
  303.3'4—dc22

                                                                    2004015679

FIRST EDITION
        10 9 8 7 6 5 4 3 2 1

Contents

Foreword

Why Servant-Leadership Matters

Warren Bennis

Leadership studies haven't paid enough attention to the range of leaders, particularly the area of bad leadership. In the last twenty years of business leadership writings, certain exemplary leaders have been lionized, even deified. Unfortunately, though, it has been ignored that some of these leaders are destructive narcissists who put themselves first. In these days—and for good reason—the world is more and more concerned about leadership that is evil and destructive—leadership in which the leaders try to win at any cost, leadership where the leaders act primarily for themselves.

One of the things that Robert K. Greenleaf's work on servant-leadership does very well is that it keeps reminding us what's really important. It is so easy for an organization to get completely consumed with the bottom line; with pleasing only the *financial* stakeholder, not the community, not the workers, not the entire cartography of people whose lives are affected by that organization. Servant-leadership is akin to a superego conscience prod: it keeps in view the very thing we should not lose sight of. We're there primarily to serve the people who have a connection to and are affected by the institution. It is *very* easy to forget that.

But there's another factor to the importance of servant-leadership. The whole idea of value-based leadership is central to Greenleaf's work. We recognize more and more that servant-leadership serves as a check; a counterbalance to the glorification, deification, and lionization of leaders who have actually neglected or forgotten why they're there: to serve the people who are affected by the organization. *That's why servant-leadership matters*.

Four Crucial Thought-Leaders: Mary Parker Follett, Douglas MacGregor, Peter Drucker, and Robert K. Greenleaf

The entire field of leadership practice and leadership studies has grown tremendously over the years. I think it is of critical importance that we recognize those who have come before us, those upon whose seminal ideas so much of what we practice today has been built. I'd like to briefly trace this intellectual thread through mention of four people: Mary Parker Follett, Douglas MacGregor, Peter Drucker, and Robert K. Greenleaf.

Mary Parker Follett was a remarkable woman. She was prescient, before anybody's time, of the value of constructive, creative conflict. Her writings had an absurd lucidity to them that hasn't been fully acknowledged, even to this day. She influenced—without our knowing it—almost everyone in the field of leadership. Much of what is written in leadership today was first written by Mary Parker Follett.

Doug MacGregor was my mentor, my role model, someone I tried very much to emulate. He wrote very little, yet his influence is widely acknowledged. I think that's because of his incredible *personal* touch. He had an amazing empathy with the reflective manager, speaking his language, as it were. And in that language he could ask, "What is your view of human nature?" and get people to look at themselves for the answer. That was Doug's real contribution— what he wrote about in "Theory X, Theory Y"—that your leadership behavior, style, and character are determined by how you view people. If you view people as being intrinsically lazy and requiring coercion to get the job done, then you'll lead a certain way. But if you think of people as having the capacity to learn and the desire to bring out their best selves in doing their jobs, then your style of leadership is going to be totally different.

Peter Drucker, thank goodness, continues to teach and write. Peter really made the study of leadership, the discipline of leadership, respectable. He made it possible for us to continue to work with a degree of legitimacy. Drucker also made the study of management a legitimate pursuit.

Bob Greenleaf's work on servant-leadership was unique. His great contribution was in making us aware that the role of the leader, to a great extent, is *value* based. And the *main* value is that the leader is not simply someone who is in it for the recognition, but someone who works to create the social architecture that benefits the cartography of the people for whom that organization is responsible.

Doug MacGregor brought Bob Greenleaf to MIT in the early 1960s, when Bob was in the higher echelons at AT&T. I remember Bob as a guy who had a deep intellectual curiosity, a marvelous sense of optimism and hope. He was a radiant human being, a very open, positive man, very eager to learn. I think that period of time was formative for him in gestating the ideas that became *The Servant as Leader*. I also think it's interesting that he and MacGregor were drawn to each other's methods. The world of management education, and of schools like MIT, had little connection to the real world of practice, and Doug's bringing Bob to MIT was a clear example of their courage and bravery in doing something quite new. Kurt Lewin made a famous statement that "There's nothing so practical as a good theory," and I think that influenced Greenleaf's vision.

Key Attributes in Forming Effective Caring Leadership

I wish there were some kind of a blood test for the thing we call a moral compass, that powerful discernment of right and wrong. I'm not a cultural relativist or contingency theorist; in fact I'm opposed to them. I think that leaders have to have a strong ethical basis and a clear and explicit basis for their leadership. This is another key factor of Bob Greenleaf's work: You have to be clear and explicit about *how* you lead and what the *value* is of what you believe. I think that one aspect of effective and moral—let me call it *just* leadership—is a sense of moral compass, and not just authenticity. Some of the most evil people in the world are authentic. Adolph Hitler was authentic. Osama Bin Laden is authentic. Both, certain of doing "the right thing." Yes, authentic, but in terms of a moral compass, both evil.

The major attributes of effective leadership today are integrity, trustworthiness, *and* authenticity. That is what people most want from their leaders, and that moral compass is, of course, what Bob Greenleaf would focus on. The most important thing to keep in mind is this: *never let your ambition surpass your moral compass.*

I think we in business schools, and in education in general, have sometimes played down the value basis of leadership because it has to do with faith and personal values and belief systems. That threatens us. They should be the *key* attributes of leadership. Yes, you have to have adaptive capacity and you must set a direction. You must have business literacy—don't get me wrong. You can't lead any organization or any corporation without knowing a fair amount about corporate finance, marketing, and any number of other things that have to do with business. But those things are *easy*. Those things are perishable. I know that business systems will change, but character, values, and belief—those are not perishable. And it is your character, values, and belief systems that form the basis of how you lead, however aware or unaware you are.

Resolving Conflict—Between People, Within Organizations, and Beyond

I can't help but think of our current crisis in Iraq. A lot of what goes into resolving conflict has to do with trust. You can communicate to warring elements that you're interested in the welfare of both, whoever the competing, conflicting elements are; that you as a peace and bridge builder are interested in an agenda that would benefit both, that has the self-interest of all sides, including yourself, involved.

Let me give you an example that would be quite important at the moment. George Herbert Walker Bush, the first President Bush, made fourteen separate trips to Europe and Asia before the Gulf invasion of 1991—fourteen separate trips. The current President Bush did not even start to go abroad until our potential allies were thoroughly dyspeptic and totally distrustful of U.S. motives and behavior. War is the most destructive event that can occur between nations. The only way you can bring sides together is to show that you have a profound belief in the continuing welfare of all, that there will be a winning situation for all parties as much as possible, or at least some compromise that you all can accept. That is the basic factor. If people suspect your motive, you don't have a chance.

I'm not any kind of expert on conflict resolution. But I do know that you cannot resolve any conflict with threats or by playing a bluffing game of poker. Servant-leadership teaches us that you have to lay your cards on the table. I think you've got to show that you're interested in resolving things to the benefit of all sides, which means that all sides have to give up something. The important thing that I've discovered personally, about conflict and about resolving conflict, is to try as much as you can to not make anybody wrong.

That sounds too simple, doesn't it? It sounds like a banal, very superficial thing to say: "to not make anybody wrong." And yet, just look at what the U.S. relationship is right now with North Korea. If I were the paramount leader of North Korea, I'd be quite frightened. I would do the very best I could to get as much defensive stuff going as I could, because of the way the United States has been playing its cards, refusing to go there and talk with the people. (There is some hope that China and Japan can rescue us all from the current impasse.)

Moving from the cosmic level of foreign relations to the business level of organizations, we always find turf battles and competition for resources. To resolve these conflicts, I think that leaders have to put the overarching goal of the organization before the interests of either party and get both parties to understand that. Clark Kerr, former president of the University of California, once said that a university is a loose collection of departments, schools, divisions, centers, institutes, and so on, held together only by a central heating system. How do you as a servant-leader create the central heating system, the overarching point of view that will bring people together? That's one of the chief challenges for those servants who aspire to lead.

Servant-Leadership—A Question and Some Encouragement

Let me close with one question, and an encouraging word, for aspiring servant-leaders. *Do you really want to lead?* That is a *very* big question. Do you really want to do this? Who said it was easy? It is tough. But what more challenging, more responsible, more life-giving, more important thing can you do, than to be able to create a life for others that can bring about joy and creativity, that can elicit learning and the opportunity to be your best self, that can ultimately bring about human betterment, than being a servant-leader? But you have to ask yourself, is that what you want to do? Do you want to abandon *your* ego to the talents of others to create that kind of community that will bring out the very best in people? That's a big question—why?

In the end, if you choose to lead others as a servant-leader, then my best advice is this:

Be brave. Be kind.

Preface

Practicing Servant-Leadership owes much to the growing body of literature that has emerged around the art and practice of servant-leadership by both individuals and organizations. The idea for this book was initially born of the realization that The Greenleaf Center had recently received a great many essays on servant-leadership—many of them focused on organizational practices and written by some of today's leading practitioners and writers on servant-leadership—and that each of them deserved to be shared with as wide an audience as possible.

The unifying thread throughout the twelve essays that form the chapters of this book is to be found in the wisdom and insights provided as to best practices of servant-leadership by organizations and by individuals. Within these chapters you will find that a broad range of organizations are addressed—businesses, nonprofits, churches, schools, foundations, and leadership organizations are among them.

Structure of the Book

As an aid to the reader, the following provides a brief thumbnail description of each of the chapters contained in this volume.

1. Who Is the Servant-Leader?

This short excerpt from Robert K. Greenleaf's seminal essay "The Servant as Leader" contains an essential understanding of the origin and definition of servant-leadership. He starts by asking, "Servant and leader—can these two roles be fused in one real person, in all levels of status or calling? If so, can that person live and be productive in the real world of the present?" Greenleaf said the answer is yes, and in this chapter he explains *why* and suggests *how*.

2. The Understanding and Practice of Servant-Leadership

In countless for-profit and nonprofit organizations today we are witnessing traditional autocratic and hierarchical modes of leadership yielding to a different way of working—one based on teamwork and community, one that seeks to involve others in decision making, one strongly based in ethical and caring behavior, and one that is attempting to enhance the personal growth of workers while improving the caring and quality of our many institutions. This emerging approach to leadership and service is called *servant-leadership*. The idea of servant-leadership, now in its fourth decade as a concept bearing that name, continues to create a quiet but powerful revolution in workplaces around the world. This chapter, by Greenleaf Center President and CEO Larry C. Spears, is intended to provide a broad overview of the growing influence this inspiring idea is having on people and their workplaces.

3. The Unique Double Servant-Leadership Role of the Board Chairperson

John Carver asserts that boards control most group undertakings in the world—whether governmental, nonprofit, or business. They are our most ubiquitous, visible, powerful instance of group servant-leadership—or lack of it. With respect to legal and moral ownership, the board is a kind of group servant-leader. With respect to the board, the chair is a servant-leader. The chair, therefore, holds a "double servant-leader" role. The proper exercise of this twofold servant-leader function is crucial to resolving the problem of agency, particularly as embodied in honoring owner prerogatives and achieving organizational effectiveness. And because of that unique double leverage, the role of board chairperson properly construed is the most pervasive instance of institutional servant-leadership in our culture.

4. Love and Work

What questions would you pose to a man who ran a magazine publishing empire, was a jet fighter pilot, and writes best-selling business and poetry books, including *Love and Profit*? Larry Spears and John Noble asked these and others in their wide-ranging interview with James Autry: What does servant-leadership mean to you? How do you talk about it to others? What are some of the cultural changes that have made it more acceptable? How do you develop a servant's heart? What are some of the traits of the effective leader? What is the key to being able to say "I did it well today"? What are your thoughts on poetry, on editing, on the creative process? James Autry answers these and other questions candidly and warmly, sharing his astute observations and recommendations from a lifetime of leading and serving.

5. Servant-Leadership and Philanthropic Institutions

John C. Burkhardt (director of The Kellogg Forum) and Larry C. Spears (president and CEO of the Greenleaf Center for Servant-Leadership) outline ten key characteristics identified with the servant-leader, and explore the applicability of these characteristics to the special role and practices of foundations in our society. They pose challenging questions and offer helpful insights for all who would pursue philanthropy as servants first—for example: Can foundations view their work as an investment in the growth of people rather than as the solution to a problem? Can they have a healing role in society? Should they listen to the voices of those they serve?

Answers to these and other issues are addressed in this penetrating look at servant-leadership and philanthropy.

6. On the Right Side of History

In 1974, John C. Bogle founded the Vanguard Group, one of the two largest mutual fund organizations in the world, with current assets totaling more than $550 billion. Here, he outlines the impact of the servant-as-leader concept on the competitive world of U.S. business. He notes that in the mutual fund industry, and through-out the business world, the central idea of first serving others is being proven in the marketplace. He contends that servant-leadership is on the "right side" of history, and that its power and influence continue to grow.

7. Anatomy of a Collaboration: An Act of Servant-Leadership

Wendell J. Walls, former CEO of the National Association for Community Leadership, chronicles and analyzes a two-year collaboration between The Greenleaf Center and COMMUNITY LEADERSHIP, which culminated in the 1999 joint conference *Navigating the Future: Servant-Leadership and Community Leadership in the 21st Century*. In this insightful essay, Walls examines the many facets of practicing servant-leadership that went into the process of interorganizational collaboration, and maintains that effective collaboration requires an attitude embodied by Robert Greenleaf's test of servant-leadership.

8. Servant-Leadership Characteristics in Organizational Life

Don DeGraaf, Colin Tilley, and Larry Neal bring their organizational and university experience to this chapter, which expands our understanding of ten important characteristics of servant-leadership: listening, empathy, healing, awareness, persuasion, conceptualization, foresight, stewardship, commitment to the growth of people, and building community. The authors examine each of these characteristics in the context of organizational life, demonstrating how each characteristic can be applied to management and service delivery. The chapter is full of examples, suggestions for workplace servant-leadership practices, reflections, questions, and encouragement. A great aid in making the leap from personal servant-leadership to organizational servant-leadership.

9. Toward a Theology of Institutions

David Specht and Richard Broholm carefully explore Greenleaf's call for a "theology of institutions" and his conviction about the important role that religious congregations and seminaries might play in developing organizational trust around the exercise of their power and prerogative. The authors identify key dimensions of Greenleaf's thinking about how faith-based communities might mobilize resources around this task, reflect on key learnings emerging from a ten-year effort to develop a working theology of institutions (Seeing Things Whole), and suggest some next steps for continuing this exploration.

10. Foresight as the Central Ethic of Leadership

In this rigorous, clear, and concise chapter, Daniel H. Kim lays solid groundwork for understanding foresight as the central ethic of leadership. Kim, a founding member of the Society for Organizational Learning, brings to this work his deep understanding of system dynamics as he guides us through the differences between forecasting, predicting, and foresight; helping actions versus meddling actions; the relation between levels of perspective and action modes; understanding how vision and choices relate to foresight; and calling us to a deeper level of service to others and to self.

11. Servant-Leadership, Forgiveness, and Social Justice

Shann R. Ferch maintains that one of the defining characteristics of human nature is the ability to discern one's own faults, to be broken as the result of such faults, and in response, to seek meaningful change. Forgiveness and reconciliation draw us into a crucible from which we can emerge more refined, more willing to see the heart of another, and more able to create just and lasting relationships. The will to seek forgiveness, the will to forgive, and the will to pursue reconciliation (instead of retribution) is a significant part of developing the kind of wisdom, health, autonomy, and freedom espoused by Greenleaf in his idea of the servant-leader, for ourselves, for our families, and for our communities.

12. The Servant-Leader: From Hero to Host

In this chapter Margaret Wheatley, renowned author of the groundbreaking book *Leadership and the New Science*, issues a clarion call to move from the idea of "leader-as-hero" to one of "leader-as-host." Wheatley encourages servant-leaders to become convenors of people, and to work to develop a "fundamental and unshakeable faith in people." Why? Because, she believes, "the only way to lead when you don't have control is to lead through the power of your relationships." With clarity and empathy, Wheatley addresses servant-leadership in relation to spirit, science, organizational development, and love.

The richness of this collection has been further deepened by the addition of Warren Bennis's Foreword. Warren Bennis is widely known as the author of dozens of articles and more than thirty books on leadership, including the classic *On Becoming a Leader*, and his words help place Greenleaf's articulation of the "servant as leader" principle into a larger historical context, while calling us to be servant-leaders of character, integrity, and courage.

We view the growing trend toward servant-leadership as a reflection of the slow but ongoing maturation of humankind. It reflects a deep yearning in the hearts and minds of many people to find a better, more caring way of working together. This sometimes conscious, sometimes unconscious seeking of wisdom owes much to the original writings of Robert K. Greenleaf, and to the countless practitioners, teachers, and writers who continue to carry forward and to expand upon his crucial idea of "the servant as leader."

If you are intrigued or inspired by what you discover herein and wish to learn more, or if you would like to get involved with other servant-leaders around the world, we invite you to contact us through The Greenleaf Center's Web site (www.greenleaf.org). In the meantime, we thank you for your interest in servant-leadership, and in this book.

Indianapolis, Indiana   Larry C. Spears
July 2004   Michele Lawrence

Acknowledgments

We are particularly indebted to the staff and board of The Greenleaf Center, past and present. Through them we have grown in our own understanding and practice of servant-leadership. Thanks, too, to the tens of thousands of members, customers, program participants, donors, and other supporters of The Greenleaf Center worldwide.

Larry Spears would like to offer his special thanks to his family, friends, and colleagues around the world who have enriched his life, and especially his wife, Beth Lafferty; their sons, James and Matthew Spears; and his mother, Bertha Spears. Special thanks also go to Michele Lawrence for her good spirit, hard work, and personal encouragement over the past ten years and around this book.

Michele Lawrence would like to offer her special thanks to her husband, Joe Lawrence, and their daughter, Alexandra Lawrence, who bring such joy and meaning to her life. She would also like to acknowledge the love and influence of her late father, A. L. Richmond (Dad, this one's for you). Thank you also to Larry Spears, who is a continual inspiration and a pleasure to work with; and to my colleague Geneva Loudd, whose wisdom enriches my life in ways she doesn't dream of.

Larry and Michele want to especially thank Beth Lafferty, whose delightful company and countless hours spent on this manuscript are both very much appreciated!

We are grateful to our good friend and colleague, John Noble, for his deepening of the initial conversations that led to the two chapters by James Autry and Margaret Wheatley.

Finally, we would like to express our deepest appreciation for the many servant-leaders working within countless organizations around the world. Your efforts in growing servant-leadership point the way to the future of humankind.

—L.C.S. and M.L.

The Editors and The Greenleaf Center
for Servant-Leadership

Larry C. Spears is president and CEO of The Greenleaf Center for Servant-Leadership. He is also a writer and editor and has published the following books: *The Servant-Leader Within* (with Hamilton Beazley and Julie Beggs), 2003; *Servant Leadership* (25th Anniversary Edition), 2002; *Focus on Leadership* (with Michele Lawrence), 2002; *The Power of Servant-Leadership*, 1998; *Insights on Leadership*, 1998; *On Becoming a Servant-Leader* (with Don Frick), 1996; *Seeker and Servant* (with Anne Fraker), 1996; and *Reflections on Leadership*, 1995. His essays are also included in the following books: *Cutting Edge: Leadership 2000*, 2000; *Stone Soup for the Soul*, 1998; and *Leadership in a New Era*, 1994. He is series editor for the *Voices of Servant-Leadership Essay Series* (published by The Greenleaf Center); and he is the founder and senior editor of The Greenleaf Center's periodic newsletter, *The Servant-Leader*. Spears has also published more than three hundred articles, essays, and book reviews.

Spears was named president and CEO of The Greenleaf Center for Servant-Leadership in 1990. Under his leadership The Greenleaf Center has grown dramatically in size and influence. Larry Spears shared several experiences in common with Robert Greenleaf: In addition to their mutual interests in servant-leadership and writing, both men grew up in Indiana and migrated to major cities after college (Greenleaf to New York City, Spears to Philadelphia); they were deeply influenced by their experiences within the

Religious Society of Friends (Quakers); and they shared an abiding interest in how things get done within organizations.

A frequent traveler, Spears has spoken on servant-leadership to groups in North America, Europe, Australia, and Asia. He is a long-time member of the Association of Fundraising Professionals and has written many successful grant proposals, and he is a Fellow of the World Business Academy. His personal interests include spending time with his family, reading, writing, and vacations in his beloved Cape May, New Jersey.

Michele Lawrence has been with The Greenleaf Center since 1993. She currently directs the annual international conference; acts as editor of The Greenleaf Center's quarterly newsletter, *The Servant-Leader*; is involved in design and marketing of the Center's catalog of resources; and performs the functions of finance director of The Greenleaf Center. She was the original webmaster of the Center's Web site, bringing it online in May 1996. She was coeditor, with Larry Spears, of the 2002 anthology *Focus on Leadership*.

Her personal interests include spending time with her family, reading, watching basketball (as played by the Purdue Boilermakers and the Indiana Pacers), and occasional vacations by the ocean.

The Greenleaf Center for Servant-Leadership, headquartered in Indianapolis, Indiana, is an international nonprofit educational organization that seeks to encourage the understanding and practice of servant-leadership. It has offices in Australia–New Zealand, Brazil, Canada, Japan, Korea, the Netherlands, the Philippines, Singapore, South Africa, and the United Kingdom. The Center's mission is to improve the caring and quality of all institutions through servant-leadership.

The Greenleaf Center's programs and resources include the worldwide sale of books, essays, and videotapes on servant-leadership; research and publications; an annual International Conference on Servant-Leadership, held each June in Indianapolis; a speakers bureau; as well as a membership program, institutes and consultative services, and other activities around servant-leadership.

The Contributors

James A. Autry retired from a distinguished career at Meredith Corporation, where he was senior vice president and president of its Magazine Group, a $500 million operation with more than nine hundred employees. He directed the operation of twenty-two special interest publications and fourteen magazines, including *Better Homes and Gardens*, *Ladies' Home Journal*, and *Metropolitan Home*.

He is the author of seven published books, including the well-known business-related book *Love and Profit: The Art of Caring Leadership* (1991), which has been published in Japanese, Swedish, Chinese, Spanish, and Russian. *Love and Profit* won the prestigious Johnson, Smith & Knisely Award as the book with the most impact on executive thinking in 1992.

Autry fulfilled his military service as a jet fighter pilot in Europe during the cold war. He holds three honorary degrees, and in 1991, the University of Missouri-Columbia awarded him the Missouri Medal of Honor for Distinguished Service in Journalism, an award given for a long track record of excellence. Autry has also been active in many civic and charitable organizations, and most notably has worked with disability rights groups for twenty-five years.

Autry is a long-time member of The Greenleaf Center, and was a featured speaker at the Center's International Conference on Servant-Leadership in 1995, 2001, and 2002.

He lives in Des Moines with his wife, Sally Pederson (who is lieutenant governor of Iowa), and their youngest son. Currently he is a business consultant with top corporations and has an active speaking schedule.

Warren Bennis is Distinguished Professor of Business Administration at the University of Southern California and Founding Chairman of the USC Leadership Institute. He is also a visiting scholar at the Center for Public Leadership at Harvard University, and currently serves as chair of the Center's Advisory Board. In addition to Harvard University and USC, he has been on the faculties of MIT, Boston University, INSEAD, IMD, and the Indian Institute of Management at Calcutta. He has also served as provost of the State University of New York at Buffalo and president of the University of Cincinnati. He is a consultant for many Fortune 500 companies and multinationals, and has served on four U.S. Presidential Commissions.

Bennis is the author of dozens of articles and more than thirty books on leadership, including *Geeks and Geezers*, *Learning to Lead*, *Organizing Genius*, and *On Becoming a Leader*. His 1985 book *Leaders* was recently designated by the *Financial Times* as one of the top fifty business books of all time. He lives in Santa Monica, California.

John C. Bogle is founder of the Vanguard Group, one of the two largest mutual fund organizations in the world, and president of the Bogle Financial Markets Research Center. He created Vanguard in 1974 and served as chairman through 1997 and senior chairman through 1999. He had been associated with a predecessor company since 1951, immediately following his graduation from Princeton University, *magna cum laude* in economics.

He is the author of *Bogle on Mutual Funds: New Perspectives for the Intelligent Investor* (1993), a best-selling investment book since publication, and three other much-acclaimed books. A book about him, *John Bogle and the Vanguard Experiment: One Man's Quest to Transform the Mutual Fund Industry*, by Robert Slater, was published in 1996.

A longtime advocate of servant-leadership, he was a featured presenter at The Greenleaf Center's 1998 International Conference on Servant-Leadership. He serves as chairman of the board of the National Constitution Center, and is a director of Instinet Corporation and a member of The Conference Board's Commission on Public Trust and Private Enterprise. A trustee of Blair Academy, he served as chairman 1986–2001. He also serves on the Investment Committee of the Phi Beta Kappa Society. He has received honorary doctorate degrees from seven universities.

Bogle was born in Montclair, New Jersey, on May 8, 1929. He now resides in Bryn Mawr, Pennsylvania, with his wife, Eve. They are the parents of six children and the grandparents of twelve.

Richard R. Broholm joined the staff of MAP (Metropolitan Associates of Philadelphia) following seven years as director of The Faith and Life Community at the University of Wisconsin. MAP was an ecumenical action-research project of the World Council of Churches designed to examine how Christian laypeople could participate in the renewal of their city through the organizations in which they were employed. Among other things the staff of MAP developed theory and resources for church-based support groups linked to change agent teams within secular organizations.

At the conclusion of this work, Broholm moved to Boston, where he served as a management consultant with Hay Associates before launching an action-research project on workplace ministry and the role of the congregation at Andover Newton Theological School. This five-year effort led to the establishment of The Center for the Ministry of the Laity, where he met Robert Greenleaf and helped establish what eventually became The Greenleaf Center for Servant-Leadership. During these years, Broholm and his colleague David Specht began work to develop a theology of institutions. Following several years of work as an evaluator of leadership grants with Lilly Endowment, Broholm again joined forces with Specht to work on a theology of institutions through Seeing Things Whole, an action-research project devoted to bridging the

gap between theology and organizational performance, with participating organizations scattered across the country. Some of the
results of that action-research are reflected in Chapter Nine.

John C. Burkhardt is a professor of higher education and director of
the Kellogg Forum on Higher Education for the Public Good at the
University of Michigan. From 1993 through 2000, Burkhardt was
program director for leadership and higher education at the
W.K. Kellogg Foundation, where he led several major initiatives
focused on transformation and change in higher education and participated in a comprehensive effort to encourage leadership development among college students.

Burkhardt is coauthor of *The Guide to Student Success* (with
Ronald Lippit and Laurence N. Smith, 1989) and *Leadership in the
Making* (with Kathleen Zimmerman-Oster, 1999), and he was a
contributing author for *Leadership Reconsidered* (edited by Alexan-
der and Helen Astin, 2000). Burkhardt serves on the editorial
board of the *Journal of Leadership Studies*, is a senior fellow at the
James McGregor Burns Academy for Leadership at the University
of Maryland, and has served on The Greenleaf Center for Servant-
Leadership's board since 2002. He is married to Janis (Ross)
Burkhardt, an elementary school teacher who works with children
requiring special assistance in reading and with children for whom
English is a second language. They are the parents of one son,
John.

John Carver is the world's most published author on the governing
board role, having authored or coauthored five books and more than
170 articles on the topic. Among his books are *John Carver on Board
Leadership: Selected Writings from the Creator of the World's Most
Provocative and Systematic Governance Model* (2001), *Corporate
Boards That Create Value: Governing Company Performance from the
Boardroom* (coauthored with Caroline Oliver, 2002), and *Boards
That Make a Difference: A New Design for Leadership in Nonprofit and
Public Organizations* (1990, 1997).

As creator of the groundbreaking Policy Governance model, he is widely considered the most provocative international authority on governance (www.carvergovernance.com). He has consulted with business, nonprofit, and governmental boards on every populated continent. Carver is adjunct professor in the Schulich School of Business, York University, Toronto, and the Institute for Nonprofit Organizations, University of Georgia, Athens. He earned a B.S. degree in business and economics from the University of Tennessee and a Ph.D. in psychology from Emory University. He and his wife, Miriam Carver, also an author and governance consultant, live in Atlanta. He is a long-time member of The Greenleaf Center, and a featured speaker at The Greenleaf Center's International Conference in 1998 and 2004.

Don DeGraaf is a full professor in the Health, Physical Education, Recreation, Dance, and Sports (HPERDS) Department at Calvin College in Grand Rapids, Michigan. DeGraaf has coauthored four textbooks, including *Leisure and Life Satisfaction: Foundational Perspectives* and *Programming for Parks, Recreation, and Leisure Services: A Servant Leadership Approach*, written more than seventy-five articles, and made more than eighty presentations on the local, state, national, and international level dealing with leadership, management, and recreation programming.

DeGraaf is also a faculty member of the World Leisure and Recreation Association's International Center of Excellence (WICE) in the Netherlands. WICE is an international graduate program in the study of leisure, recreation, and related subjects. This international experience, along with the experience of being a U.S. Peace Corps volunteer in the Philippines, working four summers in the Republic of Korea, and serving as a program adviser to TREATS, a youth-serving organization in Hong Kong, has fostered a deep appreciation for other cultures and a global perspective on such issues as leadership, management, recreation, and leisure.

His professional and community service includes serving on the boards of Hostelling International, American Youth Hostels, and

Camp Tall Turf. He and his wife Kathy enjoy traveling, water sports, camping, reading, and hanging out with their family. Together they have two children, Isaac and Rochelle.

Shann R. Ferch grew up in Alaska and Montana, and lived on the Northern Cheyenne Reservation in southeast Montana. From this he gained the much-needed perspective of living as a minority in a Cheyenne culture that faces societal pressures with courage and dignity. Basketball and the inherent nuances of leadership in environments of intensity, rising from the basketball experience, became a significant life passion. He played college basketball at Pepperdine University and professional basketball in Germany.

Ferch also attained a B.A. in organizational communications and an M.A. in clinical psychology from Pepperdine. In his doctoral work at the University of Alberta in Edmonton, Alberta, Canada, the focus of his research was touch, forgiveness, and reconciliation among people who have suffered a breach in beloved relationship. He attributes his own love for people, landscape, and the divine possibility of the human heart to his good father, Tom, and his good mother, Sandy. His wife, Jennifer, weaves the garment of praise instead of the spirit of despair, and his two daughters, Natalya and Ariana, shine like the sun.

Ferch is chair of the Doctoral Program in Leadership Studies at Gonzaga University (www.gonzaga.edu/doctoral), a program that employs servant-leadership as one of its central leadership theories. He is also a research psychologist with the U.S. Centers for Disease Control and a marriage and family psychologist in private practice. His work regarding leadership and the human will to forgive and reconcile has appeared in scientific journals internationally.

Robert K. Greenleaf coined the term *servant-leadership* in his seminal 1970 essay, "The Servant as Leader." The servant-leader concept has had a deep and lasting influence over the past three decades on many modern leadership ideas and practices. Greenleaf spent his first career of forty years at AT&T, retiring as director of management research in 1964. That same year Greenleaf founded The Center for Applied Ethics (later renamed The Greenleaf Center for Servant-Leadership). He went on to have an illustrious second career that lasted another twenty-five years as an author, teacher, and consultant. Greenleaf, who died in 1990, was the author of numerous books and essays on the theme of the servant as leader. His available published books now include *The Servant-Leader Within* (2003), *Servant Leadership* (2002, 1977), *The Power of Servant-Leadership* (1998), *On Becoming a Servant-Leader* (1996), and *Seeker and Servant* (1996), along with many other separately published essays that are available through The Greenleaf Center.

Daniel H. Kim is an organizational consultant, facilitator, teacher, and public speaker committed to helping problem-solving organizations (reactive) transform into learning organizations (generative). For more than ten years, Kim has worked closely with Peter Senge in putting into practice the five disciplines of the learning organization—shared vision, personal mastery, mental models, team learning, and systems thinking.

Kim is the originator of a number of frameworks now in widespread use across many organizations. Among these are the Vision Deployment Matrix, the Core Theory of Success Loop, and the Systemic Quality Management model. He has written extensively on the topics of systems thinking and organizational learning and has been published in many journals, including the *Sloan Management Review*, the *Healthcare Forum Journal*, and *The Systems Thinker* newsletter, as well as in several anthologies.

He has worked with a diverse range of organizations, including Arthur Andersen, Chrysler, DuPont, Ford Motor Company, General Electric, Harley-Davidson, Hewlett-Packard, Xerox, and a number or organizations in the Singapore government. Kim was a featured presenter at The Greenleaf Center's International Conference on Servant-Leadership in 2000.

Kim has an electrical engineering degree from Massachusetts Institute of Technology and a Ph.D. in Management from MIT's Sloan School of Management. He is founder and publisher of *The Systems Thinker*, a newsletter that helps managers apply the power of systems thinking in their organizations. He is also a founding member of the Society for Organizational Learning (formerly the MIT Organizational Learning Center).

Larry Neal has served as an associate professor at the University of Oregon in Eugene for more than thirty years. During this tenure, Neal has contributed more than two hundred articles and presentations in the areas of leadership and management of leisure service organizations, employee motivation, and tourism.

Neal has been recognized for his international work in improving people's quality of life through recreation and leisure by being named the Distinguished Scholar of the International Council for Health, Physical Education, Recreation, Sport, and Dance. He is also a faculty member of the World Leisure and Recreation Association's (WLRA) International Center of Excellence (WICE) in the Netherlands. Neal's professional and community service has been diverse and includes involvement in the American Association for Leisure and Recreation, World Leisure and Recreation Association, Hostelling International: American Youth Hostels, and the National Recreation and Park Association. He and his wife, Pat, live in Eugene, Oregon.

Larry C. Spears was named president and CEO of The Greenleaf Center for Servant-Leadership in 1990. He is also a writer and an editor, having edited or coedited nine books on servant-leadership and published more than three hundred articles, essays, and book reviews.

Under his leadership The Greenleaf Center has grown dramatically in size and influence. Spears shares several experiences in common with Robert Greenleaf: In addition to their mutual interests in servant-leadership and writing, both men grew up in Indiana and migrated to major cities after college (Greenleaf to New York City, Spears to Philadelphia); they were deeply influenced by their experiences within The Religious Society of Friends (Quakers); and they shared an abiding interest in how things get done within organizations.

A frequent traveler, Spears has spoken on servant-leadership to groups in North America, Europe, Australia, and Asia. He is a long-time member of the Association of Fundraising Professionals, has written many successful grant proposals, and is a Fellow of the World Business Academy. He and his wife Beth live in Indianapolis with their two teenage sons, James and Matthew.

David L. Specht serves as director of Seeing Things Whole, an action-research effort that has worked in association with The Greenleaf Center since 1993, and in partnership with a network of theologians and organizational leaders to explore the implications of religious belief for organizational life and performance. During the early 1980s, he collaborated with Dick Broholm in an earlier action-research effort focused on workplace ministry at Andover Newton Theological School's Center of the Ministry of the Laity, where Broholm served as executive director and Specht as director of publications and editor of *Centering*. During this period, at the encouragement of Robert K. Greenleaf and Jitsuo Morikawa, Specht and Broholm began working on the development of a theology of institutions. Following several years of work as mediator and conflict management consultant, Specht resumed his collaboration with Broholm on the development of theology of institutions through their new initiative, Seeing Things Whole.

Specht also serves on the faculty of the Mediation and Conflict Management Program at Woodbury College in Vermont. He lives with his wife Clare and their two teenagers on a farm in the northern Berkshires of western Massachusetts.

Colin Tilley is currently a freelance consultant based in the United Kingdom. Prior to that, he was a founding partner in the U.K.-based leisure consultancy Whiteley International, which was acknowledged as being one of the leaders in its field, providing consultancy services and advice to government and voluntary sector agencies. He is also a founding codirector of an event management and sports development and management agency, Creating Excellence, which develops and delivers events and sports management programs for a range of clients, provides motivational speakers for engagements, and provides personal management services to a number of athletes, especially women and athletes with disabilities.

Tilley has coauthored a book titled *Leisure and Finance*. He has also coauthored with Larry Neal some twenty-five articles on management motivation and principles of management for *Leisure Management* magazine, and has written various articles and publications with a leisure and sports management theme. Tilley's professional and community service includes serving on local school and hospital boards and coaching youth rugby. He is also currently on the board of the World Leisure Organization.

He and his wife, Maxine, live in Hertfordshire, England, where they enjoy most sports, reading, and watching their children's fledgling careers develop.

Wendell J. Walls, CAE, is the proprietor of Walls & Associates, a consultancy focusing on organizational development and program evaluation. A native of Indiana, Walls has a diverse management background in developing organizations, both large and small. From 2000 to 2002, he served as director of development at The Greenleaf Center for Servant-Leadership. He served as president and CEO of the National Association for Community Leadership (now the Community Leadership Association, or CLA) from 1988 to 1998. Prior to that, he was president of the Indianapolis Public Schools Education Foundation.

Walls has served on numerous federal, state, and local boards including the Governor's Task Force on Cost Reduction, the Indiana Advisory Council on Vocational-Technical Education, the Indianapolis Private Industry Council, and the Key School Organization. He served on the steering committee of the Centers for Disease Control's STD Prevention Task Force. He has served on the boards of both the Indiana Society of Association Executives (ISAE) and its foundation and is a past president of ISAE. He served on the board of the International Leadership Association, and on the education committee of the American Society of Association Executives. He is a two-time jurist for the National Civic League's All-American Cities Award. He is also a graduate of the Stanley K. Lacy Executive Leadership Series, sponsored by the Indianapolis Chamber of Commerce, and is active in its graduate organizations.

Wendell and his wife, Dianne Wagner, live in Zionsville, Indiana, and are the parents of four children.

Margaret J. Wheatley writes, teaches, and speaks about radically new practices and ideas for how we can live together harmoniously in these chaotic times. She is president of The Berkana Institute (www.berkana.org), a charitable global foundation supporting life-affirming leaders around the world. Since 2000, Berkana's initiative, "From the Four Directions: People Everywhere Leading the Way," has been organizing conversations among people in their local communities in more than thirty countries.

Wheatley has been an organizational consultant since 1973, as well as a professor of management in two graduate business programs. She received her doctorate in organizational behavior from Harvard University, an M.A. in systems thinking from New York University, and has been a research associate at Yale University. She has been a public school teacher and administrator in inner cities, as well as a Peace Corps volunteer in Korea. She has been recognized by several awards and honorary doctorates.

Her work appears in two award-winning books, *Leadership and the New Science* (1992, 1999) and *A Simpler Way* (1996), plus many videos and articles. A powerful advocate for servant-leadership, she has contributed articles to two previous Greenleaf Center anthologies, *Focus on Leadership: Servant-Leadership for the 21st Century* (2002) and *Insights on Leadership: Service, Stewardship, Spirit, and Servant-Leadership* (1998). Wheatley was a featured presenter at The Greenleaf Center's annual international conferences in 1995 and 1999, and she served as distinguished speaker at The Greenleaf Center's annual Leadership Institute for Education from 2000 to 2002.

Practicing Servant-Leadership

Who Is the Servant-Leader?

Robert K. Greenleaf

Servant and leader—can these two roles be fused in one real person, in all levels of status or calling? If so, can that person live and be productive in the real world of the present? My sense of the present leads me to say yes to both questions. This chapter is an attempt to explain why and to suggest how.

The idea of the servant as leader came out of reading Hermann Hesse's *Journey to the East*. In this story we see a band of men on a mythical journey, probably also Hesse's own journey. The central figure of the story is Leo, who accompanies the party as the servant who does their menial chores, but who also sustains them with his spirit and his song. He is a person of extraordinary presence. All goes well until Leo disappears. Then the group falls into disarray and the journey is abandoned. They cannot make it without the servant Leo. The narrator, one of the party, after some years of wandering, finds Leo and is taken into the Order that had sponsored the journey. There he discovers that Leo, whom he had known first as servant, was in fact the titular head of the Order, its guiding spirit, a great and noble leader.

This short excerpt from Robert K. Greenleaf's essay "The Servant as Leader" contains an essential understanding of the origin of the term and definition of "servant-leader." Here Greenleaf relates how his reading of Hermann Hesse's *Journey to the East* led to his developing the servant-as-leader terminology.

One can muse on what Hesse was trying to say when he wrote this story. We know that most of his fiction was autobiographical, that he led a tortured life, and that *Journey to the East* suggests a turn toward the serenity he achieved in his old age. There has been much speculation by critics on Hesse's life and work, some of it centering on this story, which they find the most puzzling. But to me, this story clearly says that the great leader is seen as servant first, and that simple fact is the key to his greatness. Leo was actually the leader all of the time, but he was servant first because that was what he was, deep down inside. Leadership was bestowed on a man who was by nature a servant. It was something given, or assumed, that could be taken away. His servant nature was the real man, not bestowed, not assumed, and not to be taken away. He was servant first.

I mention Hesse and *Journey to the East* for two reasons. First, I want to acknowledge the source of the idea of *the servant as leader*. Then I want to use this reference as an introduction to a brief discussion of prophecy.

In 1958 when I first read about Leo, if I had been listening to contemporary prophecy as intently as I do now, the first draft of this piece might have been written then. As it was, the idea lay dormant for eleven years during which I came to believe that we in this country were in a leadership crisis and that I should do what I could about it. I became painfully aware of how dull my sense of contemporary prophecy had been. And I have reflected much on why we do not hear and heed the prophetic voices in our midst (not a new question in our times, nor more critical than heretofore).

I now embrace the theory of prophecy which holds that prophetic voices of great clarity, and with a quality of insight equal to that of any age, are speaking cogently all of the time. Men and women of a stature equal to the greatest prophets of the past are with us now, addressing the problems of the day and pointing to a better way to live fully and serenely in these times.

The variable that marks some periods as barren and some as rich in prophetic vision is in the interest, the level of seeking, the responsiveness of the hearers. The variable is not in the presence or absence or the relative quality and force of the prophetic voices. Prophets grow in stature as people respond to their message. If their early attempts are ignored or spurned, their talent may wither away.

It is seekers, then, who make prophets, and the initiative of any one of us in searching for and responding to the voice of contemporary prophets may mark the turning point in their growth and service. But since we are the product of our own history, we see current prophecy within the context of past wisdom. We listen to as wide a range of contemporary thought as we can attend to. Then we choose those we elect to heed as prophets—both old and new—and meld their advice with our own leadings. This we test in real-life experiences to establish our own position.

One does not, of course, ignore the great voices of the past. One does not awaken each morning with the compulsion to reinvent the wheel. But if one is servant, either leader or follower, one is always searching, listening, expecting that a better wheel for these times is in the making. It may emerge any day. Any one of us may discover it from personal experience. I am hopeful.

I am hopeful for these times, despite the tension and conflict, because more natural servants are trying to see clearly the world as it is and are listening carefully to prophetic voices that are speaking now. They are challenging the pervasive injustice with greater force, and they are taking sharper issue with the wide disparity between the quality of society they know is reasonable and possible with available resources and the actual performance of the institutions that exist to serve society.

A fresh, critical look is being taken at the issues of power and authority, and people are beginning to learn, however haltingly, to relate to one another in less coercive and more creatively supporting ways. A new moral principle is emerging, which holds that the only authority deserving one's allegiance is that which is freely and knowingly granted by the led to the leader in response to, and in proportion to, the clearly evident servant stature of the leader.

Those who choose to follow this principle will not casually accept the authority of existing institutions. Rather, they will freely respond only to individuals who are chosen as leaders because they are proven and trusted as servants. To the extent that this principle prevails in the future, the only truly viable institutions will be those that are predominantly servant-led.

I am mindful of the long road ahead before these trends, which I see so clearly, become a major society-shaping force. We are not there yet. But I see encouraging movement on the horizon.

What direction will the movement take? Much depends on whether those who stir the ferment will come to grips with the age-old problem of how to live in a human society. I say this because so many, having made their awesome decision for autonomy and independence from tradition, and having taken their firm stand against injustice and hypocrisy, find it hard to convert themselves into affirmative builders of a better society. How many of them will seek their personal fulfillment by making the hard choices, and by undertaking the rigorous preparation that building a better society requires? It all depends on what kind of leaders emerge and how they—we—respond to them.

My thesis, that more servants should emerge as leaders, or should follow only servant-leaders, is not a popular one. It is much more comfortable to go with a less demanding point of view about what is expected of one now. There are several undemanding, plausibly argued alternatives from which to choose. One, since society seems corrupt, is to seek to avoid the center of it by retreating to an idyllic existence that minimizes involvement with the "system" (with the system that makes such withdrawal possible). Then there is the assumption that since the effort to reform existing institutions has not brought instant perfection, the remedy is to destroy them completely so that fresh, new, perfect ones can grow. Not much thought seems to be given to the problem of where the new seed will come from or who the gardener to tend them will be. The concept of the servant-leader stands in sharp contrast to this kind of thinking.

Yet it is understandable that the easier alternatives would be chosen, especially by young people. By extending education for so many so far into the adult years, normal participation in society is effectively denied when young people are ready for it. With education that is preponderantly abstract and analytical it is no wonder that a preoccupation with criticism exists and that not much thought is given to "What can I do about it?"

Criticism has its place, but as a total preoccupation it is sterile. In a time of crisis, like the leadership crisis we are now in, if too many potential builders are completely absorbed with dissecting the wrong and striving for instant perfection, then the movement so many of us want to see will be set back. The danger, perhaps, is to hear the analyst too much and the artist too little.

Albert Camus stands apart from other great artists of his time, in my view, and deserves the title of prophet, because of his unrelenting demand that each of us confront the exacting terms of our own existence, and, like Sisyphus, accept our rock and find our happiness by dealing with it. Camus sums up the relevance of his position to our concern for the servant as leader in the last paragraph of his last published lecture, entitled "Create Dangerously":

> One may long, as I do, for a gentler flame, a respite, a pause for musing. But perhaps there is no other peace for the artist than what he finds in the heat of combat. "Every wall is a door," Emerson correctly said. Let us not look for the door, and the way out, anywhere but in the wall against which we are living. Instead, let us seek the respite where it is—in the very thick of battle. For in my opinion, and this is where I shall close, it is there. Great ideas, it has been said, come into the world as gently as doves. Perhaps, then, if we listen attentively, we shall hear, amid the uproar of empires and nations, a faint flutter of wings, the gentle stirring of life and hope. Some will say that this hope lies in a nation, others, in a man.

I believe rather that it is awakened, revived, nourished by millions of solitary individuals whose deeds and works every day negate frontiers and the crudest implications of history. As a result, there shines forth fleetingly the ever-threatened truth that each and every man, on the foundations of his own sufferings and joys, builds for them all.

Who Is the Servant-Leader?

The servant-leader is servant first—as Leo was portrayed. Becoming a servant-leader begins with the natural feeling that one wants to serve, to serve first. Then conscious choice brings one to aspire to lead. That person is sharply different from one who is leader first, perhaps because of the need to assuage an unusual power drive or to acquire material possessions. For such people, it will be a later choice to serve—after leadership is established. The leader-first and the servant-first are two extreme types. Between them are the shadings and blends that are part of the infinite variety of human nature.

The difference manifests itself in the care taken by the servant—first to make sure that other people's highest priority needs are being served. The best test, and most difficult to administer, is this: Do those served grow as persons? Do they, while being served, become healthier, wiser, freer, more autonomous, more likely themselves to become servants? And what is the effect on the least privileged in society; will they benefit or at least not be further deprived?

All of this rests on the assumption that the only way to change a society (or just make it go) is to produce people, enough people, who will change it (or make it go). The urgent problems of our day—the disposition to venture into immoral and senseless wars, destruction of the environment, poverty, alienation, discrimination, overpopulation—exist because of human failures, individual failures, one-person-at-a-time, one-action-at-a-time failures.

If we make it out of all of this (and this is written in the belief that we will), the system will be whatever works best. The builders will find the useful pieces wherever they are, and invent new ones when needed, all without reference to ideological coloration. "How do we get the right things done?" will be the watchword of the day, every day. And the context of those who bring it on will be: All men and women who are touched by the effort grow taller, and become healthier, stronger, more autonomous, and more disposed to serve.

Leo the servant, and the exemplar of the servant-leader, has one further portent for us. If we assume that Hermann Hesse is the narrator in *Journey to the East* (not a difficult assumption to make), at the end of the story he establishes his identity. His final confrontation at the close of his initiation into the Order is with a small transparent sculpture: two figures joined together. One is Leo, the other is the narrator. The narrator notes that a movement of substance is taking place within the transparent sculpture.

> I perceived that my image was in the process of adding to and flowing into Leo's, nourishing and strengthening it. It seemed that, in time . . . only one would remain: Leo. He must grow, I must disappear. As I stood there and looked and tried to understand what I saw, I recalled a short conversation that I had once had with Leo during the festive days at Bremgarten. We had talked about the creations of poetry being more vivid and real than the poets themselves.

What Hesse may be telling us here is that Leo is the symbolic personification of Hesse's aspiration to serve through his literary creations—creations that are greater than Hesse himself—and that his work, for which he was but the channel, will carry on and serve and lead in a way that he, a twisted and tormented man, could not—as he created.

Does not Hesse dramatize, in extreme form, the dilemma of us all? Except as we venture to create, we cannot project ourselves beyond ourselves to serve and lead.

To which Camus would add: *create dangerously!*

2

The Understanding and Practice of Servant-Leadership

Larry C. Spears

*The servant-leader is servant first. It begins with the
natural feeling that one wants to serve. Then conscious choice brings one to aspire to lead. The best
test . . . is this: Do those served grow as persons?
Do they, while being served, become healthier, wiser,
freer, more autonomous, more likely themselves to
become servants?*
                                    —Robert K. Greenleaf

The mightiest of rivers are first fed by many small trickles of
water, and that is an apt way of conveying my belief that the
growing number of individuals and organizations practicing servant-
leadership has increased from a trickle to a river. Servant-leadership
is also an expanding river, and one that carries with it a deep current of meaning and passion.

The servant-leader concept continues to grow in influence and
impact. In fact, we have witnessed an unparalleled explosion of
interest in and practice of servant-leadership in the past fifteen
years. In many ways, it can truly be said that the times are only now
beginning to catch up with Robert Greenleaf's visionary call to
servant-leadership.

The idea of servant-leadership, now in its fourth decade as a
concept bearing that name, continues to create a quiet revolution

in workplaces around the world. This chapter is intended to provide a broad overview of the growing influence this inspiring idea is having on people and their workplaces.

In countless for-profit and nonprofit organizations today we are seeing traditional autocratic and hierarchical modes of leadership yielding to a different way of working—one based on teamwork and community, one that seeks to involve others in decision making, one strongly based in ethical and caring behavior, and one that is attempting to enhance the personal growth of workers while improving the caring and quality of our many institutions. This emerging approach to leadership and service is called *servant-leadership*.

The words *servant* and *leader* are usually thought of as being opposites. When two opposites are brought together in a creative and meaningful way, a paradox emerges. And so the words *servant* and *leader* have been brought together to create the paradoxical idea of servant-leadership. The basic idea of servant-leadership is both logical and intuitive. Since the time of the Industrial Revolution, managers have tended to view people as objects; institutions have considered workers as cogs in a machine. In the past few decades we have witnessed a shift in that long-held view. Standard practices are rapidly shifting toward the ideas put forward by Robert Greenleaf, Stephen Covey, Peter Senge, Max DePree, Margaret Wheatley, Ken Blanchard, and many others who suggest that there is a better way to lead and manage our organizations. Robert Greenleaf's writings on the subject of servant-leadership helped to get this movement started, and his views have had a profound and growing effect on many.

Robert K. Greenleaf

> *Despite all the buzz about modern leadership techniques, no one knows better than Greenleaf what really matters.*
>
> —Working Woman *magazine*

The term *servant-leadership* was first coined in a 1970 essay by Robert K. Greenleaf (1904–1990) titled "The Servant as Leader." Greenleaf, born in Terre Haute, Indiana, spent most of his organizational life in the field of management research, development, and education at AT&T. Following a forty-year career at AT&T, Greenleaf enjoyed a second career that lasted twenty-five years, during which time he served as an influential consultant to a number of major institutions, including Ohio University, MIT, Ford Foundation, B. K. Mellon Foundation, the Mead Corporation, the American Foundation for Management Research, and Lilly Endowment Inc. In 1964 Greenleaf also founded the Center for Applied Ethics, which was renamed the Robert K. Greenleaf Center in 1985 and is now headquartered in Indianapolis.

As a lifelong student of how things get done in organizations, Greenleaf distilled his observations in a series of essays and books on the theme of "The Servant as Leader"—the objective of which was to stimulate thought and action for building a better, more caring society.

The Servant as Leader Idea

The idea of the servant as leader came partly out of Greenleaf's half-century of experience in working to shape large institutions. However, the event that crystallized Greenleaf's thinking came in the 1960s, when he read Hermann Hesse's short novel *Journey to the East*—an account of a mythical journey by a group of people on a spiritual quest.

After reading this story, Greenleaf concluded that the central meaning of it was that the great leader is first experienced as a servant to others, and that this simple fact is central to the leader's greatness. True leadership emerges from those whose primary motivation is a deep desire to help others.

In 1970, at the age of sixty-six, Greenleaf published "The Servant as Leader," the first of a dozen essays and books on servant-leadership. Since that time, more than a half-million copies of his books and essays have been sold worldwide. Slowly but surely, Greenleaf's servant-leadership writings have made a deep, lasting impression on leaders, educators, and many others who are concerned with issues of leadership, management, service, and personal growth.

What Is Servant-Leadership?

In his works, Greenleaf discusses the need for a better approach to leadership, one that puts serving others—including employees, customers, and community—as the number one priority. Servant-leadership emphasizes increased service to others, a holistic approach to work, promoting a sense of community, and the sharing of power in decision making.

Who *is* a servant-leader? Greenleaf said that the servant-leader is one who is a servant first. In "The Servant as Leader" he wrote, "It begins with the natural feeling that one wants to serve, to serve first. Then conscious choice brings one to aspire to lead. The difference manifests itself in the care taken by the servant—first to make sure that other people's highest-priority needs are being served. The best test is: Do those served grow as persons; do they, while being served, become healthier, wiser, freer, more autonomous, more likely themselves to become servants? And what is the effect on the least privileged in society? Will they benefit or at least not be further deprived?"

It is important to stress that servant-leadership is *not* a quick-fix approach. Nor is it something that can be quickly instilled within an institution. At its core, servant-leadership is a long-term, transformational approach to life and work—in essence, a way of being—that has the potential for creating positive change throughout our society.

Characteristics of the Servant-Leader

> *Servant leadership deals with the reality of power in everyday life—its legitimacy, the ethical restraints*

upon it and the beneficial results that can be attained
through the appropriate use of power.
                                            —New York Times

After some years of carefully considering Greenleaf's original writings, I have extracted a set of ten characteristics of the servant-leader that I view as being of critical importance. The following characteristics are central to the development of servant-leaders:

  1. *Listening:* Leaders have traditionally been valued for their communication and decision-making skills. While these are also important skills for the servant-leader, they need to be reinforced by a deep commitment to listening intently to others. The servant-leader seeks to identify the will of a group and helps clarify that will. That means listening receptively to what is being said (and not said!). Listening also encompasses getting in touch with one's own inner voice and seeking to understand what one's body, spirit, and mind are communicating. Listening, coupled with regular periods of reflection, is essential to the growth of the servant-leader.

  2. *Empathy:* The servant-leader strives to understand and empathize with others. People need to be accepted and recognized for their special and unique spirits. One assumes the good intentions of co-workers and does not reject them as people, even while refusing to accept their behavior or performance. The most successful servant-leaders are those who have become skilled empathetic listeners.

  3. *Healing:* Learning to heal is a powerful force for transformation and integration. One of the great strengths of servant-leadership is the potential for healing one's self and others. Many people have broken spirits and have suffered from a variety of emotional hurts. Although this is a part of being human, servant-leaders recognize that they have an opportunity to "help make whole" those with whom they come in contact. In "The Servant as Leader" Greenleaf writes: "There is something subtle communicated to one who is being served and led if, implicit in the compact

between servant-leader and led, is the understanding that the search for wholeness is something they share."

4.   *Awareness*: General awareness, and especially self-awareness, strengthens the servant-leader. Making a commitment to foster awareness can be scary—you never know what you may discover. Awareness also aids one in understanding issues involving ethics and values. It lends itself to being able to view most situations from a more integrated, holistic position. As Greenleaf observed: "Awareness is not a giver of solace—it is just the opposite. It is a disturber and an awakener. Able leaders are usually sharply awake and reasonably disturbed. They are not seekers after solace. They have their own inner serenity."

5.   *Persuasion*: Another characteristic of servant-leaders is a primary reliance on persuasion rather than positional authority in making decisions within an organization. The servant-leader seeks to convince others rather than to coerce compliance. This particular element offers one of the clearest distinctions between the traditional authoritarian model and that of servant-leadership. The servant-leader is effective at building consensus within groups. This emphasis on persuasion over coercion probably has its roots within the beliefs of the Religious Society of Friends (Quakers), the denomination with which Robert Greenleaf himself was most closely allied.

6.   *Conceptualization*: Servant-leaders seek to nurture their abilities to "dream great dreams." The ability to look at a problem (or an organization) from a conceptualizing perspective means that one must think beyond day-to-day realities. For many managers this is a characteristic that requires discipline and practice. The traditional manager is focused on the need to achieve short-term operational goals. Managers who wish to also be servant-leaders must stretch their thinking to encompass broader-based conceptual thinking. Within organizations, conceptualization is also the proper role of boards of trustees or directors. Unfortunately, boards can sometimes become involved in day-to-day operations (something that should

always be discouraged!) and fail to provide the visionary concept for an institution. Trustees need to be mostly conceptual in their orientation; staffs need to be mostly operational in their perspective, and the most effective CEOs and leaders probably need to develop both perspectives. Servant-leaders are called to seek a delicate balance between conceptual thinking and a day-to-day focused approach.

7. *Foresight:* Closely related to conceptualization, the ability to foresee the likely outcome of a situation is hard to define but easy to identify. One knows it when one sees it. Foresight is a characteristic that enables the servant-leader to understand the lessons from the past, the realities of the present, and the likely consequences of a decision for the future. It is also deeply rooted within the intuitive mind. One can conjecture that foresight is the one servant-leader characteristic with which one may be born. All other characteristics can be consciously developed. There hasn't been a great deal written on foresight. It remains a largely unexplored area in leadership studies, but one most deserving of careful attention.

8. *Stewardship:* Peter Block (author of *Stewardship* and *The Empowered Manager*) has defined stewardship as "holding something in trust for another." Robert Greenleaf's view of all institutions was one in which CEOs, staffs, and trustees all played significant roles in holding their institutions in trust for the greater good of society. Servant-leadership, like stewardship, assumes first and foremost a commitment to serving the needs of others. It also emphasizes the use of openness and persuasion rather than control.

9. *Commitment to the growth of people:* Servant-leaders believe that people have an intrinsic value beyond their tangible contributions as workers. As a result, the servant-leader is deeply committed to the growth of each and every individual within the institution. The servant-leader recognizes the tremendous responsibility to do everything possible to nurture the personal, professional, and spiritual growth of employees. In practice, this can include (but is not limited to) concrete actions such as making

available funds for personal and professional development, taking a personal interest in ideas and suggestions from everyone, encouraging worker involvement in decision making, and actively helping laid-off workers find other employment.

10.   *Building community:* The servant-leader senses that much has been lost in recent human history as a result of the shift from local communities to large institutions as the primary shaper of human lives. This awareness causes the servant-leader to seek to identify some means for building community among those who work within a given institution. Servant-leadership suggests that true community can be created among those who work in businesses and other institutions. Greenleaf said: "All that is needed to rebuild community as a viable life form for large numbers of people is for enough servant-leaders to show the way, not by mass movements, but by each servant-leader demonstrating his own unlimited liability for a quite specific community-related group."

These ten characteristics of servant-leadership are by no means exhaustive. However, I believe that the ones listed serve to communicate the power and promise that this concept offers to those who are open to its invitation and challenge.

Tracing the Growing Impact of Servant-Leadership

> *Servant leadership has emerged as one of the domi-*
> *nant philosophies being discussed in the world today.*
> —Indianapolis Business Journal

Servant-leadership principles are being applied in significant ways in a half-dozen major areas. The first area has to do with servant-leadership as an institutional philosophy and model. Servant-leadership crosses all boundaries and is being applied by a wide variety of people working with for-profit businesses, nonprofit corporations, and churches, universities, health care organizations, and foundations.

Servant-Leadership as an Institutional Model

Servant-leadership advocates a group-oriented approach to analysis and decision making as a means of strengthening institutions and improving society. It also emphasizes the power of persuasion and seeking consensus over the old top-down form of leadership. Some people have likened this to turning the hierarchical pyramid upside down. Servant-leadership holds that the primary purpose of a business should be to create a positive impact on its employees and community, rather than using profit as the sole motive.

Many individuals within institutions have adopted servant-leadership as a guiding philosophy. An increasing number of companies have adopted servant-leadership as part of their corporate philosophy or as a foundation for their mission statement. Among these are the Toro Company (Minneapolis, Minnesota), Synovus Financial Corporation (Columbus, Georgia), ServiceMaster Company (Downers Grove, Illinois), the Men's Wearhouse (Fremont, California), Southwest Airlines (Dallas, Texas), Starbucks (Seattle, Washington), and TDIndustries (Dallas, Texas).

TDIndustries (TD), one of the earliest practitioners of servant-leadership in the corporate setting, is a heating and plumbing contracting firm that has consistently ranked in the top ten of *Fortune* magazine's 100 Best Companies to Work for in America. TD's founder, Jack Lowe Sr., came upon "The Servant as Leader" in the early 1970s and began to distribute copies of it to his employees. They were invited to read through the essay and then to gather in small groups to discuss its meaning. The belief that managers should serve their employees became an important value for TDIndustries.

Thirty years later, Jack Lowe Jr. continues to embrace servant-leadership as a guiding philosophy for TD. Even today, any TDPartner who supervises at least one person must go through training in servant-leadership. In addition, all new employees continue to receive a copy of "The Servant as Leader," and TD has developed elaborate training modules designed to encourage the understanding and practice of servant-leadership.

Some businesses have begun to view servant-leadership as an important framework that is helpful (and necessary) for ensuring the long-term effects of related management and leadership approaches such as continuous quality improvement and systems thinking. It is suggested that institutions that want to create meaningful change may be best served in starting with servant-leadership as the foundational understanding and then building on it through any number of related approaches.

Servant-leadership has influenced many noted writers, thinkers, and leaders. Max DePree, former chairman of the Herman Miller Company and author of *Leadership Is an Art* and *Leadership Jazz*, has said, "The servanthood of leadership needs to be felt, understood, believed, and practiced." And Peter Senge, author of *The Fifth Discipline*, has said that he tells people "not to bother reading any other book about leadership until you first read Robert Greenleaf's book, *Servant-Leadership*. I believe it is the most singular and useful statement on leadership I've come across." In recent years, a growing number of leaders and readers have "rediscovered" Robert Greenleaf's own writings through books by DePree, Senge, Covey, Wheatley, Autry, and many other popular writers.

Education and Training of Nonprofit Trustees

A second major application of servant-leadership is its pivotal role as the theoretical and ethical basis for trustee education. Greenleaf wrote extensively on servant-leadership as it applies to the roles of boards of directors and trustees within institutions. His essays on these applications are widely distributed among directors of for-profit and nonprofit organizations. In his essay "Trustees as Servants" Greenleaf urged trustees to ask themselves two central questions: "Whom do you serve?" and "For what purpose?"

Servant-leadership suggests that boards of trustees need to undergo a radical shift in how they approach their roles. Trustees who seek to act as servant-leaders can help to create institutions of great depth and quality. Over the past decade, two of America's largest grant-making foundations (Lilly Endowment Inc. and the W.K. Kellogg Foundation) have sought to encourage the development of programs designed to educate and train nonprofit boards of trustees to function as servant-leaders. John Carver, the noted author on board governance, addresses this particular application in Chapter Three, his contribution to this book.

Community Leadership Programs

A third application of servant-leadership concerns its deepening role in community leadership organizations across the country. A growing number of community leadership groups are using Greenleaf Center resources as part of their own education and training efforts. Some have been doing so for more than twenty years.

M. Scott Peck, who has written about the importance of building true community, says the following in A World Waiting to Be Born: "In his work on servant-leadership, Greenleaf posited that the world will be saved if it can develop just three truly well-managed, large institutions—one in the private sector, one in the public sector, and one in the nonprofit sector. He believed—and I know—that such excellence in management will be achieved through an organizational culture of civility routinely utilizing the mode of community."

Service-Learning Programs

A fourth application involves servant-leadership and experiential education. During the past twenty-five years experiential education programs of all sorts have sprung up in virtually every college and university—and, increasingly, in secondary schools, too. Experiential education, or "learning by doing," is now a part of most students' educational experience.

Around 1980, a number of educators began to write about the linkage between the servant-leader concept and experiential learning under a new term, service-learning. It is service-learning that has become a major focus for some experiential education programs in the past two decades.

The National Society for Experiential Education (NSEE) has adopted service-learning as one of its major program areas. In 1990 NSEE published a massive three-volume work called *Combining Service and Learning*, which brought together many articles and papers about service-learning—several dozen of which discuss servant-leadership as the philosophical basis for experiential learning programs.

Leadership Education

A fifth application of servant-leadership concerns its use in both formal and informal education and training programs. This is taking place through leadership and management courses in colleges and universities, as well as through corporate training programs. A number of undergraduate and graduate courses on management and leadership incorporate servant-leadership within their course curricula. Several colleges and universities now offer specific courses on servant-leadership. Also, a number of noted leadership authors, including Peter Block, Ken Blanchard, Max DePree, and Peter Senge, have all acclaimed the servant-leader concept as an overarching framework that is compatible with, and enhancing of, other leadership and management models such as total quality management, systems thinking, and community building.

In the area of corporate education and training programs, dozens of management and leadership consultants now employ servant-leadership materials as part of their ongoing work with corporations. Among these companies are U.S.Cellular, Synovus Financial, and Southwest Airlines. A number of consultants and educators are now extolling the benefits to be gained in building a total quality management approach upon a servant-leadership foundation. Through internal training and education, institutions are discovering that servant-leadership can truly improve how business is developed and conducted, while still successfully turning a profit.

Personal Transformation

A sixth application of servant-leadership involves its use in programs relating to personal growth and transformation. Servant-leadership operates at both the institutional and personal levels. For individuals it offers a means to personal growth—spiritually, professionally, emotionally, and intellectually. It has ties to the ideas of M. Scott Peck (*The Road Less Traveled*), Parker Palmer (*The Active Life*), Ann McGee-Cooper (*You Don't Have to Go Home from Work Exhausted!*), and others who have written on expanding human potential. A particular strength of servant-leadership is that it encourages everyone to actively seek opportunities to both serve and lead others, thereby setting up the potential for raising the quality of life throughout society.

Servant-Leadership and Cultural Tradition

For some, the word *servant* may prompt an initial negative connotation due to the oppression that many people—especially women and people of color—have historically endured. However, upon closer analysis many come to appreciate the inherent spiritual nature of what Greenleaf intended by the pairing of *servant* and *leader*. The startling paradox of the term *servant-leadership* serves to prompt new insights.

In an article titled "Pluralistic Reflections on Servant-Leadership," Juana Bordas has written: "Many women, minorities and people of color have long traditions of servant-leadership in their cultures. Servant-leadership has very old roots in many of the indigenous cultures. Cultures that were holistic, cooperative, communal, intuitive and spiritual. These cultures centered on being guardians of the future and respecting the ancestors who walked before."

Women leaders and authors are writing and speaking about servant-leadership as a leadership philosophy that is most appropriate for both women and men to embrace. Patsy Sampson, former president of Stephens College in Columbia, Missouri, is one such person. In an essay on women and servant-leadership she writes: "So-called [service-oriented] feminine characteristics are exactly those which are consonant with the very best qualities of servant-leadership."

A Growing Movement

> Servant-leadership works like the consensus building
> that the Japanese are famous for. Yes, it takes a while
> on the front end; everyone's view is solicited, though
> everyone also understands that his view may not ulti-
> mately prevail. But once the consensus is forged,
> watch out: With everybody on board, your so-called
> implementation proceeds wham-bam.
>
> —Fortune

Interest in the philosophy and practice of servant-leadership is now at an all-time high. Hundreds of articles on servant-leadership have appeared in various magazines, journals, and newspapers over the past decade. Many books on the general subject of leadership have been published that recommend servant-leadership as a holistic way of being. And there is a growing body of literature available on the understanding and practice of servant-leadership.

The Greenleaf Center for Servant-Leadership is an international nonprofit educational organization that seeks to encourage the understanding and practice of servant-leadership. The Center's mission is to fundamentally improve the caring and quality of all institutions through a servant-leader approach to leadership, structure, and decision making.

In recent years, the Greenleaf Center has experienced tremendous growth and expansion. Its growing programs include the worldwide sales of more than 120 books, essays, and videotapes on servant-leadership, plus research and publishing, a membership program, a speakers bureau, and its annual International Conference on Servant-Leadership. A number of notable Greenleaf Center members have spoken at our annual conferences, including James Autry, Peter Block, Max DePree, Stephen Covey, Margaret Wheatley, M. Scott Peck, and Peter Senge, to name but a few. These and other conference speakers have spoken of the tremendous impact that the servant-leader concept has played in the development of their own understanding of what it means to be a leader.

Paradox and Pathway

The Greenleaf Center's logo is a variation on the geometrical figure called a "Möbius strip." A Möbius strip, pictured here, is a one-sided surface constructed from a rectangle by holding one end fixed, rotating the opposite end through 180 degrees, and applying it to the first end—thereby giving the appearance of a two-sided figure. It thus appears to have a front side that merges into a back side, and then back again into the front.

The Möbius strip symbolizes, in visual terms, the servant-leader concept—a merging of servanthood into leadership and back into servanthood again, in a fluid and continuous pattern. It also reflects The Greenleaf Center's own role as an institution seeking to both serve and lead others who are interested in leadership and service issues.

Life is full of curious and meaningful paradoxes. Servant-leadership is one such paradox that has slowly but surely gained hundreds of thousands of adherents over the past thirty-five years. The seeds that have been planted have begun to sprout in many institutions, as well as in the hearts of many who long to improve the human condition. Servant-leadership is providing a framework from which many thousands of known and unknown individuals are helping to improve how we treat those who do the work within our many institutions. Servant-leadership truly offers hope and guidance for a new era in human development, and for the creation of better, more caring institutions.

3

The Unique Double Servant-Leadership Role of the Board Chairperson

John Carver

I t is common knowledge that the position of board chairperson is an important position, indeed. Its importance is due, of course, to the considerable authority wielded by the governing board being chaired. I believe that the chairing is not so crucial a topic as that which is chaired. If I am correct, any discussion of the chair's role must rest upon a prior discussion of the board's role. I want to make the case that the role of board chairperson is, if I may say so, "servant-leadership squared." But to do that, I must begin with the play in which the chair is merely an actor: the setting called governance.

Governance can mean a number of things, but for the moment, it will be defined merely as the kind of leadership appropriate for a governing board, that is, defined as a governing board's proper job. I have some peculiar ideas about what *proper* means in the board context, ones that radically challenge the conventional wisdom, a "wisdom" that is actually a hodgepodge of tradition-blessed practices with little managerial respectability and no conceptual coherence. The governance job is the weakest link in enterprise, the least well designed, the least studied, the least modeled.

But I don't stand alone with that sad diagnosis. Consider a few brutal comments. Peter Drucker said in 1974 that all boards have one thing in common—they don't function. In 1984 Harold

Geneen complained that the boards of 95 percent of America's top five hundred companies are not doing what they are legally, morally, and ethically supposed to do—and couldn't, even if they wanted to. A Danforth Foundation report in 1992 charged that many school boards are an obstacle to—rather than a force for—fundamental education reform because of their tendency to become immersed in day-to-day administration. In a gentler vein, a 1994 article in Canada's *Maclean's* magazine noted that the time is long past when corporate directors can remain imbued with what a British judge once characterized as "lovable dimness."

But, in fact, *Maclean's* is wrong. The time is neither long past, nor even recently past. The time is with us still. To be sure, you and I have seen a few bright moments, for sometimes boards do rise to leadership. But it is an inescapable conclusion that standards for governance are appallingly low, that mediocrity is the norm. Trivia and empty ritual abound. What should give us pause is that if the most powerful role in enterprise is not up to its task, what hope can we have for our institutions?

Robert Greenleaf beat me to that distressing opinion. Unfortunately, my Policy Governance model and my 1990 book came into existence without the benefit of knowing about Robert Greenleaf. I would love to have known his work and even to have shared my emerging governance model with him. That is my loss.

In *Trustees as Servants*, he observed that there is "an abundance of literature on contemporary institutions, but most of it is concerned with 'fine tuning' within the limits of conventional language and wisdom." He eschewed merely helping "trustees do just a little better with their roles as now defined." In the parlance of today, we would call his aim a full paradigm shift, for he said his vision was not boards as we know them, but "*a substantially new institution* [italics mine], one that serves society much better, far ahead of anything that now exists or that is now dreamed of as possible."[1]

Transformation Toward a "Substantially New Institution"

I'd like to examine with you the role of the chairperson as that shows up within my vision of effective governance. This vision, that I have codified as the Policy Governance® model of board leadership, applies to any governing board of anything, anywhere. That is, it is a generic model applicable in nonprofits, business, and government—in large or small organizations. This broad applicability has been tested in quite a few parts of the world.

But allow me to position Policy Governance with respect to Greenleaf's work. Peter Senge has observed that "recent books on leadership have been about what leaders do and how they operate." "By contrast, Greenleaf," Senge says, "invites people to consider a domain of leadership grounded in a state of being, not doing." The choice of servant-leadership, he explains, is "not something you do, but an expression of your being." Policy Governance is an operational definition (in its scientific meaning) of leadership in a specific setting—that of the governing body. In some ways, the difference Senge points out is like that between philosophy and strategy or between basic research and technology.

If the judgment of history is kind, the Policy Governance model may merit being seen as a technology of servant-leadership. At any rate, it is a carefully crafted prescription for how boards can operate—boards that are committed to being servant-leaders.

My consulting practice using this model has been largely confined to the United States, Canada, Britain, and the Netherlands, though it has also extended in a very limited way to every populated continent. It has been applied in widely varying cultures, from North American aboriginal tribes to Dutch colleges and independent schools in Australia. While today's discussion of the chairperson's role could focus equally well on city councils, trade associations, foundations, business corporations, professional societies, or airport authorities, most of my references will be to the public or quasi-public domain. So let's look more closely at what the model sets out to do and, in good time, how that relates to the servant-leadership role of the board chairperson.

Greenleaf's dream of a substantially new institution cannot be achieved by cosmetic changes to the kind of governance we all know so well. Such a lofty goal calls for a true paradigm shift. This endeavor isn't a matter of improving our personnel committees, sprucing up the agenda, getting more fundraisers on the board, or getting board members more involved in the organization's work. Nor is it addressed by more board training—an exercise often best described as teaching boards how to do the wrong things better. No. Leadership, as said so well by A. Bartlett Giamatti, late president of Yale, is essentially a moral act, one of moral courage, vision, and intellectual energy.

John Gardner asked us a compelling question: "Do we have it in us to create a future worthy of our past?" It is embarrassing that the answer is not so evident. Tom Peters, in his trademark in-your-face style, has said that "we must move beyond change and embrace nothing less than the literal abandonment of the conventions that brought us to this point. Eradicate 'change' from your vocabulary. Substitute 'abandonment' or 'revolution' instead. . . . Much of what ails corporations today is traceable to a failure of nerve in every part and at every level of the organization." Making that leap from yesterday's trapeze to tomorrow's, however, requires not only innovation but boldness and risk.

Governance has been long overdue for a theory. But even if Kurt Lewin tells us, "There is nothing so practical as a good theory," introducing a new order will not be easy, for familiar poison grabs at every weakness in our confidence. So until the new order grows familiar enough to be the new old order—at which time we'd better get started on its successor—fundamental change will be an uphill battle. Many counter any new vision of how things can be with a tired appeal to human nature. I am sure that at some point the idea that a court system would be largely free from bribery, or that a population could actually choose its own leaders, was preposterous, patently "contrary to human nature." And before Roger Bannister, so was the four-minute mile. "Some . . . say that, human nature being what it is, the recommendations here are too idealistic and therefore impossible. They should be reminded that we got where we are by doing the impossible, and future progress in the quality of our major institutions, which is both inevitable and imperative, will be by the same route!" Those aren't my words, they belong to Robert Greenleaf.

When I was engaged in creating the Policy Governance model twenty-eight years ago, I wasn't sure what to do with lofty sentiments like those. But I was sure of one thing: leadership, particularly leadership at a high level, must be concerned with—perhaps I should say *obsessed* with—values: the importances of life, the commitments of life, and, yes, the swap-offs of life. Leaders must be able to speak the language of values and, if there is no such language, they must create one that connects our sometimes rather soft and fuzzy insides with hard and precise operational utility. For the organizational context, there has long been a need for a technology of values. And, in fact, making a successful marriage of the seemingly oxymoronic juxtaposition of "technology" and "values" is exactly what is demanded to connect *who we are* to *what we can do.*

For governing boards, the context in which those values would be sought out, explicated, debated, and decided would have to be a context of trusteeship. For boards, as traders in values, do so not for themselves, but for others. The creed expressed in the short phrase "on behalf of" is integrally attached to every motion, every debate, every vote. If the board fails to act powerfully, it cheats those for whom it is in trust of a voice. If it acts self-servingly, it fails to act on their behalf. It must be powerful and deferential at the same time, for both timidity and high-handedness defraud the trust. The contemplation of and theory-building for governing boards—these vessels of leadership—must recognize that *proper governance is a*

logical impossibility if it does not include the concept of servant-leadership.
Let's look a bit more closely at the nature of a board's servanthood.

Where Servanthood Begins: Fidelity to the Ownership

The governing role of any board is not to administer an institution
but to be an owner-representative. Whether the owners are shareholders, trade association members, or a political constituency, the
governing board stands in for them. The board is a microcosm of
the ownership. That is true even when the ownership is only a convenient fiction, such as when the general public is the owner of a
local mental health center or family planning clinic. Indeed, in the
case of most public or quasi-public organizations, most owners do
not even know they are owners.

I have stubbornly insisted on using the term *ownership* in dealing with such boards simply because it forces consideration of an
important role, a role either omitted from the usual governance
equation or defined without the clarity or forcefulness that befits its
importance. We do this, for example, by diluting it in the popular
but less specific *stakeholder* concept. After all, if a board is operating
on someone's behalf, it is rather crucial to know who the someone
is. In the absence of a compelling concept of ownership, pretenders
to that crown move in to fill the vacuum. Many public organizations, for example, operate as if the staff owns the enterprise more
than the public. In other cases, a vocal consumer group grasps that
high ground when a cowardly board bends to its every wish. These
phenomena are not rare but routine. They can be observed every
time a city council pays more attention to the few insistent citizens
who demand the council's collective ear than it does to the other
99 percent of citizens who do not descend upon the council cham-
bers or tie up officials' home phone lines each evening.

In any event, the ownership for a board to concern itself with
may well be a moral rather than legal matter. In my own mission-
ary zeal as a reformer, I have coined the term *moral ownership* to

underscore the nature of owners in the public and quasi-public sectors, occasionally confusing people who thought my term had something to do with moral majority or, in a more serious vein, that I simply meant *stakeholder*. No—on both counts. The ownership to which I refer is a very special subsection of stakeholders. It is the legitimacy base that closely parallels the role of shareholders for an equity corporate board, the membership for an association or federation board, or the municipal residents for a city council. So let me place that important group into an accountability scheme.

Although we are accustomed to using the board-staff relationship as the point of departure in describing the board's own peculiar role, it is really the wrong place to start. The board's role is more properly described from the other direction: the board is an organ of ownership. Its relationship with owners should be the more intimate relationship and the one it spends more time on, not its relationship to staff.

And from that vantage point, the board forms an important link between owners and operators. For that link to have accountability, the board must actually use its authority, not default upon it as nonprofit boards rather commonly do. As the great psychologist Rollo May taught us, failing to lay claim to the power we have is a certain path to irresponsibility in its use. Power must be used. But, as we have been warned by Lord Acton, and as every day's newspaper proves, power corrupts. Only servanthood tempers the power and makes it incorruptible. Servant-leadership, in other words, enables incorruptible power. To get ahead of my story, that protection is further represented in a properly construed chair's role, but more on that later.

So the board is servant to the owners. Of course, the servanthood of a board is neither weak nor passive, for the board is also a leader with respect to the owners. The board of a health clinic may be servant to the public, but it is also obligated to inform, educate, and lead that public with respect to the issues of health. The trade association board is servant to the membership, but must also lead the membership to confront issues of the trade, trends not to be ducked, and even the duties of responsible ownership. Leading those to whom one is first a servant is, experience shouts at us, tricky business. Let's look at one familiar aspect of this phenomenon.

A board's role as servant to the ownership requires that the board find out what owners want before it decides what the institutional outputs shall be. Goal-setting, in other words, is not a closeted activity, emerging full-blown from board members' own foreheads. Knowing this, boards frequently reach out for input using public hearings, polls, and surveys. But being a proper servant does not mean the board is a mere poll-taker. If it were, we would not need boards; we would only need polls and pocket calculators.

Owners have a right to expect a board operating on their behalf to know more than the owners themselves do about the subject matter of the institution. For example, a school board operating on behalf of citizens of a jurisdiction should know more about what is possible in education, what the future holds, and what knowledge young persons are likely to need twenty years from now. Therefore, while by no means unmindful of ownership opinions, the board is obligated to bring specialized judgment to the situation. I hasten to add that this is not necessarily professional judgment—nor is it an uninformed judgment. As Greenleaf said, it is "not a *lay* judgment. It is a unique thing, *trustee judgment*, and it stands on a par in importance with any other judgment within the institution."[2] It is on behalf of the owners, but more informed than the owners. That quality can easily become elitism, if not tempered with considerable stewardship. A Texas legislator put it this way: "I vote the way my constituents would vote if they knew what I know."

Tricky though the task might be, the board as a group is both servant and leader and has no responsible choice to be otherwise.

The Discipline of Leadership

Using one's judgment on behalf of someone else introduces what legal scholars would call the *problem of agency*—the difficulty of an agent subjugating personal needs in the service of the principal.

Board members, frail humans all, have a special authority to act on behalf of the interests of an ownership that they rarely see. Board members do not hold their considerable trust in order to get perks, or to "be involved," or to engage in whatever they'd like to do. A given board's role, in other words, should not be defined as the laundry list of trustees' individual interests. It is a job. Like any real job, it has obligatory outputs and disciplines, though in the absence of a coherent model, those outputs and disciplines are more a product of anecdotal experience than a conceptually sound wisdom. And those elements must amount to the board's behavior being always in the service of the ownership it represents, not the service of board members' own individual needs.

So we ego-driven, flawed individuals must somehow rise to the occasion of fulfilling a bigger-than-life role wherein the mantle we take on is that of many. We speak for hundreds or even millions. When board members take their seats, a transformation must take place wherein they become the vessels through which the multitudes dream, form intentions, debate, and decide. If not mystical, this phenomenon is at the very least impressive and inspirational. Robert Bellah explains de Tocqueville's experience of this transformation. Citizens, he found, got involved in local civic associations out of self-interest, yet the resulting mindfulness of public responsibility caused them to transcend that very self-interest.

Any approach that we design for the governance task must aid in making this transformation that de Tocqueville either observed or idealized. It is common, however, to speak of board strategies that cater to board members' individual interests rather than to the satisfaction of their servanthood obligation. Staffs are known to turn flips trying to find ways to keep the volunteers happy, or keep them involved, or satisfy their individual needs to partake in one or another part of the organization's work.

A question I confronted recently is illustrative of this "please the board members" phenomenon. A journalist called to interview me about a number of governance articles being run in the inaugural issue of a new Canadian magazine, an issue focusing on my work.

In her research she uncovered some criticisms of my work and called to give me the opportunity to respond. That is an opportunity I always love, partly because I love to explain governance, but also because after this many years there aren't many questions I haven't heard. But one question surprised me. She said one source thought the Policy Governance model is flawed in that it doesn't allow some board members to do what they want to do. That is, the board job as I have defined it may not be of interest to every board member. The discipline required would not allow all board members to follow their specific interests.

It speaks volumes about how we have trivialized and cheapened this pivotal servant-leadership role in our society that a significant number think that the job of a governance model is to enable current board members to use their platform of trust as a protected province for following their own interests—or in more than a few cases I have encountered—to use the privilege of board position to provide a permissive playground. An example from last month: A questioner recounted his board's struggle with whether to allow board members to volunteer within the staff organization, that is, to be operational volunteers at the same time as being governing volunteers. They ultimately decided to allow it, in part because they felt it would be wrong to "deny board members the opportunity to participate as volunteers"! The distressing aspect of that position is not that it came up or even that it won the day in this particular board. The distressing aspect is that so many boards' members—as well as those who work for them, write about them, and consult to them—would not notice anything awry about it!

One would have hoped for this board and all others that the first consideration, perhaps the obsessive one, be "what is our governance obligation to those who morally own this organization"—a question I believe must be answered in servant-leadership terms. Then the board might have asked what must we do and be to fulfill that trust as a board, and what behaviors, processes, or failures of discipline will jeopardize our fulfillment of that trust. But this board showed itself more concerned about trustee rights than about right trusteeship.

As an aside, many of our so-called voluntary organizations are at risk for the damaging confounding of volunteer roles. It is common for persons active in voluntary health organizations, for example, to "graduate" to a governing board level because of their years of conscientious service. Robert Greenleaf, three decades ago, was prescient and bold enough to say that volunteers who govern should stay out of operational work. Rather less boldly than he, I have warned only that they should be scrupulous in wearing these two very different hats separately. The problem is obvious. Board members inappropriately drag their operational interests, proclivities, and ways of thinking into the boardroom, dooming governance to a short-term mentality, to interference in staff work, and to fragmentation of that all-important big picture. Operational details are not inconsequential if one is in operations. But they certainly are if one is on the board.

A character in a novel by Lee Gruenfield put it well: "It's human nature, this propensity in the face of the profound to be distracted by the trivial." Since trivia in the boardroom can consist of merely dealing with topics that are perfectly appropriate in an operational setting, failing to make the transition from operations to governing virtually cripples board leadership. Greenleaf felt that making the necessary switch would be difficult, in part because "one is apt to make any position one holds fit one's habitual way of working." Board members whose interpretation of board leadership consists largely of dragging operational behavior into the boardroom remind me of the old saw about a kid with a hammer: Everything comes to look like a nail. Long-term conceptual problems are met with short-term operational solutions.

When discussing the mix of conceptual and operating skills and talents, Greenleaf observed, "Leadership, in the sense of going out ahead to show the way, is more conceptual than operating."[3] So trustees must be conceptual people, persons capable of envisioning a world that isn't, rather than being captured by a world that is. But beyond their intellectual and visionary equipment, those who would be our leaders at the board level must have a commitment to discipline, for the board job is a real job, not just a ceremonial position. And, of course, their commitment must be one of servant-leadership. A proper governance model, then, is merely a structure for fulfillment of the servant-leadership obligation of intelligent, caring, committed persons.

Let me add here that the tradition-blessed practice of reserving a board position for an accountant, a lawyer, a public relations person, a human resources person, or, in some cases, a physician, an educator, or other specialty also falls into the same trap. If an organization is quite small, these provisions may make some sense. But in an organization large enough to have a CEO and active staff, the practice is outmoded and dysfunctional. It persists because boards feel it is their responsibility to furnish experts to guide their staff in staff work. Board-as-expert-collection is quite different, however, from board as responsible servant-leader for an ownership.

Don't get me wrong on this point, please. Lawyers, accountants, physicians, and others can be wonderful governing board members—if, in fact, that is what they are charged to be. But they will not be if they are recruited so that the board can load onto them responsibilities that should have been shouldered by the full board. With the entire group taking responsibility, it can entertain whatever wisdom should be heard, make appropriate policies using that wisdom, then have something of substance to delegate to the CEO. (At that point, if the CEO wishes to use experts from *any* source to help fulfill the board's expectations, that is completely the CEO's business.) How commonplace is the refrain, "Our fiduciary responsibility is too complicated for us; we have Sally, CPA on the board to take care of that for us."

What would I say to Sally? You are a board member first and an accountant second. You may bring your knowledge and wisdom to the table for the board to use in accomplishing its job. But never save the board from being the board. Leave pigeonholes to pigeons. Your portfolio is the same as that of all other board members: to participate in the group responsibility of governance. What would I say to the board? To fulfill your responsibility, you must learn to use experts to inform your wisdom, never to substitute for it.

But—back to the role of a conceptually coherent framework to embrace this thing we call governance. My point is that a respectable governance model is not designed to make trustees happy—though their happiness is by no means a bad thing—but to see to it that trustees taken as a body fulfill their trusteeship responsibly. Board members who can only meddle might just have to leave the board. Board members who can only rubber-stamp might be left behind. This job of governing isn't for everyone. We need to define the job and let the chips fall where they fall, not define the job to fit board members as they have, by accident of history, been appointed in the past. "There are able people," Greenleaf said, "who ought not to be trustees." He was comfortable that a better approach would "more quickly and sharply expose those who should not be in institutional leadership at all."[4]

From Responsible Individuals to Responsible Boards

But as important as it is that trustees be capable servants, being so *individually* is not good enough to transform this institution of governance—not sufficient to the task of creating a servant-leadership group. Boards can easily be incompetent groups of competent people, untrustworthy groups of trustworthy people, and far more often than even I sometimes imagine, cruel groups of good-hearted people. The transformation of responsible individuals into a responsible group is not an automatic product of good people with good intent. Greenleaf noted that the servant-leadership role of the board is optimized only if the board learns to act as a *unitary* body. He said, "If trustees . . . [are] to be influential in raising the performance of the institution to the optimal . . . they confront a difficult problem: how to carry that role *as a group*. It is one thing to carry a trustee role as an individual. It is quite another to function effectively as part of a group process."[5] The board *as a body* has the authority to act on behalf of the ownership, not trustees taken one at a time. Another way to say this is that no one board member has any rights at all over the organization governed.

No one argues with this in theory. But in practice, this tenet is violated regularly. Staff members can be seen scrambling to do what one board member wants done. Individual board members can be found expressing criticisms of staff performance against criteria the board has never stated—criteria that emanate from the one trustee alone. Subgroups of the full board—committees—regularly do the same things. In practice, boards have rarely learned to discipline themselves in this regard. As a consequence, the leadership of most boards is seriously flawed, because the integrity of group authority is not strictly maintained. (Existing popular and reputable expert sources actually teach governance methods designed with these flaws built in.)

Let me assure you that my allegation that "most boards" are caught in the pervasiveness of this phenomenon is not lightly made. I have personally dealt with thousands of boards directly and tens of thousands indirectly through their members' participation in my workshops. I truly mean, given experience that is admittedly not "research" in a scientific sense, *most* boards. Try a simple test: any board that truly means its authority will be exercised only as a group will tell its CEO "when we speak as individuals in or out of board meetings, you never have to pay attention to any of us." Try to find such a board.

Perhaps this is a good place to point out that proper exercise of the board's group challenge enables the board to delegate cleanly and powerfully to a CEO. There is never a need for the board chair to be in that loop. The chairperson helps the board get its job done, but does not interfere between the employer (the board) and its employee (the CEO). Contrast this with the common practice in which boards allow or even require their chair to supervise the CEO or, similarly, to require that certain CEO actions have chair approval, and other such dilutions of the CEO's role. Each dilutes the board's integrity as a body and seriously weakens the board's ability to hold the CEO accountable to it and to it alone. A properly construed chair role has virtually nothing to do with CEO activities, decisions, or performance. In fact, the only excuse for the chair's becoming, if you will, the super-CEO is the board's failing to do its own job—that is, to make governance decisions as a group so crafted that delegation to the CEO is direct and unobstructed by any intervening authority, including that of a chair or of committees.

This is to say that the board's relationship with the chair is circular, while its relationship with the CEO is linear. Consider two scenarios: Number one, I meet with my personal physician, accepting that I am responsible for my own health but enlisting my doctor in helping me do that well. Number two, as owner of my manufacturing business, I tell the plant manager what I want, after which the manager instructs the shift managers, who in turn instruct their various supervisors.

Allow me to amateurishly misappropriate from physics and hypothesize a "plasma" that flows in these relationships, a plasma composed of both instructing and "acting upon," quite apart from the more familiar concept of feedback. Mindful of the difficulty of group discipline, the board charges the chair with the task of keeping the boss on track, *not* with personally taking over and becoming the boss. The "flow" of governance plasma, if you will, is back and forth between the board and the chair, a closed-system, two-party interaction that does not go beyond the dyadic. In contrast, mindful of the impracticality of the board itself accomplishing the organization's work, the board charges a CEO with the task of getting that job done, *not* with keeping the board on track. The flow of executive plasma is from board to CEO to sub-CEO staff, a linear progression that may have as many parties as the organizational size accommodates.

An analogy in more familiar management terminology can be found in the concepts of line and staff. Although there is some variation in the way the words are used in the management literature, I will define them in this way: *Line* positions are those on a direct line that can be drawn from the highest authority through to the lowest person engaged in producing the organization's output to customers or clientele. Thus, the board, the CEO, the plant manager, and the product installer all hold line positions. *Staff* positions, on the other hand, assist or counsel one or more line positions; their authority is always granted and controlled by some line position and they have no direct command authority of their own over line positions. As an aside, violating this principle results in dismaying problems in many nonprofit organizations when, for example, a program head is expected—in practice if not on the organization chart—to work for the finance officer.

At any rate, given this distinction between line and staff that management tradition has given us, it can be seen that the board chairperson is staff, while the CEO is line. The board chairperson is staff to the board, much as the finance officer is staff to the CEO. This highly visible staff position, no matter how important it is to the board, can have no legitimate authority over line personnel— including the CEO and the other employees.

Whether you find it more convenient positing a fictional plasma or seeing things in terms of line and staff, it is inescapable that the role assigned here to the chairperson is impossible if the board is incapable of speaking with one and only one voice. It must be so, for the chairperson's authority can only derive from a group decision—and the chair's obligation is, similarly, to group expectations. "One voice" in this context does not imply unanimous votes, but does require the mindset that if the board hasn't spoken as a group, it hasn't spoken at all. Contrary to common belief, the great impediment to this one-voice simplicity is not that some boards have members who differ widely and almost violently.

The impediment is simply lacking the discipline to say that, until a motion passes, the board exercises absolutely no authority over anyone.

Quite often, however, boards are not sufficiently committed to their trusteeship to require this discipline of themselves. But nature abhors a vacuum, including the vacuum of leadership. When the board as a group fails to be the originating seat of leadership, the vacuum gets filled anyway. Sometimes, of course, boards fly off in all directions—so that the vacuum is filled with uncoordinated individual actions—but more commonly, they settle into the indolent comfort of letting someone just tell them what to do.

That someone might be the chair. But even more commonly it is the board's employed executive who moves into that vacuum. Ask any board where its last agenda came from. Although our rhetoric celebrates the board as the source of vision and strategic leadership, it has to have someone else tell it what to talk about at the next meeting! I submit that the only reason this phenomenon doesn't sound absolutely daft is because it has historical momentum on its side. Board agendas provided by management is just the way we've done it. It is common for a board to expect its CEO to be more responsible for at least the appearances of governance than the board is. And, credit to their cordiality more than their judgment, CEOs oblige.

As illustration of the unquestioning acceptance of this inversion, almost every article on boards that appears in the popular periodical *Nonprofit World* tells CEOs how to see to it that their boards do the right things. No one ever publishes articles about how vice presidents should make their presidents do the right things. Governance can only have the needed integrity when boards, not their CEOs, assume the responsibility for governance. Wouldn't it be a breath of fresh air if board meetings truly became the board's meetings, not the CEO's meetings for the board?

The Chairperson: Servant-Leader to the Servant-Leaders

But how can a leaderless board determine its own agenda, its own role, its own discipline? It can select a chairperson who can help the board be what it means to be. But in this familiar practice lies a trap. Boards can easily default to their chairs rather than delegate to them. For chairs can help rob a board of its group strength quite as quickly as CEOs can. The traditional strong chair might run a tight ship but does not develop a strong board. In fact, it is not uncommon for a strong chair to become more the board's boss than its servant. Yet strength is needed, so how is the dilemma to be settled?

The solution, of course, is servant-leadership. The chair, in fact, works for the board. If we remember that the organizational authority begins with the board as a group, then no one can have any authority that the board as a body has not given out. That includes the chair quite as much as it includes the CEO. The board begins by accepting that it and it alone has the responsibility to govern—there is no whining that holds up at this point. Failure to govern well can never be blamed on the CEO or the chair or a committee. The buck truly stops with the group. Understanding this, the board then admits that fulfilling its role will be difficult without enlisting someone to help it stick with the task.

The CEO is a very bad choice for that job, hence the role for one of the board's own: a chairperson. But the logical sequence is crucial. In the beginning was the board. There is no chair until the board empowers a chair, which means the chair works at the pleasure of the board and has whatever authority the board chooses to give. And the value-added assigned to this newly created servant is the job of leadership! "Lead us to be what we've decided to be. Lead us to produce what we've decided to produce. Impose upon us the discipline we've committed ourselves to." The authority of the chair, in other words, comes from the board. The visible, dynamic, sometimes insistent leader is first servant.

You may have come across a greeting card that reads "A friend is someone who learns the words of your song, then sings them back to you when you forget." That is a beautifully simple description of the role of board chair at its best. And in this role, the chairperson can be inspiring, encouraging, enlightening, challenging, and often cajoling—all within the servanthood that calls for just this kind of tough-love leadership.

But while I am describing a good chair, let me warn against the problem I am myself at this moment exacerbating. Charging the chair with responsibility for meeting-by-meeting and even minute-by-minute board discipline risks letting other board members off the hook for that discipline. Group responsibility is tricky business and negotiating its unfamiliar twists and turns is not second nature to us yet.

Let me put it this way: If board hegemony is to make sense, the point of departure must be the board's *group* responsibility for governance, including the discipline necessary to make governance work. The board exercises that responsibility in three ways. It first *describes* the discipline to which the board *as a body* will be committed. Second, it pins the fulfillment of that discipline on the chairperson, simultaneously granting the chairperson the authority over board process that will be necessary to keep discipline on track. Third, the board also prescribes for itself the discipline that *individual trustees* are to observe—this can take the form of a code of conduct that goes beyond the usual conflict-of-interest provisions.

As the real work of board meetings takes place, the chairperson plays a role we might describe as the board's "point person" for discipline. The term is borrowed from the old army term "point man." Everybody will get shot, but the point person will get it first. Although the chairperson has been given authority to keep the board in line and should do so, board members must not be released from their individual responsibility to object if the board is not on track. Any time a board is doing things it said it wouldn't do, making decisions it said it would leave to the CEO, judging the CEO on criteria it never set—or any of a myriad strayings from its stated discipline commitment—*every* board member whose hand does *not* go in the air to correct the straying *is culpable*. In other words, waiting for the chair to be responsible is not itself responsible.

There is irony in group responsibility wherein the group charges and empowers one of its own to help it be true to its self-defined responsibility. Your experience and mine is that who the chairperson is makes a big difference to board effectiveness, the tone of interpersonal interchange, the board's relationship with its staff, and, yes, the board's relationship with the ownership. But we have garnered that experience in the environment of traditional governance. The irony to which I refer is this: the more a board really learns how to embrace group responsibility and to express that responsibility through a coherent governance model, the less it makes any difference who the chairperson is!

I am not convinced that the most perfect board composition and board process will ever be *completely* unaffected by who the chairperson is. The power of personal modeling and inspiration are too great for me to see that far ahead if, indeed, that perfection does lie ahead. And I certainly do not want to make the case that we are closer to that nirvana than we are. So I, too, have a list of personal qualities I believe will lead to a chair's being able to fulfill the "servant-leadership squared" role I have described.

- *Personal integrity.* It is important that the chair deal straightforwardly with trustee relationships and commitments, neither engaging in interpersonal games nor playing favorites. This person's conduct is guided more by principles than politics.

- *Ability to leave the CEO alone.* A good chair candidate must have no need to interfere with chief executive prerogatives granted by the board. A chair who covets the type of executive authority vested in the CEO may well encroach upon that role. Although chair intervention between the board and its CEO can satisfy a board's anxieties in the short term, it inevitably causes deterioration in the proper board-CEO relationship.

- *Intelligence and conceptual flexibility.* Since board members should all be leaders, it is hard to imagine a chair who can lead their process who is not their intellectual caliber. Because of the especially conceptual nature of leadership at this level, the ability to deal with concepts and constructs and principles is crucial.

- *Mindfulness of group process.* Living by principle, however, need not mean unawareness of interpersonal and political realities. A candidate for the chair should be comfortable with group process, especially the ability of a group to capitalize on the talents of its members. This capability should extend to dealing calmly and appropriately with the occasional group process that goes awry. When Kipling wrote of keeping "your head when all about you are losing theirs and blaming it on you," he spoke to board chairs.

- *A disposition of servanthood.* The chair is servant to the board and must never forget it, particularly when tough times call upon the chair to lead. The chair can never forget on whose behalf he or she works and by whose grace he or she exercises authority. The chair's compelling ambition is only to influence the board toward greater integrity and leadership.

- *Ability to confront and lead.* The chair must be able to act with the authority the board has granted, for not to do so cheats the board process. That includes the ability to confront individuals and the group with their or its own behavior. "We committed ourselves to do X,

yet we at this moment are doing Y. We must either stop
or change our commitment. Which shall it be?" I
alluded earlier to the analogy of learning the board's
song, then singing it back when board members forget.
I suppose that the most effective singing might on
some occasions better be described as bellowing!

These characteristics are those of a person who is capable of
being *modestly in command*. The task of board chairperson calls
for leadership that is both compassionate and compelling, as self-
disciplined as it is obliging others to be self-disciplined. It means
servant-leadership practiced by a highly capable person. It
means fulfilling what Robert Greenleaf conceptualized so purely for
us: that the most morally justifiable leadership is founded in, legit-
imized by, and, yes, even sanctified by servanthood.

Summary

The chair is servant-leader of the board. The board is servant-leader
of the ownership. The chair is, therefore, servant-leader of the
servant-leaders. The chair thus holds a unique servant-leadership
role. The woman or man in this role is ideally situated to make
servant-leadership work, for this role is crafted to be an institutionalized embodiment of servant-leadership, a visible and practical model for others.

This kind of chair is guardian of group integrity, not worker of
any personal agenda. This kind of chair nurtures the ability of his
or her boss—the board—to truly be and stay the boss. This kind of
chair is a reflector of board discipline, like the moon shining by a
light no less spectacular because it is only reflected. This kind of
chair never forgets that the conductor doesn't make the music.

4

Love and Work

A Conversation with James A. Autry

On October 20, 2000, Larry Spears, president and CEO of The Greenleaf Center for Servant-Leadership in Indianapolis, and John Noble, director of the Greenleaf Centre-United Kingdom, met with James A. Autry in Des Moines, Iowa. What follows is a record of the conversation that took place.

JOHN NOBLE: *Jim, you have had a profound effect on the attitudes and actions of huge numbers of people through your work. What were the markers in your life, the people and events that have helped shape your thinking?*

JAMES AUTRY: I feel that everything is connected, every experience and relationship is connected, and somehow they all point in the same direction. So I go back to people in my childhood who were people of good values who had a great influence on me in a very difficult situation—my parents were divorced, and I lived in a federal housing project in Memphis with my mother. These were some of the personal influences that shaped my values along the way.

And then I learned in the Air Force—which we all think of as a hierarchical structure—that the best leaders, the ones who seemed to achieve the best results, weren't the ramrod-straight, "kick 'em in the rear" sort, but the ones willing to get out among the people to identify with them. The best squadron commanders were the ones who regularly flew, who didn't just sit behind a desk, who mingled with the pilots and had a more personal relationship with them. I also found that they didn't have any more problems with discipline than the ramrod-straight ones did, and that had an influence on me.

Later, when I went into business, it was very clear to me that the people who were the most effective managers were those who were thought of as the weakest by higher management. This always troubled me, because if the objective was to achieve results, why was there such an emphasis on behaving a certain way? It was as if the results themselves were worthless if the managers didn't conform to what was perceived to be a management attitude. I think I learned from that. When I became a manager—at twenty-nine, I think I was the youngest managing editor in the history of *Better Homes and Gardens*— I thought the way to do it was to adopt the hierarchical attitude. It didn't work for me. I tried, but it wasn't me and it didn't work.

Then along came a man named Bob Burnett, the CEO of the Meredith Corporation. In 1968 he made a speech about self-renewal. This was a top corporate manager—one of the most courageous ones I ever saw—and he made a speech to the management group about self-renewal. As he went through the list of all the things about self-renewal, he said, "The most important thing is love." That was the first time I had ever heard the word *love* used in the context of corporate life. This was 1968, and he spoke of love—love of what we do together, love of ourselves, love of our customers, love of our products. He said we could not renew ourselves without love. The company really was in need of renewal, and I saw his leadership turn the company around. He became a mentor to me, and that probably marked the beginning of the end of my transformation.

That's when I completely let go of the old ways. In the next several years I tried to integrate that love into the corporate setting. And it just kept working: I just kept getting results. We went from

$160 million in revenues to $500 million; we went from four magazines to seventeen magazines during that period, and it was all about supporting people, being a resource to people and letting the vision evolve from the organization, rather than enforcing the "top down" vision. These were my markers. They started with values. I'll tell you something else I've learned: there's something about being at the bottom of the economic totem pole, and it seems to me it goes one of several ways. With the grace of God, a good mother, and several other influences, I went in a good direction. I learned that if you can retain the feeling of what it feels like to be a "have not" in a society of "haves," to be down in the hierarchy, you can carry that with you into leadership positions. I think it makes you a more effective leader. So don't forget where you came from. In *Love and Profit* there's an essay called "Management from the Roots."

LARRY SPEARS: *Can you tell us about three or four authors or books about leadership that you have found particularly useful?*

JAMES AUTRY: I'm not just saying this because you're here, but Robert Greenleaf's work has had a great influence on me. Before discovering that, I was influenced a good deal by Warren Bennis, not just by his writing but by the man himself, in his seminars and workshops. I'm taken by Peter Block and Peter Vaill, especially Vaill's book *Managing as a Performing Art*. These are the people that just jump to mind. I have a library full of leadership books. And it's interesting, I get something out of a lot of them, and yet I find that the totality of the work often doesn't appeal to me, but something in there does. But Warren Bennis's work, Peter Vaill, and, although it's a lot to work through, Peter Senge's *Fifth Discipline* and his whole learning organization work I've found very helpful. I've used some of the exercises in Senge's books to help achieve some honesty in a community setting. I've never met him, but I've seen videos of him, and he seems to be what his work reveals. I guess that's what jumps to my head. Oh! Of course! Margaret Wheatley for *Leadership and the New Science*, that whole notion of everything in relationships and everything affecting everything else, the model from quantum physics. And then there are people who've not written on leadership but whose work has had an influence on me, like Joan Borysenko and Scott Peck. I've enjoyed Joan's work, and Scott Peck's original *The Road Less Traveled*, and subsequently meeting him and working with him has been a very positive influence on some of the things I've done on leadership.

LARRY SPEARS: *Leadership concepts, including servant-leadership, values-based management, learning organizations, and similar ideas are being learned, taught, and practiced more than ever before. What do you see as the cultural changes that have caused these ideas to be more widely accepted?*

JAMES AUTRY: Well, we have to qualify the answer by saying that there are still some industries where none of this is being done, like in Detroit, the oil industry, and some of the heavier manufacturing industries. I don't think it's because they have union people; I think it's just that the culture hasn't shifted. Now, it may be that within departments or within groups you'll find these values. I work all the time in companies you wouldn't think of as being particularly servant-leader oriented or values-based oriented, and yet within a group it's very much alive. So I see it as a positive virus in these businesses. But there are companies that are wholly committed. I am not a sociologist, only an amateur social observer, and anything I say on the subject will be obvious, but clearly one of the cultural shifts has been the increasing number of women in the workforce. There are two factors that come into play. One is the impact of motherhood and women's need to balance this, and the other is scientifically based, the idea that women socialize by affiliation, whereas men socialize by separation. That makes a profound difference on how their work styles will be manifested. These are generalizations, of course. You will find women who are hard-edged and tough, and men who are sensitive and supportive, so I don't want to overgeneralize, but I do think these differences have had a major impact in the development of workplace culture, especially in helping to create a medium in which concepts that are more affiliative and communal and more supportive of workers and less hierarchical can grow. I think the presence and influence of women is certainly a factor.

I think another factor is that so many people have seen that the old ways simply don't work as well as this stuff. There's been a feeling of frustration that "I can't get the results that I want to get" that leads to an openness to writings and influences from the media about another way to do it, so that's been a factor. The challenge of how to get results has permeated management generally as compensation systems have shifted for CEOs and have created a downward pressure from CEOs to enhance stock price. *Stockholder value* has become the mantra, and in the end that is defined as stock price. So the emphasis on results has created fear and frustration on one hand, and a desire to try almost anything to get better results on the other hand. And that creates an approach to change that's phony: "Well, I think I'll try the soft approach now and get them to work a lot harder." You have to be careful about that; it's got to really come from the inside of a person. But it does seem to me that society is more open to it.

Many company leaders are concerned about loyalty and turnover. This also creates an interest in values-based leadership. What's been proved over and over again is that people are not going to work where they feel driven or unhappy. They work hard (and I think people are working way too hard doing unnecessary things), they're putting in a lot of hours, but they're not doing it because managers are kicking them in the rear and making them do it. What does that mean if you're trying to hang on to people in a highly mobile culture? How do you create culture, how do you do things that bind them, that make them want to stay someplace? What works is creating community, even if people say "Yeah! But they're not going to be here very long." This is a lesson I learned in the Air Force: People rotate in and out of squadrons and highly intensive settings all the time. Personnel are changing all the time; in fact, the most you get is a three-year tour. There's a very intense and intentional imperative toward creating a community, then people come into these communities, they're brought into it, and immediately become a part of it. They may be only there six months, but they're no less a member of this community and they feel no less committed to it. I have seen it work in that kind of setting, and I know that it can be done. And the businesses that are building community are the ones who are holding on to employees the longest, regardless of what the compensation structure might be.

JOHN NOBLE: *One situation I think we are familiar with is that in which the CEO of a company is very willing to make the change toward more values-based management. The junior managers are gung ho for the whole idea, but it is in the ranks of middle management where the resistance, not surprisingly, exists. What advice or guidance do you offer companies in this situation?*

JAMES AUTRY: I think the situation starts with an analysis. Part of the analysis is this: The reason is fear. So what are the middle managers afraid of? They are afraid of the loss of power, perceived power, the loss of their jobs. If everything goes well, they might not be needed. In order to make this change, you have to address the fear issue in the middle manager. Let's face facts—in the great wave of white-collar layoffs, it was the middle managers who got the axe, so they've got good reason to be afraid in view of what's been happening in the last fifteen years or so. If the CEO is gung-ho on it, it's on the CEO to bring it about.

I think it has to be done by building a sense of community based on trust. The middle managers have to feel that they are a part of bringing this about, that it's not being foisted on them. It's a huge education process for them because a lot of them got where they are under the old ways. "The old ways worked for me; why change?" So there's a reeducation and a reorientation process needed, and at the same time there has to be a reaffirmation that they got there because of their knowledge and competence, not because of their management style, not because of authoritarianism. What we're going to change is the culture, the social architecture, the interpersonal relationships. We're not going to change the positions, the accountability. We're not going to change the results we want. But the fear has to be taken out, and that's an education process.

I've been involved in this in three companies and, I'll tell you, it's a tough nut to crack. Managers have been brought up in an atmosphere of "They don't trust people, they don't feel trusted, they don't trust the company." It's a long process and it's a difficult challenge. I think it takes community building, it takes personal attention and commitment from the CEO, because on the one hand he's saying "I'm going to need these results" and on the other hand he's saying, "We want to be this kind of company." He's got to somehow communicate that "I think that creating this kind of company is going to give us these even better results. Trust me on this, let's do it." This takes leadership from the top. You can't delegate this kind of cultural change.

JOHN NOBLE: *Thinking more about these young leaders, what are two skills or characteristics you would wish them to have?*

JAMES AUTRY: Let's call them characteristics, because I never try to tell people what to do, I try to tell them how to be. I think they have to be empathetic, that's one of the characteristics. Can I give you five? The five are be authentic, be vulnerable, present, accepting, and useful. And by *useful* I mean, be servants. Those are the five characteristics. And underneath all that they have to be courageous, they have to show that vulnerability and authenticity, and empathize and listen—that's all part of it. One of the first things I say to groups when I speak to them is: "I'm not here to tell you what to do. You know what you should do much better than I could ever know."

JOHN NOBLE: *One of the things I often find myself talking to colleagues about is the joy of what you once called leaving work and being able to say, "I did it well today." What were the circumstances that usually led you to be able to say that?*

JAMES AUTRY: It's always been relationships. It's always been somehow if at the end of the day I've managed to create a sense of community, and have either resolved conflicts or created circumstances in which they got resolved. It's always been about personal relationships. Now, am I really happy when we start a new magazine, or we got a good sales result, or we turned the corner and made a profit? Yes, I really am, and that gives me an enormous sense of satisfaction. But I have always seen those results—even my own salary—as simply the tangible measurement of the real work. That's not the real work, making profits. This is one of the great distortions in American business life. The real work is not making profits; making profits is the result of the real work. So I get enormous satisfaction from that, and great satisfaction from the doing that's done. But when I felt *I did it well today*, it's always been relationships, even if it was just convening a good meeting filled with ideas and energy. That could make me feel good because I realize that people felt confident enough to be able to say things, knowing that they might not work, without fear of ridicule or fear of being shouted down.

Lately, in the last several years, the greatest feeling of satisfaction I've gotten is when I've been called to go into a company to resolve conflict between people. I've done a lot of what's now called executive coaching and counseling, and a lot of this is listening to people talk about the things that trouble them most deeply in their personal relationships. But conflict resolution is getting people who are at odds with one another—vociferously and sometimes angrily at odds with one another—bringing them together and getting them to make a human connection. You realize that underneath the differences in ideas, they are more similar than dissimilar. They have joys, fears, griefs, and celebrations that are more similar than dissimilar. Because they have different views of how the work has to be done does not make them enemies.

And it's that old dualism, and we fight the dualism all the time—you know, "If you're not for me, you're against me." We know from Biblical scholarship that that's not exactly what Jesus meant, but it gets quoted all the time. "If you're not with me, you're against me." That dualism of defining myself by the other, by who I'm not, permeates business. People have disagreements over all kinds of things like budgets or sales presentations. Some things that require disagreements, perhaps to shape them to the most effective way of doing business, turn into personal warfare. Well, it gives me an enormous sense of satisfaction to help people accept one another as human beings, even uneasily at first, and know that they can disagree about ideas without demonizing one another as fellow human beings. Sometimes I let these discussions become heated because it's necessary to get some of the feelings out on the table where they can be dealt with.

JOHN NOBLE: *I'd like to ask you about one of the old chestnuts, "I don't have to be liked to be an effective leader." What are your views on that?*

JAMES AUTRY: The way you hear it in America often is, "Look, management is not a popularity contest." When a manager would say that to me, I'd say, "Well, to a certain extent, it is." It's not that you have to be the jolly, well-liked, "hail fellow well met," but if people don't respect you—and that's the operative word—if they don't respect you and your abilities as a person, it's not going to work for you. What I think and what I've often said is, we don't really have to love one another to work together. In fact we really don't have to like one another. We don't have to walk out the building and commingle, have drinks or party or anything. But in this kind of place we have to care about one another. That's kind of an interesting concept, to say we don't have to love one another, just care about one another. Because you have to care about what we do together, because what we do together is interdependent. We need to care about one another in the context of what we do together. That's a difficult concept sometimes for people. If people like one another and care about one another—genuinely—outside, then so much the better. I've always promoted that sort of personal connection. I've always been against the idea that "I have to remain aloof from the people, and it doesn't matter if they like me or not, because I might have to fire one of them." So I may use a different vocabulary in saying this, but respect and caring in the context of what we do together is essential. Whether you have personal likes or not is neither here nor there.

LARRY SPEARS: *In* Confessions of an Accidental Businessman *you wrote, "The commitment to act out beyond ego, to recognize when we are in denial, to retain humility, to correct our mistakes and to learn from others, regardless of their so-called status, is the commitment to grow personally and spiritually through the work we've chosen to do." To me that really captures the essence of servant-leadership, at least in my own understanding of what servant-leadership is about. Would you talk about how one goes about overcoming ego in a leadership position?*

JAMES AUTRY: That's a good question: How do you overcome ego? The first step toward overcoming acting out of ego, I think, is to recognize that you do it, and to be able to identify when you are doing it. I think the only way to get out of the ego is to get into yourself. You have to have some sort of spiritual discipline— meditation, prayer, yoga. I am always recommending to people that they do something to nurture the inner life, that they try to do something every day that is reflective or meditative, even if they do it while they're jogging or walking. In order to get out of the ego you have to somehow get deeper into your own inner life. And I think you do that through the spiritual disciplines of silence and prayer and meditation. Or by reflective and meditative action, and by that I mean you can jog meditatively. I do it. I walk that way. You could also do psychotherapy or counseling, or meet with groups or just meet sometimes like with these groups where high-level busi-nesspeople meet to discuss their mutual problems.

Once you recognize it and begin to work on it, you have to stop throughout the day and examine what your actions are. In order to be able to admit mistakes and to learn from others, no matter what their status, the piece of advice I give to everybody—in fact, it's the same advice I offer every manager, new or old—is this: Whenever you attempt to make a statement, ask a question. Instead of saying "Here's what you should do," you say, "What do you think we should do?" That's a huge leap for a lot of people. It seems simple to say it, doesn't it? But it's difficult for us to fathom how challenging that is for some people who act out of ego. Because you are saying, "Put my ego in the drawer and I'm gonna ask how you think it should be done; you, who are seventeen layers down in the hierar-chy from me."

The next step is to do that not just as a technique, but to rec-ognize that you're open to learning, and that other person may know the thing to do. My attitude about this is, if an employee comes in and says, "Jim, here's the situation and this is the problem and I'm laying it out and what do you think we ought to do?" then I know that person already knows what to do. They've got the sit-uation surrounded, they have the problem defined, and they, whether it's a group, or just a he or she, they know what to do—probably. If not, they've got a good first step. And I may know what to do, too, because I've been in this long enough, I can see all the pieces, it fits together, and I know what has to happen. And I know they have a step. They know that I know. But as soon as I fulfill the expectation that I'm going to be "Big Daddy"—you know, I'm going to make a pronouncement and they're gonna go do it—I've destroyed any possibility, one, to learn something from them and, two, to recognize their own power, which is their knowledge and their skill and which is real empowerment. Empowerment is not about "I take some of my power and give it to you." That's the myth.

Real empowerment is recognizing that you, by your skill, your knowledge, your commitment, you already have power. What I'm trying to do is take the leashes that I've put on, off.

So by that simple technique of asking a question instead of making a pronouncement, we can start to come out of ego. Another step toward acting beyond ego is to let go of my solution and embrace someone else's. Any number of solutions may work. They may not work as well as I think mine would work, but if one will work and achieve the result, then let go of ego and embrace the other solution. All our management structure traditionally is built on the basis of the person up here who has all the answers. What I keep saying is, don't be the person who has all the answers; be the person who has the best questions. And then you'll get better answers!

LARRY SPEARS: *You mentioned doing work in the governor's office, and your wife is lieutenant governor of the State of Iowa. I was curious to know whether past experience, or even more recent experience, has led you to any sense regarding whether there are differences between leadership as practiced in politics versus business or organizations. You've written a great deal about effective leadership in the business setting. Do you see any differences when it comes to that kind of leadership within the political structure?*

JAMES AUTRY: I think leadership in public service is more difficult. It is a good place to practice servant-leadership. American people seem to want a field general in their leadership positions, yet the most effective leaders have been the ones who really practiced community and consensus building. It's really the only way to get anything done—I've learned that from the inside, just seeing this process. I realize that the most effective public servant-leaders are those who know how to get people together and build a consensus; who interpret and articulate what they are trying to accomplish; and who tell why and how they are doing it for the people, for the voters.

It's a much more challenging kind of leadership than in business, because in business, the objectives are very clearly defined. One, the most imperative objective is survival; not survival at any cost, not sacrificing your values for survival—though some have done that—but survival. Second, you need to achieve the objectives of the business, which some people define as *stockholder value*. Once you define the objectives of the business, they are pretty concrete, they don't shift very much. There may be factors and market changes and things like that, but you're still trying to achieve these objectives. The constituency you have may be millions of stockholders, but they're represented by a board of directors of twelve or fourteen people, and they're the ones you have to convince. So finding the leadership of the employee group is, I think, less challenging in business because you have such flexible tools. You have compensation systems; you have hours and benefits; you can try all sorts of modes of structuring the office, from the virtual office to flextime. You find you have a vast array of tools that you can use, if you're courageous enough to use them and smart enough to use them.

In public service, all the employee rules have been set by legislation, and are managed by agencies and work under legislative oversight. It's a very complex management challenge. There are posts that the governor comes in and appoints, then these appointees hire more positions, and then agencies get permeated with people with one political philosophy. Legislation changes, political philosophy changes, and it's very difficult. We've heard that democracy's messy. Democracy's very messy! It's a good system, I like the checks and balances. I think that it generally serves the people, but it could serve them better if we could get better public perception and understanding of what the real objectives are, what we're really trying to accomplish, rather than all the peripheral things. And, in that, I blame my old business, the media. They are forever doing an injustice to the system by jumping on things that are of relatively little consequence when it comes to governance and the objectives of society. So, yes, I think political leadership is far more difficult. Yet there are some good people on both sides of the aisle. They're good leaders, they're good about the vision, they're good about consensus, they don't let their egos paint them into a corner, and they don't demonize others.

In politics there's a lot of demonizing. Having grown up a fundamentalist Christian, I understand those folks and what they want. But, as I say to my relatives in Mississippi, the U.S. Constitution is about equality and justice and opportunity. It's not about righteousness. There was no intention for us to become a righteous nation, but a nation governed by people whose values, perhaps even whose righteousness, was based on their faith—probably. Wouldn't have to be. You can be moral without religious faith, you can be an atheist, but for the most part, these values are based on faith. But the objective of the Constitution is not to be a righteous country; even George Washington said that America is by no means a Christian nation. But these folks say America is a Christian nation. When this kind of thing happens—when the objective becomes righteousness and not good moral governance—we begin to demonize people who don't agree with us. To me that's the great malignancy in American politics. It's not new, of course, but it seems to be particularly virulent right now. I don't think they'd put up with that attitude in companies, because the governance is much more tightly focused. Yet, because of that tight focus, it does allow egomaniacal top-down management to have free rein, whereas that only goes so far in politics before you throw them out. There are shadow sides to both!

LARRY SPEARS: *Do you recall when you first discovered Greenleaf's writings and what it was you first read?*

JAMES AUTRY: I think it was in the mid to late 1980s, at the Foundation for Community Encouragement, which was Scott Peck's organization. I met several people, and one of them, Will Clarkson was his name, first recommended Greenleaf's work to me.

LARRY SPEARS: *Can you speak briefly to your understanding of servant-leadership and what it means to you?*

JAMES AUTRY: First, understand that when I talk about servant-leadership I usually pair it—because I'm bringing it to business audiences who may have never heard of it before, who don't know The Greenleaf Center—I usually pair it with these terms: *being useful* and *being a resource.* The leader's responsibility, or one of them, is to ensure that the people have the resources that they need to do the work to accomplish the objectives, and the principal resource of the people is you, the leader. You have to serve the people and to think of yourself as a resource, as a servant to them. That's almost exactly the language I use when I'm talking to them.

So, I never stand up and say, "I'm going to speak now about servant-leadership." For one, I find that people who are biblically literate immediately think of the Bible, which is okay. Some, who are more literate than biblically literal, tend to think of it in ways that I don't think are particularly helpful. And others who connect it to the Bible begin to think, "Oh, it's going to be about religion." So I don't say I'm going to talk about servant-leadership. Instead I talk about leadership, and then I use what I think are the precepts of being a servant-leader.

The number one precept is, "I am here to serve, to create the community in which you can do the work that you do in order to achieve the objectives and results we are all trying to achieve together. My principal job is to serve you." What does that mean? That means, in my view, to be the kind of leader who does the five things I said before. Project authenticity and vulnerability, be present, be accepting, and see your role as being useful, as being the servant. I think it's all the techniques we talk about; it's always operating, making every decision from a basis of values, what's the right thing to do, not what's the expedient thing to do. Perhaps not even what's the most profitable thing to do, but what's the right thing to do. To me, it is a confluence of morality, which derives for the most part from my faith. Incidentally, I often find that atheists respond to the word *spirituality*. So it's a confluence of spirituality and work.

I don't usually try to go beyond that. For one, I wouldn't know how, and two, the imperative of my work is always making myself useful to the people I'm presenting to. I don't think of myself as there to entertain them or tell them what to do, but to be helpful and useful. When people hire me, what I say to them is, "Look, I want to be useful, so I want to know what your objectives for me are." And I always say—and this is not bravado—"If at the end of it all I haven't been useful, don't pay me!" Everything I write about, everything I talk about in these books is servant-leadership, but I don't know if I can come up with a nifty, clean definition of it. But that's the general realm of vocabulary that I work in when I'm talking on these subjects. And I always recommend your books.

JOHN NOBLE: *I wanted to ask you something about your poetry, and the process of writing your poems. How much is inspiration and how much perspiration? Do you have an idea that you write a poem about, or do the words form and you write the poem?*

JAMES AUTRY: The answer is "d": all of the above! Sometimes I get a good line and it just comes to me. Other times it's an idea, and other times it's a theme that I want to do something about that kind of percolates, percolates, percolates. It always emerges as an idea or a line. That's the inspiration part.

The greatest discovery that I made about poetry, back in the 1970s when I first started writing it, is that it yields to good craftsmanship, it yields to editing and to all the mechanics I learned as a journalist and a writer. For years I thought it just came, that it's very mystical, you get it down on paper, and you don't mess with it very much. But you do. You sometimes turn it upside down and write it in five or six different ways. I've thrown out whole sections of a poem. One of the things you learn about poetry is the least said the better. It's not about how many words you can use; it's about how few words you can use, how can you get the message, evoke the idea, the imagery, the emotion in as few words as possible.

William Faulkner once said that the most difficult thing to write is poetry, and the next most difficult is short stories. The easiest is the novel. I've never written a novel, so I've not found that to be true. I sometimes carry slips of paper around in my pocket, and I'll write lines of poetry on them and carry them around. I work on a poem and carry it in my pocket. I write my prose on a word-processor, but I always write poetry by hand. There's something about the click, click, click that destroys the rhythm of the poetry, the words. I lose the rhythm of the words. So I write poetry by hand.

JOHN NOBLE: *What do you think are the poems that you've written that folk will remember you by?*

JAMES AUTRY: Well, I guess I have to choose several. The poem I'm going to be most remembered by in business is "On Firing a Salesman." It's been anthologized in more books in more different languages, appeared in more settings than any poem I've ever written, and I always read it because it seems to grab people. Second in the business world would be "Threads." The one I'll be most remembered for in the South comes from my first book, *Nights Under a Tin Roof*, and it's called "Death in the Family." I think in the disability community, where I've written a lot of poetry, the one I'll be most remembered for is "Leo."

JOHN NOBLE: *At the beginning of* Love and Profit *you quote Rabindranath Tagore. Has he been an influence in your work?*

JAMES AUTRY: I wouldn't say he's been an influence. It's hard to say who is and who isn't, because almost everything I read has some influence, down deep somewhere. But Tagore I admire, his work and philosophy and a lot of what he's written and said. I love the mystical poetry. I love Rumi's work very much, I'm very taken with it. His work is both love poetry and mystical spiritual poetry, and he talks about the beloved. He's often talking about God, the mystery, and the ineffable, and he mentions Jesus by name in a lot of his poetry, even though he's a Sufi poet. He writes a good deal about religion. I love Rumi's work; it is so spare.

I continue to write poetry. I've gotten back into it a lot more lately, and I've written quite a bit about my son and his autism, as well as other matters. But my work seems to be moving very much more toward the spiritual relationship with God. It's not direct. I've written a new poem called "Death Bed Meditation." My beloved sister-in-law died this year very suddenly from cancer, and that poem is all I really know about life that I can say in a few words.

Death Bed Meditation

All I really know about life I can say
in a few lines:
In April the small green things
will rise through the black Iowa soil
whether we're ready or not.
The Carolina wren will make her nest
in the little redwood house
my son built from a kit.
Daffodils, tulips, irises will get the attention as usual
while purslane, pig weed, and lamb's quarters
will quietly take over a place
while no one is watching.
In June the corn shoots
will etch long green lines
across the dark loamy fields
and the greenest of all green grasses
will crowd into the ditches and line the roads.
In August the early bloomers
begin to burn themselves out,

but in September the late yellows appear,
luring the bumblebees and yellowjackets
into a frenzy of pollination.
You already know about October,
the color, the last burst of extravagant life.
And then all at once it seems
everything retreats, pulls into itself, rests,
and prepares for the inevitable resurrection.

JOHN NOBLE: *Is there a song or a poem, or even a line that someone else wrote that you wished you had written?*

JAMES AUTRY: Oh, gosh. You know, it's popular to say, "I wish I'd written that" or "I wish I'd said that," but it gets a little close to envy. What I'm more likely to say is I wish I could write *like* that, I wish I could achieve that sense of excellence and the ability to polish my words, find the right word, put them together in such a way to evoke the emotional response in other people that that person has evoked in me. But sure, I've said, "Gosh! I wish I'd written that sentence" about Rumi's work, the work of Yeats, and my current favorite contemporary American poet, Mary Oliver. "The Summer Day"—now there's a poem I wish I'd had the talent to write. Genius stuff. So, yes, there are poets whose work and talent I immensely admire and I hope that I can achieve work that is of this quality.

LARRY SPEARS: *Do you have a different approach in writing poetry rather than prose? And do you have greater satisfaction in doing one or the other?*

JAMES AUTRY: I really don't. I get a great deal of satisfaction out of doing either one well. If I've crafted an essay that I think is particularly satisfying and good, I get as much satisfaction from that as I do from poetry. So I don't have a preference. Sometimes the message determines the form. I was going to write an essay about the experience of taking Communion to the shut-ins for the church.

One of our jobs as elders was to take it out to the shut-ins, these elderly people, and I was going to write an essay about it, but it turned into a poem almost on its own.

LARRY SPEARS: *You spent the better part of a lifetime as an editor. Did you have any kind of philosophical approach to the art of editing in a general sense that you have followed?*

JAMES AUTRY: There are certain parallels with being a manager and being an editor, in that the fundamental objective is to bring out the best of people's own work, not to impose your own work on it. That goes right back to asking the question "What would you do?" So, there's that parallel.

But I think my philosophical approach as an editor was to do no harm, to try to find the essence of the good work there, and to help lead people to making their work the best it could be without my rewriting it. Sometimes I've had to just go in and rewrite something because the writer was blocked, or tunnel-visioned about it, or something, but my philosophy generally was to try to see the essence of what the work was and to bring this out. Sometimes it took a little bit of fiddling, or sometimes going back and conferring with the writer, and sitting down and discussing it and having the writer redo it. But always my objective was to have the writer himself or herself bring out the best that was in there. A good editor—and I think I was a competent editor, I certainly don't think I was a great editor, on the other hand the kind of editing I was doing was not heavy literature—I think the good editor has the ability to see into that work, has to get through the words and see what's there, and then determine whether the words are adequately bringing out what is there.

Words are filters, really. Once you put a word on something, you fix it. If I say something is superb or something is good, that may mean it's superb or good, but it also means it is only that. What else is it? Put more words on it, and pretty soon you put new words on it, and then it doesn't mean anything anymore. It's nothing because it's everything, and you can't be everything. It is a constant frustration for writers to realize that words are filters. Yet we don't have another way to get the emotions of my heart into your heart, except through words. So I've got to use words, realizing that they're always going to be inadequate for what I really want to achieve, but I'm trying to make them the best they can be. Oftentimes a writer falls so in love with his filters that the essence of what the writer is trying to accomplish gets mangled or camouflaged or overfiltered. The good editor will see through these filters, see what's really there, and help the writer bring it out. So my philosophy is that editing is very much like management: helping people do their best work. It's in there, look for it, give them the tools, help them, and on the rare occasions, do it for them. Sometimes I had to rewrite something. Most often it wasn't because of a writer's lack of talent, it was frustration or blockage. Who knows? Writers are like everybody else— funny creatures!

LARRY SPEARS: *What's your sense on how a leader gets better at developing a servant's heart, and how to view oneself as a servant to others?*

JAMES AUTRY: To me, the road to servanthood has to be, almost by definition, a road away from ego. I think developing the servant's heart—you know if we want to, we could shift this over to Buddhism and say *path* of heart—that path of heart, that move to the servant's heart is a move away from ego. I think it has to be done in the context of one's own spiritual development, spiritual growth, the spiritual disciplines I mentioned before, and by reading other spiritual disciplines and picking heroes, picking people you think are the spiritual heroes, those who emulate how you would like to be, and following these models, letting them be mentors, even though they may have lived hundreds of years ago.

I think Jesus is a terrific model, but I think a lot of the interpretations of Christianity distort that model of servant-leadership. We see it manifest as judgment, manifest as trying to control people's lives, how they live, and what they believe. Here's what Jesus says to me as a role model: The strictures and structures of orthodoxy and hierarchy work against the human spirit, they work against the relationship with God, with the ultimate, with the mystery, the ineffable. And I think he said that, and lived that, over and over again, and he died for that. I like to tell the story of the Good Samaritan to people who want to listen because I want to tell it the way I really think it is, in a way I don't think biblical scholars might say it.

This person lying by the side of the road is ignored by the high priests and the church people, not because they're not compassion-ate people, but because the purity code prohibited even being in the same room as a dead person or touching a dead person, and you were unclean if you touched a dead person under the Hebrew purity code. Jesus was saying, "Look, you take the code so far, you lose all your compassion and connection. For fear of breaking the rule you won't even save a person's life." Along comes the Samaritan—and you know who the Samaritan would be today? The good Samaritan could be the good Communist, the good Nazi, the good Ku Klux Klan member, the good whore: whoever you perceive to be the very opposite of you. The Samaritan was the very opposite of the people Jesus was telling the story to. This is a powerful message to me about not letting the rules keep you from doing the compassionate thing, the right thing, the thing from your heart.

I think there are lots of other examples of the beatitudes being a wonderful message for us all. I think Jesus is a wonderful role model for servant-leadership, and he was a teacher. That's another thing I've left out of being a servant-leader. You don't hand down the poli-cies; you are a good teacher and a good mentor. Jesus was a teacher. He wasn't anybody's boss. He got angry a couple of times, said some sharp things, and I think that's proof of his humanity. You could also look to the Buddha, to the prophet Mohammed, or to Moses; there are leaders and role models in all these faith traditions. My point is, whatever your faith, whatever your spiritual orientation, whatever your interest in wisdom literature, there are heroes there, there are lessons there, there are teachings there. I think you have to be active and intentional about exploring them—in the right way—not to become indoctrinated but to become educated. It's not about trying to find something to help you be a more effective leader. It's about trying to be a better person. The other will follow.

Any time people want to focus on my work, servant-leadership, or other values as a way to get better results, it's critical to start from the right place. You sincerely have to start with what *you yourself are wanting to become*, the being and becoming of you. To me that's what the servant's heart is about. I think it's like every other spiritual discipline or interest, I think it's all a matter of becoming. I like the scholars who say that if we really translated the first verse of the Bible, grammatically in English, it can't be done, there's no grammatical parallel. It's written in the present continuing tense, not the past tense. It's not "In the beginning God created the Heavens and the Earth," it's "In the beginning God is creating the Heavens and the Earth." It changes the whole context when you think about it that way. So I think that the path to the servant's heart is a never-ending path. You don't ever get there, but the journey is the objective.

5

Servant-Leadership and Philanthropic Institutions

John C. Burkhardt, Larry C. Spears

Consider the following list of leadership authorities: James Autry, Warren Bennis, Ken Blanchard, Peter Block, Stephen Covey, Max DePree, Peter Drucker, Frances Hesselbein, Joe Jaworski, Jim Kouzes, M. Scott Peck, Peter Senge, Peter Vaill, Margaret Wheatley, and Danah Zohar. What do these authors have in common? All of them have been explicitly or implicitly influenced by the writings of Robert K. Greenleaf, and these and many other leadership authors are increasingly calling attention to the growing influence of Greenleaf's concept of servant-leadership.

The concept of servant-leadership sounds so paradoxical. What is it, and how can it enhance our understanding and practice of philanthropy as we enter a new century? Over the past decade we have experienced a significant trend toward values, ethics, and service-based leadership within many philanthropic organizations. A growing number of leadership education programs now focus on servant-leadership. A few of the notable advocates of servant-leadership in philanthropy and fundraising are James Gregory Lord (author, *The Raising of Money*), John Lore (former board chair, National Society of Fund Raising Executives), Milton Murray (Philanthropic Service for Institutions), Betty Overton (former staff member, W.K. Kellogg Foundation), Robert Payton (The Center on Philanthropy), the late Henry Rosso (The Fund Raising School),

Janet Haas (William Penn Foundation), the late James Shannon (Council on Foundations), and Susan Wisely (former staff member, Lilly Endowment).

Characteristics of the Servant-Leader

The following characteristics are considered central to the development of servant-leaders.

1. *Listening:* Leaders have traditionally been valued for their communication and decision-making skills. Servant-leaders reinforce these important skills with a focus on listening intently and reflectively to others in order to identify and clarify the will of a group of people.

2. *Empathy:* Servant-leaders strive to understand and empathize with others. They accept and recognize others for their unique gifts and spirits, assuming the good intentions of coworkers and not rejecting them as people.

3. *Healing:* Learning how to help heal difficult situations is a powerful force for transforming organizations. Servant-leaders recognize that they have an opportunity to help make whole those people and institutions with whom they come in contact.

4. *Persuasion:* Another characteristic of servant-leaders is a reliance upon persuasion rather than positional authority in making organizational decisions. Servant-leaders seek to convince others, rather than coercing compliance. They are effective at building consensus within groups.

5. *Awareness:* General awareness, and especially self-awareness, strengthens servant-leaders. Awareness aids them in understanding issues involving ethics and values, and it enables them to approach situations from a more integrated, holistic position.

6. *Foresight:* The ability to foresee the likely outcome of a given situation is a characteristic that enables the servant-leader to

understand the lessons from the past, the realities of the present, and likely consequences of a decision for the future. It is deeply rooted within the intuitive mind.

7. *Conceptualization:* Servant-leaders seek to nurture their abilities to dream great dreams. This means that they must be able to think beyond day-to-day management realities.

8. *Commitment to the growth of people:* Servant-leaders believe that people have an intrinsic value beyond their tangible contributions as workers. Accordingly, servant-leaders are deeply committed to the personal, professional, and spiritual growth of everyone within an organization.

9. *Stewardship:* Greenleaf's view of organizations was one in which CEOs, staff members, and trustees all play significant roles in holding their institutions in trust for the greater good of society. In effect, everyone has a responsibility for being a good steward within an organization.

10. *Building community:* Servant-leaders seek to build a sense of community among those within an organization. Greenleaf said in "The Servant as Leader," "All that is needed to rebuild community as a viable life form for large numbers of people is for enough servant-leaders to show the way, not by mass movements, but by each servant-leader demonstrating his or her own unlimited liability for a quite specific community-related group."

Servant-Leadership and the Moral Responsibilities of Philanthropic Organizations

What are the implications of Greenleaf's writings for the work of philanthropic organizations? This is not a new topic to either the servant-leadership movement or to U.S. foundations. During Robert Greenleaf's life he served as an adviser to several U.S. foundations, and he practiced philanthropy on a personal basis as well. Not only have his writings inspired many within the field, it is clear that many of his writings were themselves inspired by the problems, the processes, and the responsibilities of organized philanthropic work.

But the field of philanthropy is growing and changing, along with the society it seeks to serve. Philanthropic resources and efforts have expanded for most of the last decade and the types of issues addressed by philanthropies, and the approaches to address them, have become more complex and, in many ways, more aggressive. There has also been an increase in the number of new foundations established, and many of these have been started by individuals new to philanthropy. Beginning in the 1980s, U.S. foundations began to take a closer look at the impact of their efforts. Program evalua- tion became more common and more sophisticated. Social prob- lems that had been identified in the preceding twenty to thirty years still loomed and the trustees of philanthropic organizations began to question the efficacy of quasi-charitable investments. Within the foundation community (and within government policy circles as well) the reliance on demonstration models as catalysts for larger social change objectives came into question. Increasingly, founda- tions began to focus efforts on defined initiatives through which spe- cific changes would be sought for identified issues.

This new direction, while not a universal trend, substantially describes the field. Moreover, it raises some questions about the role that philanthropic institutions play as leaders in a changing society. The trend suggests a need to examine the writings of Greenleaf and others who have thought about the roles of service and leadership as being intertwined and interdependent. Characteristics of servant- leadership hold special meaning when applied by philanthropic institutions.

Listening

It begins with listening. Greenleaf reminds us that leaders have a special responsibility to remain attentive to the voice of those they serve. Philanthropies must make extra efforts to minimize the barriers to communication that separate them from the constituencies and communities in which they work. This is a special challenge given the perceptions held—and the realities, too—of the relative distribution of power in relationships with potential and current grantees.

As the work of philanthropic institutions becomes increasingly focused on strategic initiatives, a great deal of effort has been placed on "getting the message out" about foundation efforts within society. To support this work, several major foundations have recruited talented individuals to serve as communication consultants, or have developed in-house communication capacity to support their programming initiatives. Greenleaf offers us something to think about in this regard in his essay "The Servant as Leader," drawing upon the prayer of St. Francis of Assisi, "Grant that I may not seek first to be understood, but to understand."

Listening, as Greenleaf pointed out many times, is an attitude. It is rooted in a genuine interest in the viewpoints and perspectives of those served. This observation has two very real implications for philanthropic work. One can be seen in the internal practices of the philanthropic process as found in many established institutions; the other is a challenge to the role that philanthropy plays in the larger society. The process by which philanthropic organizations come to decisions is often based on a series of questions framed and raised by the institution, to which grantees are invited to respond (invited in the sense that if the grantee stops responding the relationship is ended). Throughout this interaction, the philanthropy sets the pace and the context of the discussion, poses the questions, and evaluates the responses. If this is a process of dialogue, it hardly constitutes listening in the sense that Greenleaf describes. Instead, he challenges us to maintain "an openness within the widest possible frame of reference" when it comes to interaction with those we seek to lead and serve.[1]

Philanthropies have a special responsibility that goes beyond listening for themselves: to lift up and amplify the voices of those who are unheard within society. The unique circumstances of established philanthropic organizations give them a place and a stature in American society. This privilege comes with a responsibility to make sure that the dialogue that creates our public consensus is inclusive of voices that are often lost. At the end of Greenleaf's essay in which he speaks of the responsibilities of trustees in philanthropic organizations, he quotes Abraham Joshua Heschel, "All worlds are in need of exaltation, and everyone is charged to lift what is low, to unite what lies apart, to advance what is left behind." Or, as suggested by the Tuscarora Indian proverb, "Man has responsibility, not power."[2]

Empathy

It is entirely appropriate that Greenleaf begins his description of servant-leadership with a discussion of the importance of listening. Only through that act can we access the other qualities important to servant-leadership, most notably that of empathy. In his essay "The Servant as Leader," Greenleaf combines a discussion of the importance of empathy by building a contrast with the idea of acceptance.

> These are two interesting words, acceptance and empathy. If we can take one dictionary's definition, *acceptance* is receiving what is offered, with approbation, satisfaction, or acquiescence, and *empathy* is the imaginative projection of one's own consciousness into another being. The opposite of both, the word *reject*, is to refuse to hear or receive—to throw out.[3]

Philanthropic organizations are, to a large extent, organized around rituals of acceptance and rejection. Prospective grantees approach foundations with proposals in hopes of having them accepted. Foundation officials review proposals with the responsibility to recommend either acceptance or rejection. The very word *grant* implies a relationship between foundations and their primary constituencies (grantees) that is far more closely associated with Greenleaf's observations about acceptance in contrast to empathy.

It is a matter of fact that foundations receive far more proposals than can possibly be funded, and therefore program staff and trustees are unavoidably in a position to make judgments about the relative merits associated with ideas. This occupation with judging ideas can easily (and some may say necessarily) lead to a preoccupation with judging people. And when one is limited to seeing people solely in terms of the needs that they bring, as opposed to their values, assets, and strengths, it is predictable that one would begin to see them as self-interested, self-serving, and weak.

In a talk with faculty at Barnard College in 1960, Greenleaf spoke to the importance of maintaining an empathetic connection between those in positions of influence and those whom they are required, by circumstance, to judge. While his contextual reference is the classroom, the concept translates easily enough to the work of philanthropic organizations. Referring to the cultivation of servant-leadership under conditions in which power is unevenly distributed within a relationship, he said: "Finally there is a developing *view of people*. *All* people are seen as beings to be trusted, believed in, and loved, and less as objects to be used, competed with, or judged."

As a former director of human resources at AT&T, Greenleaf spoke frequently of the importance of empathy as a quality at work inside organizations as well. He admonished organizational leaders to trust in their own employees and to organize work in ways that created conditions in which employees learned to respect, trust, and value one another. It is difficult to expect foundation staff to identify and empathize with others when they experience leaders and organizational cultures that fail to treat them as worthy and valuable individuals.

Healing

Can philanthropic organizations really make claim to a healing role in the societies they serve? Only if they enact this healing role in the context of involvement and engaged partnership described previously. Society's characterization of healing and the role of the healer often suggest, at best, a dispassionate and detached outsider whose views of health are imposed on the stricken. But worse, as Ivan Illich argues in *Medical Nemesis*, the healer can be a most serious threat to health by fostering a relationship of false dependence or by contributing to "an industry of despair."[4] Greenleaf acknowledges this risk of "giving as a potentially immoral act" in his essay on the role of trustees in foundations, a dynamic directly at odds with his view of leadership as service to promote the autonomy of those served, and his view of healing, as well.[5]

Greenleaf's challenge to serve in a healing role is meant in a very different way and begins with a commitment to heal one's self. The best efforts of philanthropy to deal with racism, improve opportunity, promote peace, or build community can not succeed unless those efforts are reflected internally as well as externally. The implications for foundation hiring practices, trustee selection, strategic orientation, decision-making procedures, and communication approaches are obvious. Less clear but equally important are considerations about investment decisions, the style and location of corporate offices, and even the internal relationships and practices that create a sense of the organizational culture.

Foundations do have a unique opportunity to provide leadership in the ongoing process of reconciliation, which is the basis for a working civil society within the United States. As a society, we often debate the relative merits of *pluribus* versus *unum*, as if we had a choice of being either "many" or "one." Organized philanthropy in the United States has the opportunity to bridge this false dichotomy and to promote respect for differences while at the same time building connections between people, ideas, and resources.

Persuasion

Perhaps no servant-leadership role comes as naturally to organized philanthropy as that of Greenleaf's description of persuasion. Greenleaf uses this term to distinguish between leadership that relies on positional authority and coercion, in contrast to leadership that works through a process of influence, example, and moral power.

It is worth examining the role of philanthropy in terms of the classic theories of leadership that operated at the time of Greenleaf's career and during the period of his early writing. Leadership authority, as viewed in the prevailing models, was based on three sources of power: rational grounds, traditional grounds, and charismatic grounds.[6] Rational power derived from positional status within a formal (hierarchical) structure. Traditional power was rooted in cultural relationships of an "immemorial" nature. Charismatic power, the closest analog to leadership authority vested in influence rather than the status of the leader, was reserved to a "certain quality of an individual . . . set apart from ordinary men . . . endowed with supernatural, superhuman, or at least specifically exceptional powers . . . not accessible to the ordinary person, but . . . regarded as of divine origin."[7]

Greenleaf was entirely familiar with this formulation of leadership and used it as an organizing structure for his essay "The Leadership Crisis" in 1978. He goes beyond the Weberian construction of power and describes the concept of persuasive authority and also introduces the concept of the persuasive power of institutions.

Consider the role of foundations in U.S. society in light of the classic conception of authority. They enjoy no direct coercive authority over government policy at any level. Corporations have greater access to formal resources and exercise a greater influence on economic and community circumstances within society. Foundations are specifically proscribed from lobbying and do not have the power of the vote. They do not enjoy the benefits of a direct constituency, have no means to directly foster civil unrest, or even, in most cases, provide direct, hands-on, and face-to-face service to anyone. Even the amount of resources controlled by U.S. foundations is generally overstated: Of all the charitable giving that occurs in the United States each year, only about 1 percent comes from foundations. By far the largest share of philanthropy originates with gifts made by individuals.

And yet few would argue that philanthropies lack influence. The means by which this influence is actualized comes, by and large, through the persuasive power of which Greenleaf writes. The tools of philanthropy are meager in some respects: demonstration models, support for promising projects, resources to the fledgling, some research, the rare but occasional bequest for a building or institute. The power to influence society comes in part from the ideas these efforts embody and the potential they hold. The persuasive power of foundations is rooted in many small things that take on larger significance because of the way they come into being.

Awareness

Greenleaf wrote of awareness and of the need to see things as interconnected whole systems long before the current discussion on systemic leadership began. Thought leaders in the field of "the new science" of leadership—Wheatley, Senge, Jaworski, and others—all give credit to Greenleaf's perception of the essential interdependence of events and causes, problems and solutions.

But translating the concept of individual knowledge, the process of "knowing," and the role that Greenleaf describes as the "leader as seeker" to an institutional perspective requires some adaptation. How do institutions create an attitude of awareness? How would this value and behavior be expressed on an organizational basis?

Senge's often-cited description of the "learning organization" is probably consistent with Greenleaf's view of awareness as translated to a foundation setting. The learning organization is one characterized by openness, freedom of expression, and a focused curiosity in which learning becomes practiced as both a central value and a core competency. Foundations that systematically examine the impact of their own efforts and the environments in which they take place, and adjust their efforts accordingly, are examples of this commitment.

To fully accept awareness as a chosen characteristic of organizational life means to come face-to-face with uncertainty and ambiguity. These are not descriptors easily associated with the culture of U.S. foundations: in fact, often the opposite is true. If one were to plot the predisposition of foundations as we sometimes do with people, along the lines of an organizational Myers-Briggs scale, we would describe foundations as "judging" as opposed to "perceiving" in their approach to the organization of their work. Proposals are reviewed and accepted for funding—or rejected. Foundation executives and staff are often chosen and evaluated on the basis of their good judgment, as opposed to the breadth of their perceptions. Awareness is often a secondary characteristic in the foundation environment. Greater value is placed on objectivity, detachment, or expert knowledge.

Philanthropic work is absorbing, even fascinating. This fact makes it all the more important that those engaged in these efforts fight the tendency toward preoccupation with the process of making grants, or worse, an obsession with organizational issues that comes at the expense of an awareness of those who are to be served. If anything, the emphasis on strategy and alignment as the basis for effectiveness on the part of organized philanthropy can blind us to real conditions and real challenges that exist in the larger society.

Foresight

Philanthropic organizations lead a rather divided existence as relates to the concept of time. In many cases, particularly among the nation's most established foundations, the resources for philanthropic work derive from a decision that was made some time in the past, often by individuals (or in many cases a family of individuals) often no longer involved in the active management of their benefaction. The bequests were made in a specific social context and guided by a set of time-related perspectives and values, sometimes with a specific set of social conditions or objectives in mind. This is the way in which many of the United States' largest foundations were created, and their names should remind us that actual, historical individuals made decisions some time ago that allow the work of these organizations to go forward: Ford, Rockefeller, Kellogg, Carnegie, Lilly, Mott, and many others.

But these gifts, while made in the past, were given with the future in mind. At the very heart of philanthropy is the responsibility to take the past and present forward into the future. Those charged with managing the resources derived from a gift made in a previous era are also charged with trying to understand and interpret the intentions and wishes of individuals who, in most cases, had no idea of the circumstances in which the philanthropies that bear their names would operate. For this reason, it is a mistake for those engaged in this work to limit their perspective to the question of how the donor's wishes might be interpreted if he or she were alive at present. The real task is to accept the challenge that the original donor took on: to commit resources now, not with the present in mind but with the future in mind.

Greenleaf speaks of this paradox in his essay "The Servant as Leader," an idea that he first articulated in his 1969 lecture to the students and faculty at Dartmouth College: "Let us liken *now* to the spread of light from a narrowly focused beam. There is a bright intense center, this moment of clock time, and a diminishing intensity, theoretically out to infinity, on either side. As viewed here, now includes all of this—all of history and all of the future."

The mechanics of philanthropic work within our largest foundations involve great use of trend and analytic data, intended to get a fix on the current environment. Great store is placed on the ability of foundation staff and trustees to understand and interpret the challenges that face the societies they serve. Greenleaf reminds us that leadership in this field is equally a creative act, prospective in nature. "Foresight is the 'lead' the leader has," and those who fail to relate their actions to the future soon lose their ability to contribute as leaders, no matter their endowment.

It is not too much to say that organized philanthropies have a special responsibility to represent and protect the future within U.S. society. They do not have to publish earnings reports or return profits to stockholders. They do not have to stand for reelection. In most cases, they have no need to appeal for public support. They have but one true constituency: the future. Philanthropy would do well to consider the test placed on decisions within the Native American tradition, a concern not merely for the present but for seven generations to come.

Conceptualization

The work of philanthropy takes place in a world that is increasingly glutted with information and yet starved for meaning. While Greenleaf's writings were based on organizational life in a very different era, he nonetheless articulated a belief that leaders have a unique responsibility to search for and articulate coherence for the groups they lead. True to the themes that run through his work, he argued that this is a process that is both intellectual and spiritual, and that rather than being the solitary gift of a leader working in isolation from peers, the process of conceptualization is rooted in relationships and shared meanings.

If Greenleaf were writing today, we could not be certain that he would have framed the distinction between conceptual and operational leadership in just the same way that he did when he wrote his essay "The Institution as Servant" in 1972. His stated view that conceptualization is the unique gift of leaders at the top of a hierarchical organization has been challenged by advances in the ways in which information becomes available and is put to use, by the pace of change within organizations, and by the general trend to flatten organizational structures, placing greater responsibility and adaptive capacity into more hands. But his central idea, that leaders effectively create the group by having a primary role in defining its central purpose, is a thought very appropriate to the current situation.

When ideas of all sorts flash through the marketplace of consciousness, the tendency is to associate no idea with much meaning, knowing that another will soon replace it. In fact, the preoccupation of the media with (literally) *news*—that is, only what is new and different—supports a culture where all ideas are transitory and hold equal nonimportance. Within this milieu, the leader's role is to help in the recognition of "a great hope held in common" (to use Teilhard de Chardin's phrase), and to literally "make meaning" with and on behalf of the group being led.

This process of meaning-making is very much related to the current preoccupation in our business and political leadership literature with the idea of "vision." Unfortunately, vision has become identified as an attribute enjoyed by leaders, rather than a process that engages leaders and followers together. Despite Greenleaf's description of conceptualization as a "prime talent" of leaders, it might be seen in its larger context to be a "way," rather than an innate quality or even a skill, one that binds individuals and ideas in a common commitment.

Philanthropic work is increasingly attentive to this responsibility of leadership. Where once the processes of grantmaking seemed reactive and distant, there are increasing attempts to engage collectively in the definition of problems and strategies. Philanthropic organizations can begin by looking at their own hierarchies and the ways in which they are infused with "common purpose," the degree to which this sense of commitment is the result of open interaction and a shared construction of meaning inside and outside the organization.

Commitment to the Growth of People

Robert Greenleaf offered a significant departure from most models of leadership when he spoke of leaders as servants to others. Previous writing in the field of leadership extant at the time of Greenleaf's essays placed the leader at the center of interaction with followers. Leaders directed, followers responded. Leaders brought unique gifts, talents, and aspirations to their interactions. Followers were agents, generally indistinguishable one from another and valued for their compliance, not their potential. In fact, given the logic of a single leader at the top of a structured hierarchy, followers with a penchant for high achievement were potential threats in the long run.

Greenleaf turned this thinking upside down. His challenge to leaders was to put the needs of followers first and to subject their leadership to this test: "Do those served grow as persons? Do they, while being served, become healthier, wiser, freer, more autonomous, more likely themselves to become servants?"

This may be the heart of Greenleaf's message, and it is a direct reflection of the choices that Robert Greenleaf made in his career at AT&T. He came to see his role, enacted over many years and in relationship with many colleagues, as a commitment to the growth of people. This was, to him, a high calling.

Foundations view their missions in the context of a similar commitment but are often challenged by the temptation to define themselves in terms of the issues they address or the aspirations they hold. It is a difficult discipline to consider philanthropic investments as commitments to people, not problems. Such a focus places an entirely different perspective on the conceptualization of the work. "Who is served? How? Is this the way in which they would choose to be served?"

And most troubling: "How do we measure the impact of what we do?" If our commitment is to the growth of individuals, our evaluation of impact will be guided by very different considerations. We would look for measurable improvement in the lives of individuals, in their opportunities, their capacities, the relief of their pain and the maximization of their potential. The work of philanthropies would be changed in many fundamental ways if individual people—not social problems, not economic, political, or environmental circumstances—were at the heart of the effort.

Stewardship

One definition of stewardship, offered by Peter Block, is "holding something in trust for another." In a very direct way, this is the exact role of philanthropies in the United States, and it plays out in multiple ways.

Those wealthy individuals who created our large foundations chose to place their wealth in the hands of a (literally) trusted organization that would in turn act on some responsibility in the founder's stead. These founders' decisions, taken at different points and by different individuals over the last hundred years, had this same fundamental intention: to establish a stewardship over the resources of the philanthropist that would outlive the benefactor. This has a direct impact—and should—on the decisions taken by officers and trustees of foundations as they act on a historic trust in a modern context.

The concept of stewardship operates in a second, arguably more important way. The wealth that created our nation's foundations was sheltered from further taxation by the decision to establish a continuing public philanthropy. In this regard, it is a resource that is held in trust for society every bit as much as it is held on behalf of the original benefactor. If taxed, most of the benefice provided by Henry Ford or W. K. Kellogg or Andrew Carnegie would have long been redistributed to others through tax policy. Bluntly, it would be gone—or at least impossible to find. No doubt it might have done some good, but the fact that it is still in an identifiable *corpus*, still associated with the work of a specific organization, is the result of an intentional provision in the public law. In this interpretation, foundations operate as stewards for a public interest. They hold resources on behalf of society.

This responsibility is complete with challenges and obligations, and as Greenleaf points out, its own moral dilemmas. In his extended parable, *Teacher as Servant*, he describes the situation of a foundation executive faced with the evidence that his organization has been less than effective and, worse yet, less than vigilant. Greenleaf makes it clear by his construction of dialogue in this lesson that the temptation to let "giving [become] a potentially immoral act" is manifest in the sin of inaction just as much as in action. The many layers of insulation that protect the foundation from its direct public accountability cannot ameliorate the moral responsibility that comes through an existential basis in stewardship.

Building Community

Even though Greenleaf spent much of his professional life in the context of one of America's largest corporations, he maintained a deep sense of the importance of community in the lives of people. Greenleaf spoke often about the influence of a sociology professor who, during Greenleaf's senior year in college, challenged him to get involved in one of the big institutions of society and to do what he could to turn the institution into a vehicle for service. Over the course of Greenleaf's career, he learned that no organization could be oriented to serve if it lacked its own sense of internal cohesion and purpose. Therefore the first challenge for an organized philanthropy is to seek community from within.

"All that is needed to rebuild community as a viable life form for large numbers of people is for enough servant-leaders to show the way, not by mass movements, but by each servant-leader demonstrating his own liability for a quite specific community-related group," wrote Greenleaf.[8]

A sense of community within a foundation is not an end in itself but rather a means of drawing upon an immediate experience in order to more plainly promote it within the larger society. The leadership that is at the heart of philanthropic work is leadership directed to the creation of community. In "The Ethic of Strength," Greenleaf speaks of requirements for leadership that should be nurtured in the young leader. Among them is the need to ask, "Am I connected?" While the question is posed in the context of a young person's self-examination, Greenleaf's elaboration is appropriate to the modern philanthropic organization. Connectedness suggests the ability to be at once "on the growing edge of the contemporary phase of history but still connected to the main body of people and events."[9]

How is this accomplished? The key maybe is found in Greenleaf's admonition to live and operate in an integrated way. Foundations must make a determined effort to be both state-of-the-art and state-of-the-heart in relationship to those they wish to lead. With access to expert staff and a world of eager consultants, they must discipline their efforts to build and honor bonds with people at all levels and from many perspectives within the society they serve. And this is only the start.

Foundations must set a vision for community that goes beyond access and contact, and approach the more difficult challenge of engagement. The sense of community envisioned by Robert Greenleaf does not tolerate much self-interest, nor does it provide much in the way of shelter from real relationships with real people in real situations.

Conclusion

Public interest in the philosophy and practice of servant-leadership is now higher than ever before. Many books and articles on servant-leadership have appeared in the last ten years, and dozens of organizations have begun to incorporate servant-leadership internally. Servant-leadership has slowly but surely gained thousands of practitioners over the past thirty-five years—both inside and outside philanthropy. The seeds Bob Greenleaf first planted have begun to sprout in many philanthropic institutions, and in the hearts of people who long to improve the human condition. Servant-leadership provides a framework out of which many people today are now working to create more caring institutions. We have written this essay for those persons and institutions who wish to accept the challenge of bringing servant-leadership more fully into the twenty-first-century world of philanthropic organizations. We invite you to reflect upon this closing thought by Robert Greenleaf:

The servant-leader may be not so much the prophetic visionary (that is a rare gift) as the convener, sustainer, discerning guide for seekers who wish to remain open to prophetic visions. The maintenance functions within all sorts of institutions may not require leaders of any sort, but seekers, of which every institution should have some, must have servant-leaders.

6

On the Right Side of History

John C. Bogle

I want to mix some corporate history and some personal philosophy, and try to impart some sense of how the idealistic vision of the servant as leader, and of the leader as servant, can have—and has had—an impact on the pragmatic, dog-eat-dog competitive world of American business. I'm going to use as my example the burgeoning mutual fund industry—next to the Internet, I suppose, the fastest-growing industry in the United States—and The Vanguard Group, its fastest-growing major firm.

What is of interest, I think, is not our mere success—a word so elusive in its connotations that I use it here with considerable reluctance—but the fact that, whatever we have achieved, it has been by marching to a different drummer. Our unique corporate structure has fostered our single focus on being the servant of our fund shareholders, our disciplined attitude toward the costs that they bear, and our conservative investment strategies and concepts (many of which we created *de novo*). In remarks that I hope will be especially relevant to all of you who are interested in servant-leadership, I plan to demonstrate how so many of those concepts have served us well—implicitly to be sure, but served us well nonetheless—in bringing us to where we stand today.

The Fund Industry and Vanguard

Hesitant as I may be to do so, I must establish my bona fides, as it were, by drawing a brief sketch of the mutual fund landscape today and identifying Vanguard's position in the scene. The mutual fund industry is booming:

- Its asset base has swelled to $4.7 trillion (in 1999), compared to just $50 billion a quarter century ago—a ninetyfold increase, equivalent to a compound growth rate of 20 percent annually.

- Cash inflow from investors is running in the range of $500 billion per year, compared to an *outflow* of $290 million in 1974. Mutual funds have become the investment of choice for American families at the moment, accounting for 100 percent of net additions to the financial assets of our households.

- In 1974 the market was tumbling, with the Dow Jones Industrial Average on its way to a twelve-year low of 578. As I write, the Dow is at the 9000 level. While the *relative* returns of the average managed equity mutual fund have fallen far short of those achieved by the unmanaged market averages, the *absolute* returns of even the most mundane funds have been little short of spectacular.

- As a result of the great bull market, common stock funds are again the driving force of the industry with 53 percent of its assets, although money market funds have had their turn as the industry's largest component (75 percent of industry assets in 1981), followed by bond funds (37 percent of assets in 1986). This is a market-sensitive industry!

- The character of the industry has changed rather radically. As investors have become better educated, more aware, and more self-reliant, the no-load (no sales commission) segment of the mutual fund industry has become its largest component—surging from just 15 percent of industry assets in 1979 to 35 percent currently. In fact, the industry's two largest firms, and five of its ten largest, offer primarily—often solely—no-load funds.

Using the conventional measuring sticks, Vanguard—a firm that did not even exist before the mid-1970s—is emerging as the industry leader. We have by far the fastest growth rate of any major firm, and as a result have become one of the two largest fund organizations in the world. A scattering of measures makes the point:

- Assets recently topped $400 billion, up from $1.4 billion in the mutual funds for which we assumed responsibility at our inception in 1974—a near three-hundred-fold increase, equivalent to a compound growth rate of 27 percent.

- Cash inflow is running at a $50 billion annual rate, compared to an outflow of $52 million in 1975, an even more extreme turnabout than the industry has enjoyed.

- Typical of the industry, Vanguard funds carried sales loads at the outset. However, we abruptly made an unprecedented switch to no-load distribution in 1977, less than two years after the firm began operations. We led the industry shift to no-load dominance, and are today that segment's largest unit.

- Our market share has risen from 2 percent of industry assets in 1980 to 8 percent today, and from 9 percent of no-load assets to 24 percent—one dollar of every four invested in no-load funds.

- And, driven by our preeminence in money market funds, bond funds, conservative stock funds, and index (market-matching) funds, we currently account for fully 50 percent of the net cash flowing into no-load funds. Our three nearest rivals account for 15 percent, 7 percent, and 6 percent respectively.

My point in presenting you this context is not merely to illustrate, with what I hope is not false pride, our position in the industry but to set the stage for how and why this situation has developed, and what it says about the important principles of business ethics—so closely aligned with the principle of servant-leadership—we have established for ourselves. Most important of all, I want to strike an important and optimistic keynote: that it is possible to do well by doing good, to succeed by serving others, to lead by having principles hold sway over opportunism. Indeed it is my deeply held conviction that our principles, by creating a corporate environment that encourages us to do the right things in the right way, have placed us on the right side of history.

Turning Back the Clock

Let me now turn back the clock. In 1925—more than three-quarters of a century ago—an aging professor said to his university class, "There is a new problem in our country. We are becoming a nation that is dominated by large institutions—businesses, governments, universities—and these businesses are not serving us well. I hope that all of you will be concerned about this. But nothing of substance will happen unless people inside these institutions lead them to better performance for the public good. Some of you ought to make careers inside these big institutions and become a force for good—from the inside."

Those words could have as easily been said today. But, as some of you here today will surely recognize, they were in fact the words that inspired a college senior named Robert K. Greenleaf to cast his lot with business as a career. On graduation, he joined American Telephone and Telegraph Company (AT&T), in important measure because it was then the largest employer in our nation. He described himself as one who knew how to get things done and as a pursuer of wisdom, and his objective was to work on organizational development for the company. He worked there for nearly forty years, until he retired in 1964.

I have no way of knowing about the influence that Robert Greenleaf exerted on the AT&T organization. But the work he did after his retirement, beginning with his brilliant 1970 essay, "The Servant as Leader," has surely brought much-needed wisdom and insight to the subject of corporate and institutional leadership in the United States. And I salute with admiration the leadership of The Greenleaf Center for its extraordinary accomplishments in carrying on his crusade.

Remarkable Relevance

I must acknowledge that I did not read "The Servant as Leader" until the early 1980s, well after it had become one of a series of a dozen related essays, published in book form under the title *Servant-Leadership*. But as I read his words then, and as I read them again in preparing these remarks, I was thunderstruck by the power and relevance of his philosophy. Not merely to the great world out there, beyond my ken, but to me. To me, directly and personally, as if this man of my own parents' generation had placed me in the crosshairs of his telescopic sight, and would not rest until he captured the mind of his quarry.

Now, I hope—and indeed I suspect—that many others who have shared in his concepts feel the same way. And that acceptance, that feeling of revelation, more than anything else suggests the force of his mind and the power of his ideas. In this sense, then, the fact that he speaks to me with such relevance may be far more important than if he had in fact been directly responsible for inculcating in me the values and principles of the enterprise I founded in 1974, years before the uncanny yet powerful reinforcement I received from his accumulated wisdom.

What I want to do now is to directly quote at reasonable length some of the words that Robert Greenleaf has written (taking only the most minimal liberties in paraphrasing them), and then describe the extraordinary parallelism their spirit holds with the spirit of Vanguard. I hope in this way that I can persuade you that his dreams of long ago can not only find their way into the hard reality of the world of business, but can form the basis for a corporate success story.

I'm going to touch on five areas: his essay "Building a Model Institution"; the linkage between foresight and caring; his reflections on the superior company and on the liberating vision; a series of powerful parallel phrases; and finally, somewhat poignantly, his "Memo on Growing from Small to Large." In each case, I'll then follow with examples of how directly Robert Greenleaf's wisdom has spoken to me, and has fortuitously been manifested at Vanguard.

Building a Model Institution

In August 1974, Robert Greenleaf spoke about building a model institution. Interestingly, he was speaking, not about a business, but about a women's college affiliated with a religious order, at the celebration of its hundredth anniversary. His blueprint identified the four cornerstones:

> First, a goal, *a concept of a distinguished serving institution* in which all who accept its discipline are lifted up to nobler stature and greater effectiveness than they are likely to achieve on their own or with a less demanding discipline.

Second, *an understanding of leadership and followership*, since everyone in the institution is part leader, part follower. If an institution is to achieve as a servant, then only those who are natural servants—those who want to lift others—should be empowered to lead.

Third, an *organization structure* (or *modus operandi*) focusing on how power and authority are handled, including a discipline to help individuals accomplish not only for themselves, but for others.

Fourth, and finally, *the need for trustees*, persons in whom ultimate trust is placed, persons who stand apart from the institution with more detachment and objectivity than insiders can summon.

As it happened, Vanguard was a month away from its creation when Mr. Greenleaf spoke to this century-old institution. But our resemblance to his model is striking. Our original concept, for example, was to transform the very focus of a mutual fund business from serving two masters—something the biblical Matthew describes as, well, impossible—the fund shareholder and the owners of the funds' external manager-adviser alike. We would be the servant of the fund shareholder alone, since the mutual funds—and thus their shareholders—would own our funds' manager, and would operate at cost. In effect, our fund shareholders would become the beneficiaries of the entrepreneurial rewards that managers traditionally arrogate to themselves. While I happen to believe that this concept lifts a fund enterprise to nobler stature, the fact that no others have chosen to follow down "the road less traveled" suggests a profound disagreement with that assessment. So be it.

But it is a fact that our concept of an institution that serves solely its own investors has provided measurably greater effectiveness. The combination of our focus on conservative equity funds, on bond and money market funds of high-quality securities within specific maturity ranges, and of stock and bond market index funds—of which we were the pioneering creators—has worked effectively. Our at-cost operation is now producing annual expense savings to our investors of—think of it—nearly $3 billion. Together, these successful strategies and these minimal costs have provided virtual across-the-board superiority in the long-term returns we have earned for the shareholders of the funds we serve, relative to their peer funds with similar objectives.

While I cannot in all honesty say that we began with an understanding of leadership and followership, the second Greenleaf rule for a model institution, I can say that I've spent much of my career developing similar concepts. For example, in one of my early talks to our tiny twenty-eight-person original crew, I said, "I want every one of us to treat everyone here with fairness. If you don't understand what that means, stop by my office." I constantly stressed the values that I wanted to distinguish Vanguard, above all the need to recognize that both we who serve and those whom we serve must be treated as "honest-to-God, down-to-earth human beings, with their own hopes, fears, ambitions, and financial goals."

Over the years, I have come to love and respect the term *human beings* to describe those with whom I serve and those whom we at Vanguard together serve. I even gave a talk at Harvard Business School on how our focus on human beings enabled us to become what they there call a "service breakthrough company." I challenged the students to find the term *human beings* in any book on corporate strategy that they had read, but as far as I know, none could meet the challenge. (Surprisingly, I do not believe that I've seen that term in any of Mr. Greenleaf's vast writings, but I'm certain that he'd love it too.)

Organization structure, or modus operandi, was also integral to our new model of an investment institution. Power and authority would rest not with the managers, as is the mutual fund industry convention, but with the fund shareholders. Of necessity, to be sure, much of the power would be delegated to the managers, but the ultimate authority would be vested in the collective power of those we serve. One rule set forth in modern-day business books is, "treat your clients as if they were your owners." It is a good rule, but it is particularly easy for us to observe it: Our clients *are* our owners.

It was obvious, of course, that our managers would require more direct oversight than a large mass of widely dispersed investors, most with moderate holdings in our funds, could provide. So we quickly determined that we needed truly independent trustees, who, as in Mr. Greenleaf's fourth and final requirement for a model institution, would be able to provide objectivity and detachment, and in whom the ultimate trust would be placed. Ever since, at least eight of our ten trustees have been unaffiliated with Vanguard in any way other than in the capacity of directors of our funds. In all, the Greenleaf model, described for a venerable institution, was to closely resemble a model created for a new company, with a new concept, that, as he spoke, was just coming to birth.

Linking Foresight and Caring

I now want to single out two subjects that, perhaps surprisingly, Mr. Greenleaf seemed to link: foresight and caring. He led into his subject with a few words about great leaders.

> Edwin M. Land, founder of Polaroid, spoke of the opportunity for greatness—not genius—for the many: "within his own field (be it large or small, lofty or mundane) he will make things grow and flourish; he will grow happy helping others in his field, and to that field he will add things that would not have been added had he not come along." But greatness is not enough. Foresight is crucial. The lead that the leader has is his ability to foresee an event that must be dealt with before others see it so that he can act on it in his way, the right way, while the initiative is his. If he waits, he cannot be a leader—at best, he is a mediator.

Foresight is the central ethic of leadership. Foresight is the lead that the leader has. Leaders must have an armor of confidence in facing the unknown. The great leaders are those who have invented roles that were uniquely important to them as individuals, that drew heavily on their strengths and demanded little that was unnatural, and that were right for the time and place they happened to be.

Caring for persons, the more able and the less able serving each other, is the basis of leadership, the rock upon which a good society is built. In small organizations, caring is largely person to person. But now most caring is mediated through institutions—often large, complex, powerful, impersonal, not always competent, sometimes corrupt.

To build a model institution, *caring* must be the essential motive. Institutions require care, just as do individuals. And caring is an exacting and demanding business. It requires not only interest and compassion and concern; it demands self-sacrifice and wisdom and tough-mindedness and discipline. It is much more difficult to care for an institution, especially a big one, which can look cold and impersonal and seem to have an autonomy of its own.

While in 1986 I had not read the essay by Robert Greenleaf from which those paragraphs were excerpted, I had read an earlier speech that must have been the source of his inspiration. It was a speech given in 1972 by Howard W. Johnson, chairman of the Massachusetts Institute of Technology. It inspired me profoundly, and as 1986 drew to a close, I quoted it amply in my speech to our crew. Note the similarity:

There is always a time when the longer view could have been taken and a difficult crisis ahead foreseen and dealt with while a rational approach was still possible. How do we avoid such extremes? How can sustainable growth be achieved? Only with foresight—the central ethic of leadership—for so many bad decisions are made when there are no longer good choices.

If foresight is needed to protect an institution, what are the requirements necessary to make it work? First, the sense of purpose and objective. Second, the talent to manage the process for reaching new objectives. Finally, and let me surprise you by emphasizing this third need, we need people who care about the institution. A deep sense of caring for the institution is requisite for its success.

The institution must be the object of intense human care and cultivation. Even when it errs and stumbles, it must be cared for, and the burden must be borne by all who work for it, all who own it, all who are served by it, all who govern it. Every responsible person must care, and care deeply, about the institutions that touch his life.

My 1986 speech was but one of many times when I spoke of the importance of caring. Then, I reminded the crew that "only if we truly care about our organization, our partners, our associates, our clients, indeed our society as a whole, can we preserve, protect, and defend our organization and the values we represent." Again, I emphasized our responsibility "to faithfully serve the honest-to-God human beings who have trusted us to offer sound investment programs, with clearly delineated risks, at fair prices. We must never let them down."

Five years later, in 1991, I returned to the same theme in a talk titled "Daring and Caring." I illustrated daring by using Lord Nelson's victory at the Battle of the Nile on August 1, 1798. That battle is part of our history (indeed at Vanguard, we celebrated its two hundredth anniversary in 1998) for Nelson's flagship was HMS *Vanguard*. Only weeks before the firm was incorporated in 1974, I had fortuitously learned of the battle, and, inspired by Nelson's remarkable triumph, chose Vanguard as our name.

At Vanguard, I reminded the crew, we dared to be different, in our unique corporate structure, in our unprecedented switch to commission-free distribution, in our decision to provide candid information to investors, and in forming the first market index fund, an idea considered so, well, stupid, that it wasn't even copied by anyone else for a full decade.

But caring quickly took center stage in my talk. I emphasized that caring must be "an article of faith," pointing out that each of those daring decisions that I had mentioned was driven by a philosophy of caring for our clients. And I reinforced the concept that caring must be also accorded to our crew, even then urging a spirit of "cooperation and mutual courtesy and respect," and reminding them that while we were so large as to require a policy manual, "it will never replace our own selves as the ultimate source of a caring attitude." Yes, a great deal of the spirit of Robert Greenleaf (and Dean Johnson, too) had found its way into our young business enterprise.

The Superior Company and the Liberating Vision

I now want to spend a few moments on Robert Greenleaf's views on the superior company and the liberating vision. Here is what he said:

> What distinguishes a superior company from its competitors is not the dimensions that usually separate companies, such as superior technology, more astute market analysis, better financial base, etc.; it is *unconventional* thinking about its dream—what this business wants to be, how its priorities are set, and how it organizes to serve. *It has a radical philosophy and self-image.* According to the conventional business wisdom, it ought not to succeed at all. Conspicuously less successful competitors seem to say, "the ideas that company holds ought not to work, therefore we will learn nothing from it."
>
> In some cases, the company's unconventional thinking about its dream is born of a liberating vision. But in our

society liberating visions are rare. Why are liberating visions so rare? They are rare because a stable society requires that *a powerful liberating vision must be difficult to deliver.* Yet to have none is to seal our fate. We cannot turn back to be a wholly traditional society, comforting as it may be to contemplate it. There must be change—sometimes great change.

That difficulty of delivery, however, is only half of the answer. The other half is that so few who have the gift for summarizing a vision, and the power to artic-ulate it persuasively, have the urge and the courage to try. But there must be a place for servant-leaders with prophetic voices of great clarity who will produce those liberating visions on which a caring, serving society depends.

I leave to far wiser—and more objective—heads than mine the judgment about whether or not Vanguard meets the definition of a superior company. Of course, I believe it does. But I have no hesi-tancy in saying it is the product of unconventional thinking about what we want to be, how we set priorities, and how we organize to serve our clients. And surely our competitors—even the most suc-cessful of them—look with a sort of detached amusement and skep-ticism at our emergence as an industry leader. We have dared to be different, and it seems to be working just fine.

I cannot responsibly describe the ideas on which I founded Van-guard as part of a liberating vision. But I can tell you that, way back in 1951, I was writing my senior thesis on a little-known industry, which *Fortune* magazine described as "tiny but contentious" in the 1949 article that first aroused my interest in an industry about which I had never before heard. In my thesis, I sketched out my ideas of how a better industry—if not a model institution—might be built. Nearly a half-century ago, I called for a fairer shake for investors, urged lower sales commissions and management fees, cautioned against claims that mutual funds' managements could produce miracles, warned that unmanaged indexes had proved tough competition for active managers, and ended up with a ringing call for fund managers to focus, not on the peripheral diversions of the business, but on the duty to provide prudent stewardship. "The principal function of investment companies," I concluded, "is the management of their portfolios. Everything else is incidental to the performance of this function."

If all of that sounds much like Vanguard today, so be it. But it was not a dream that easily became a reality. And it was most certainly not a deterministic series of linked events. Rather it was really a long and random series of happy accidents that led from 1951 to 1981, when the essential structure of today's Vanguard was finally put in place.

But it is, I think, remarkable how the original, if crude, dream hinted at in that Princeton thesis about the need to serve a single master—our investor-owners, now more than ten million human beings in the aggregate—has to this day determined our basic corporate strategies. I've often emphasized that "strategy follows structure," a relationship that has logically led to business decisions that are shaped around our unique shareholder-owned structure. It is what makes our enterprise work. Belying the competitors to whom Greenleaf referred when he pictured them as saying "it ought not to work," putting the shareholder in the driver's seat "ought to work." And it does.

For example, as nearly all now concede, cost is a factor in shaping long-term investment returns. If a firm achieves low-cost provider status, its bond and money market funds can follow lower-risk strategies and still offer higher yields than their peers. If low cost is the key to a successful index fund (and it obviously is), index funds can appropriately be a major focus of development. If money spent on marketing consumes shareholder assets while offering no countervailing benefit, it would seem foolish to spend much money on marketing. And all of these things are what aware investors should want. *It turns out that they do.* In the world of investing, in fact, it turns out that a superior company can be built on these strategies, all of which flow from a structure in which service to shareholders is the watchword.

Powerful Parallel Phrases

I've now touched on three broad areas of commonality between Robert Greenleaf's thinking and my own—building a model institution, foresight and caring, and the superior company and the liberating vision—as I've tried to manifest them in Vanguard's development. In this fourth section, I want to briefly describe some particularly powerful phrases that I observed in his writing that paralleled those that I have used at Vanguard forever, or so it seems. I do so because it suggests once again that his idealistic visions can in fact be successfully incorporated into a caring, sharing, serving business.

"Everything begins with the initiative of an individual." So reads the second subhead in "The Servant as Leader." "The very essence of leadership," Mr. Greenleaf says—and I am confident that he was referring not only to a sort of grand idea of corporate leadership but to the infinite number of tasks where less sweeping forms of leadership are required if an enterprise is to succeed—"is going out ahead to show the way, an attitude that is derived from more than usual openness to inspiration. Even though he knows the path is uncertain, even dangerous, a leader says: 'I will go, come with me.'"

Almost uncannily, my words about the importance of the individual leader convey the same idea. "Even one person can make a difference" has become a Vanguard article of faith, and is in fact engraved on the Awards for Excellence that we make each quarter to individuals who have met the highest standards of service, initiative, and cooperation. And even as Mr. Greenleaf defines individual initiative as "showing the way," Vanguard's very name suggests the same idea, for the motto on the HMS *Vanguard* ship badge is "leading the way."

And then there is the matter of the dream. Greenleaf speaks of the need for a leader to state and restate the goal, using the word *goal* "in the special sense of the overarching purpose, the visionary concept, the dream. Not much happens without a dream. And for something great to happen, it must be a great dream. Much more than a dreamer must bring it to reality, but the dream must be there first."

And I've talked often about Vanguard's dream. In particular, my 1975 speech to the crew was entitled "The Impossible Dream." In it, I said:

> The issue, it seems to me, is no longer how to make Vanguard a bigger company, but rather how to make Vanguard a better company, provide greater convenience and enhanced investment performance, all in the name of better service for the human beings who have turned over to us the responsibility for their investment assets. A dream it may be—getting bigger only by being better— even an impossible dream, but a thrilling dream. And we must reach for it.

I don't mind at all being a bit of a dreamer, if I can share the attribute with the likes of Robert Greenleaf.

Finally, I was struck by a third powerful parallel, nautical in derivation. Mr. Greenleaf gave this advice: "No matter how difficult the challenge or hopeless the task may seem, if you are reasonably sure of your course, just keep on going!" Leaving aside the obvious similarity with the words from "The Impossible Dream" ("no matter how hopeless, no matter how far"), his words come remarkably close to my often-repeated theme, "Press On Regardless," which was in fact the subject of a speech I gave to a graduating class at Vanderbilt University. But "just keep on going" is also a statement of what may well be the most universal of all the nautical themes we use—and sometimes perhaps even abuse—at Vanguard: "Stay the Course." It is wonderful advice for a career, superb wisdom for a project, and probably the best single piece of investment advice ever offered: "Establish a sound balance of bond funds and stock funds in your portfolio. Then, no matter what the financial markets do, stay the course."

Memo on Growing from Small to Large

In about 1972, Robert Greenleaf wrote this memorandum at the request of the head of a small company that had achieved the reputation for unusual quality of products and service, which had grown rapidly to its present size, and was in the process of becoming a distinguished large institution:

> The line that separates a large business from a small one might be drawn at that point where the business can no longer function well under the direction of one individual. If the company has been built largely on one person's drive, imagination, taste, and judgment, as yours seems to have been, it may be difficult to recognize when that point has been reached. The greatest risk may be that the company cannot grow and keep its present quality.
>
> I suggest that you begin to shift your personal effort *toward building an institution* in which you become more the manager of a process that gets the job done and less the *administrator of day-to-day operations*. This might be the first step toward the ultimate optimal long-term performance of a large business that is *managed* by a board of directors who act as trustees and *administered* by a team of equals who are led by a *primus inter pares*—first among equals. The result would be an institution that would have the best chance of attracting and holding in its service the large number of able people who will be required to give it strength, quality, and continuity if it is to continue to do on a large scale what you have been able to do so well on a smaller scale.

I am suggesting that a person like you who has been so successful in taking a distinguished business from a small size to large size might, at your age, find an even more exciting challenge in transforming a one-person business into an institution that has autonomy and creative drive as a collection of many able people, one that has the capacity for expansion without losing, and perhaps even enhancing, the claim to distinction it has already achieved.

To say that I found this memorandum both relevant and poignant when I first read it, as I was preparing these remarks, would be quite an understatement. For what struck home to me was that, while there was much that I thought of when I decided in 1996 to relinquish my position as head of Vanguard, I had not seriously considered abandoning the traditional route of simply recommending to the directors a qualified successor to replace me. The directors agreed without hesitation, perhaps in part because my weak heart was quickly deteriorating and because of my age (I was sixty-seven at the time), and, in fairness—although they did not suggest this—perhaps because they had tired of my leadership style.

In any event, within a year I had undergone a remarkably successful heart transplantation, miraculously receiving an infusion of new energy and confidence that had to be seen to be believed. A second chance at life is not to be taken lightly! But my decision had been made, and only time will tell whether it was the correct one. But whatever the case, I have no doubt that the service-caring-ethical principles of Vanguard will remain in place for as far ahead as one can see.

In the Vanguard structure, of course, the entrepreneur is not the owner. (The stock in the company is held by the funds for *their* shareholders.) When one leaves office, then, power devolves to another. And, as Robert Greenleaf wrote:

In an imperfect world, some abuse of power will always be with us. In 1770, William Pitt said to the House of Commons, "unlimited power is apt to corrupt the minds of those who possess it." One hundred years later, more famously, Lord Acton (in opposing the doctrine of papal infallibility) said, "power tends to corrupt and absolute power corrupts absolutely." That corruption is reflected in arrogance. For example, the head of a large corporation, when asked what made his job attractive, listed first, before monetary reward, prestige, service, and creative accomplishment, "the opportunity to build power."

The power-hungry person, who relishes competition and is good at it (meaning: he usually wins) will probably judge the servant-leader to be weak or naïve or both. But if we look past that individual to the institution which he or she serves, what makes that institution strong? I believe the strongest, most productive institution over a long period of time has the largest amount of voluntary action toward the goals of the institution. The people who staff the institution do the right things at the right time because the goals are clear and comprehensive and they know what ought to be done, and do the right thing without being instructed. It takes a strong leader to put the people who serve first, but that is the way to insure that they will deliver all that people can deliver—and to insure that the business will continue to lead in its field.

Vanguard, in my view, has been built on an extraordinary crew—now eight thousand strong—"who know what ought to be done, and who have done the right things at the right time." And while my strong leadership may well have been described as power-driven, my drive (I think) was focused on intellectual power—to devise sensible investment policies, an efficient structure through which to offer them, and a sensible strategy for their delivery—and moral power—to make certain that both structure and strategy were founded on a sound ethical base. Those kinds of powers do not vanish when one leaves office. But other kinds of power do, including the power of the purse, the power to direct people, the power to reshape values, even the power to change what lies firmly in place. But I hope and believe that our crew and my successors will continue to hold high what we have built, its structure and strategy, and the ethical foundation that is Vanguard's rock.

Where History Comes In

Vanguard has had the marvelous opportunity to test in the real-world marketplace the concept that serving is the essential ingredient of true success, and that servant-leaders—and leader-servants—can successfully dedicate their careers to serving the human beings who depend upon their services. All of that may sound idealistic—it is!—but we live in an era of consumerism (in the best sense) in which business has no recourse but to make a determined effort to build a new level of trust in consumer products and services alike. In the world of finance, if we are going to make the United States a nation of investor-capitalists, we'd best give our citizens the maximum possible proportion of the fruits of investing, rather than consuming large portions of those returns with excessive costs.

The fact is that "the Vanguard way" works. Not because our principles give us some divine right to success, but because we are creating extra value for investors. And, as the numbers I presented at the outset illustrate, the growth that Vanguard is enjoying relative to our peers makes clear that investors have clearly recognized that value advantage.

Yet it is a curious fact of competitive life in the mutual fund world that, while our investment policies—most notably in index funds and in bond funds—are being copied (albeit often with little enthusiasm), our low-cost philosophy and our focus on management rather than marketing are not. But as the investing public makes known its preferences, this industry will finally change. To use a computer analogy, all mutual fund organizations have pretty much the same software—common ways to invest in securities—but the industry must adopt a new operating system: serving the fund shareholder first.

I have no way of knowing whether the coincidence of Robert Greenleaf's philosophy and my own is merely fortuitous—a happy accident, random molecules bumping together in the night—or powerful evidence of the mysterious universality of a great idea. Perhaps it is a little of each. But in the mutual fund industry the central idea of serving is being proven in the marketplace by tens of millions of investors. I've long thought that servant-leadership is on the right side of evolving corporate history. And so too, in that small but growing corner of the financial world that is the U.S. mutual fund industry, the policies and principles that Vanguard adopted a quarter-century ago—which we continue to treasure today—are on the right side of history too.

7

Anatomy of a Collaboration
An Act of Servant-Leadership

Wendell J. Walls

In his article "Leadership as Partnership," Russ Moxley of the Center for Creative Leadership says, "Leadership is co-created as individuals relate as partners and develop a shared vision, set a direction, solve problems and make meaning of their work."[1] There is no better description of the origin of the collaboration between The Greenleaf Center for Servant-Leadership and the National Association for Community Leadership (now the Community Leadership Association) on their joint conference in the summer of 1999.

Planting the Seed

In the fall of 1988, the National Association for Community Leadership (COMMUNITY LEADERSHIP) moved its headquarters to Indianapolis from Washington, D.C., where it had been an administrative affiliate of the American Chamber of Commerce Executives. I was employed as president and CEO of the association with a staff of three to provide a variety of services to its then two hundred member organizations. COMMUNITY LEADERSHIP's members are community leadership development programs whose purpose, generally speaking, is to prepare volunteer leaders to be more effective in their civic lives. In the spring of 1990, the Robert K. Greenleaf Center for Servant-Leadership moved its offices from the Boston area to Indianapolis and engaged Larry Spears as its

CEO. Its small staff has as their mission to improve the caring and quality of institutions through servant-leadership. Servant-leadership is an approach to leadership, structure, and decision making that emphasizes increased service to others, a holistic approach to work, promoting a sense of community, and the sharing of power in decision making.

Building Relationships: A Prerequisite for Successful Collaboration

It is no coincidence that both organizations were "recruited" to Indianapolis by Lilly Endowment Inc., which has long supported the work of both organizations financially and philosophically. Nor was it only coincidence that Larry and I were each encouraged by our Lilly Endowment program officer to get to know the other. We soon discovered we had much in common personally as well as professionally. We are both originally from small communities in southern Indiana, and we both moved away for a while and returned to our Hoosier roots. We are each a bit introverted. We were responsible for unique national organizations with missions much larger than their current capacities if not their potential. This uniqueness made it sometimes difficult to explain to others just exactly what we did for a living. Last but not least, we discovered an occasional sense of loneliness at the top, which led us to meet periodically after work to commiserate over a glass of wine or two.

It's Important to Allow Time for Good Ideas to Emerge

While our interaction was not always work-related, we did spend time at each get-together exploring how we might help each other in our work. Over the years our institutional relationship evolved in parallel fashion to our personal one. We granted reciprocal membership in each other's organization, cross-promoted each organization's conferences and training, sold and advertised each other's publications, and invited each other to attend and present at our conferences. It didn't seem so remarkable, then, at one such meeting, for Larry to say to me, "What would you think about doing a joint conference?" I quickly replied, "Sounds like a good idea to me." So it was that late one afternoon, at a pub on the north side of Indianapolis, a collaboration was initiated. Now . . . if we could just get others to go along.

The Seed Takes Root

In a discussion on how our proposed collaboration might be best documented, someone wondered aloud whether any tome written about putting on a conference could be exciting enough to hold readers' interest. Regardless, for those curious about collaboration and its practical application, the experience of these two organizations is instructive and encouraging. Most important, it demonstrates a key element of successful collaboration seldom discussed: attitude as a determinant of behavior. It is my belief that this collaboration reflected a consummate act of servant-leadership by the two organizations via their staff and board leadership. Throughout the entire enterprise, the participating staff and volunteers represented their organizations by consistently and consciously demonstrating those characteristics most often associated with the servant-leader. In doing so, they provided us with an effective model for institutional collaboration.

> When organizations have integrity and are willing to build trust, they can move from a competing, win/lose attitude to a collaborative win/win position. This is what The Greenleaf Center for Servant-Leadership and the National Association for Community Leadership have done with this conference. They have put together, in a synchronistic way, the enabling art of servant-leadership with community leadership's work of building strong, vibrant communities. I commend you on this collaboration.
> —Stephen Covey, founder, Covey Leadership Center

I'm not sure when we started to routinely use the word *collaboration* to describe the envisioned joint conference, but there is absolutely no doubt that is what we had in mind from the very beginning. There are lots of other ways to conduct a joint conference: co-location, cooperation, and coordination. A number of publications provide excellent and detailed distinctions of the dynamics of each of these.[2] David Crislip and Carl Larson distinguish collaboration most succinctly in their book *Collaborative Leadership:*[3]

> As its Latin roots—*com* and *laborare*—indicate, collaboration means "to work together." It is a mutually beneficial relationship between two or more parties who work toward common goals by sharing responsibility, authority, and accountability for achieving results. Collaboration is more than simply sharing knowledge and information (communication) and more than a relationship that helps each party achieve its own goals (cooperation and coordination). The purpose of collaboration is to create a shared vision and joint strategies to address concerns that go beyond the purview of any particular party.

In practical terms, we might have merely held our respective conferences at the same place and adjacent on the calendar or lent our name and mailing list to each other's conference marketing. We could have shared speakers or other resources to make each conference more successful financially. We had something different in mind, I think, and that is why true collaboration was required and why I believe the overall effort to have been an act of servant-leadership.

Essential elements in any successful collaboration are an understanding and a high valuing of collaboration itself by all the parties. Both the Greenleaf Center and COMMUNITY LEADERSHIP brought to this joint endeavor an uncommon dedication to the concept of collaboration as defined earlier. I use the word *uncommon* because, in common usage, the word collaboration has long been tainted by societal suspicion. In the conference room of The Greenleaf Center lies the hernia-sized edition of *Webster's New World Dictionary* published in 1993. If you look up *collaboration* therein, you will find the following: "Collaborating with an enemy or an opposed group rather than struggling or resisting." Its definition of *collaborate* is only slightly milder: "To cooperate with or assist, usually willingly, an enemy; to cooperate with an agency or instrumentality with which one is not immediately connected, often in some political or economic effort."

Collaboration Need Not Wait on a Problem

Very little was written before 1990 addressing the kind of collaboration Crislip and Larson espouse as an effective approach to building community. Even when proffered as a viable if not absolutely indispensable element of community problem solving, the focus is usually on just that, *a problem*. Interestingly, several participants in focus groups of the organizations' constituents conducted at the joint conference shared various presumptions that the collaboration arose out of economic plight of one or both organizations, political motivations, or even represented a precursor of a corporate merger or takeover! There being no factual basis for any of these interpretations, they may have been conjured up by the mere act of collaboration. In hindsight, then, one of the things that makes this particular collaboration so unusual is the fact it did not arise from or address any problem whatsoever, perceived or real.

> *The idea for attempting a joint collaboration between our two organizations grew out of my friendship with Wendell Walls, as well as some real openness on our part to identify a scope of collaborative work that made sense. In time, this led to our talking about the possibilities of collaborating on something, and to our eventually hitting upon the idea of a joint conference.*

One key learning for me in all of this was the impor-
tance of building relationships and then allowing the
time for a good idea to emerge.
            —Larry Spears, president and CEO, The Greenleaf
                                Center for Servant-Leadership

When an organization knows its spirit, it can lead
itself from within. . . . Organizations need a strong
sense and conscience, a strong awareness of self.
Who are we? What are we trying to do?
            —Margaret Wheatley, president, Berkana Institute

An excellent climate existed for the idea of this collaboration
to take root. Relationships were strong and well established between
the CEOs of the two organizations. In fact, many members of their
staffs knew each other to some degree, having participated together
in various forums on leadership development. There had been periodic attendance and presentation at each other's conferences over
the years, and a general spirit of collegiality existed. After all, we
were all sort of in the same business, improving the caliber of civic
leadership in the world. Both organizations had similar organizational histories and continually faced the challenges all small organizations face, like meeting the growing needs of diverse
constituencies with limited resources. The environment was certainly enhanced by both organizations' professed valuing of collaboration itself as a skill or capacity of effective servant-leaders. In its
strategic plan, adopted in 1997, COMMUNITY LEADERSHIP set
a specific goal to "identify and support the work of the broadest
range of community leadership development efforts that share the
mission and values of COMMUNITY LEADERSHIP" and further
articulated an objective "to strengthen alliances with other national
organizations." In support of a goal "to promote the importance
of community leadership development in fostering effective,
inclusive communities," the plan states that "COMMUNITY
LEADERSHIP must model and encourage collaboration."

For each organization, the annual conference is a premier product. It represents a major source of operating support and is the main vehicle for strengthening the connections among the organizations' constituencies. It is pretty much the case that when someone attends the conference of either organization, their ongoing membership or affiliation is assured. Both organizations routinely achieved conferee satisfaction ratings in the 90th percentile. Thus it is not only an important service but also a popular one. Both organizations' conferences had gone through a period of steady growth and reached an attendance plateau that invited the question of what might be done to expand and enhance an already excellent product. Collaboration offered an opportunity for each organization to present its constituency with something new. There was mutual respect between the organizations' staffs and volunteer leadership. Each perceived the other as quite competent in the area of event and conference management. On the surface, then, it seemed the notion of a collaborative conference was an offer that no one could refuse. These attributes, however, masked a number of substantial issues and differences of culture, tradition, and logistics that argued so strongly against the collaboration that it is somewhat surprising it was undertaken at all.

> *You can't start a plant in a place where it doesn't*
> *want to grow. It's the same with people.*
> —*Andrew Morikawa, board member,*
> *The Greenleaf Center for Servant-Leadership*

Risk Is an Inherent Element in Any Collaboration

The very popularity of COMMUNITY LEADERSHIP's conference and its financial import to the organization caused some reluctance to make sweeping changes for fear of alienating its basic member constituency. The Greenleaf Center, without a captive membership audience, depended on much broader marketing and promotion strategies to attract individuals who, as a result of conference attendance, would develop ongoing affiliation with the Center.

"It's not change people fear; it is loss," says Ronald Heifetz. There is a lesson for collaborators in his suggestion. As a matter of policy, COMMUNITY LEADERSHIP moved its conferences around the country, alternating between the east, west, and central regions. By chance, its two previous conferences had been held in the central part of the country. A joint conference in Indianapolis, the traditional site of Greenleaf conferences, would make three years in a row. By tradition, the COMMUNITY LEADERSHIP conference doesn't return to the same city. Their 1986 conference had been held in Indianapolis. The organization had recently and reluctantly changed its conference from fall to spring in 1996. A joint conference would require another shift, this time to summer, perceived to be a bad time for many of COMMUNITY LEADERSHIP's members. The Greenleaf Center had just completed a shift in timing as well. Holding a joint conference in June 1999 would result in putting on a conference only ten months after their 1998 conference, creating an extreme planning and marketing challenge. Both COMMUNITY LEADERSHIP members and Greenleaf Center conferees had come to expect certain content in their respective conference programs. How might the collaboration affect the program in ways that could fail those expectations? COMMUNITY LEADERSHIP board volunteers had always played a significant role in conference planning and there was a great deal of uncertainty of how their role might be affected by collaboration. The difference in governance styles between the organizations meant a serious change for Greenleaf staff accustomed to unfettered initiative in establishing conference goals and means.

COMMUNITY LEADERSHIP's conference had always been about twice the size of the Greenleaf conference and both organizations faced uncertainty regarding proration of resources and revenue. Very significantly, host communities typically support COMMUNITY LEADERSHIP conferences financially. Communities bid competitively to host their conference. Under the collaborative conference proposal, the conference would be held in

Indianapolis without any pledge of this local support, making the conference challenging financially from the COMMUNITY LEADERSHIP point of view. These concerns challenged both organizations as they attempted to exercise responsible stewardship of their own resources as they wrestled with the idea of collaboration.

> Jack Lowe, the Greenleaf Center's Chairman, and I made a pledge to try and learn more about each other and our organizations. At one of our meetings, he asked, "What should we do?" I said, "Sit back until staff gets to us with an issue they can't decide on." We never got that call.
> —Mano Mahadeva, 1998–99 board chair, National Association for Community Leadership

In the end, however, both boards combined effective stewardship with the ability to conceptualize the collaboration's potential. In servant-leadership terms, neither governance nor differences were allowed to destroy the "great dream." Both organizations' boards joined staff in a commitment to make the collaboration work and gave staff authority necessary to proceed.

Meaningful Communication Is Critical

With the advantage of hindsight, why did this collaboration work? What things really contributed to its success? Most important, I think, was our decision early on to schedule regular meetings of key staff. Larry Spears and Michele Lawrence of the Greenleaf staff met monthly with COMMUNITY LEADERSHIP Vice President Kristin Bakke and me beginning nearly two years prior to the conference. We would have been well served to have begun them even sooner. These meetings served as a forum for regular communication and group decision making. As important, they were the mechanism whereby relationships were nurtured, creativity unleashed, concerns assuaged, and tensions alleviated. The meetings evolved into something beyond business meetings. They were often scheduled as the last meeting of the day so that other business pressures weren't so intrusive. Refreshments were served; the mood was relaxed. At the beginning of each meeting, we allowed time for decompression and venting about whatever was on someone's mind. There was always a loose agenda but it was subject to change, and any of us could add—or postpone, for that matter—agenda items. The meetings were informal in appearance, but the group developed cohesiveness with serious attributes. We listened very intently to one another as we described our concerns and represented the interests of our respective constituencies and organizations. There was a great deal of empathy for each other's point of view and a sincere desire to understand and adequately address the other's issues. Each of us maintained an awareness of the styles and priorities of the others. This was true in a professional and a personal sense as well. The meetings evolved into a comfortable and safe place to discuss virtually any subject. This is not to say that there was never a difference of opinion. But the meetings gave us time to reflect on these issues and come to mutual agreement on hard decisions in the spirit of true collaboration rather than expedient compromise. Over time, we became a community built around the collaboration's purpose. I can cite no better elucidation than in our use of the pronoun *we*. In the beginning, as we sat across the table, we used the word in reference to our respective organizations. Eventually, though, we began to routinely use *we* to refer to the collaboration itself.

Put the Hard Stuff in Writing Early

The first order of business in our meetings was to develop a written agreement that outlined the purpose of the collaboration in broad terms and dealt very specifically with the touchy subjects of expense and revenue allocation. With these issues out of the way early, we were free to focus our attention on our real purpose.

Differences Are as Important as Similarities

While our collaboration germinated in a seedbed of similarity, it was rooted in mindfulness of our differences. We spent a great deal of time talking about our respective organizations, our conferences, and our cultures. We identified many ways in which we differed. At COMMUNITY LEADERSHIP, board members were involved to a significant degree in conference planning. The Greenleaf Center's conference was totally staff-driven. As CEO, I had always been personally involved in all aspects of conferences. Larry Spears delegated many decisions to his staff. COMMUNITY LEADERSHIP engaged an outside meeting planner; the Greenleaf Center did not. Planning timetables were different. Internal procedures were different. COMMUNITY LEADERSHIP invested heavily in their single mailing of a conference brochure. Greenleaf had always used multiple mailings of a less expensive brochure. Greenleaf didn't publicly recognize volunteer contributions with awards. COMMUNITY LEADERSHIP has a tradition of such volunteer and staff recognition. COMMUNITY LEADERSHIP conferences were very casual and featured off-site entertainment as a hallmark. Greenleaf conferees dressed a bit more formally and large social functions were not part of their conference tradition. Of course, each organization had its own list of the very best suppliers and each list was totally different. These examples are hardly exhaustive of the differences, both subtle and obvious. Conscious awareness of these differences made each of us more sensitive in our deliberations and choices. We were able to consider options in light of both organizations' constituencies rather than just our own. Since both organizations had a track record of successful conferences, our choices were not between what worked and what didn't. In virtually every instance, all choices were viable. We therefore focused on what option would serve the collaboration best, based on unique strengths of each organization. Empathy and understanding gained

from candid discussion on differences gave credibility to negotia-
tion on roles and responsibilities. On reflection, we seldom failed
to play to our collective strength.

> *We need partners to exercise leadership, to compen-*
> *sate for our blind spots, to act as a sounding board.*
> —Ronald Heifetz, director, Leadership Education Project,
> Harvard University

Nor were most discussions directed at maintaining the status quo
for one constituency. Collaboration opened a window of opportunity for experimentation. Because all conferees expected—or
feared—something would be different at this conference, we felt
more comfortable experimenting. Whenever we took an approach
to some element of the conference that promised to be new and different to one or both constituencies, our standard internal line was,
"If someone doesn't like it, we can blame it on the collaboration."

> *Perhaps the most vital domain of leadership is the*
> *building and recognizing of the innate capacity we all*
> *have to sense and bring forth emerging futures.*
> —Joseph Jaworski, founder, Centre for Generative
> Leadership

Beginning with our most preliminary discussions, we talked
about creating a joint conference that would be "bigger than the
sum of its parts." Our primary goal was to encourage a significant
cross-fertilization between the concepts of servant-leadership and
community leadership development programs. We wanted to provide community leadership practitioners with a better theoretical
background on servant-leadership and servant-leadership practitioners with a better understanding of the practice of community
leadership development. For The Greenleaf Center's traditional
conference participants, this provided a window into the nature of

community leadership programs. In turn, community leadership program representatives would find a deeper understanding of servant-leadership concepts. Both could use this new insight to enhance their effectiveness in their communities. We each hoped to attract new participants to our ongoing work. At the same time, we had a good understanding of the importance of the conference to the operation and reputation of each organization. We were very conscious of the need to meet the expectations of our traditional constituencies. At the same time we presented them with something new, we had to provide them with the nuts and bolts they had come to depend on from the annual conference. We were also aware of the need for balanced programming. Members of each constituency had to see themselves and their national organization reflected in the conference agenda. This was uppermost in our minds in all programming decisions. To assure breakout sessions met these criteria, we used the traditional volunteer committee mechanism of COMMUNITY LEADERSHIP for programming directed specifically at community leadership professionals and their volunteers. The Greenleaf Center identified and arranged traditional breakout sessions as well. The collaboration chose additional "bridge sessions" from among solicited proposals and issued direct invitations. While diligence in this area resulted in a well-balanced and highly rated program, it may be instructive to provide an example of where we overdid it and where we came up short.

We managed to demonstrate that there is such a thing as too much balance. COMMUNITY LEADERSHIP operates a number of awards programs and traditionally features presentation of these awards at its conference. It also has a tradition of involving volunteer leadership in that presentation as well as in speaker introduction. Neither of these is part of the Greenleaf conference tradition. For the sake of both balance and experimentation, The Greenleaf Center decided to present special awards and give its volunteer leaders a greater role at the podium. In one general session, the attempt to include the combined number of awards, presentations, and introductions resulted in a session that ran overtime. On the other hand, we underestimated the extent to which language would be used by conferees to gauge balance. All major speakers were well briefed on the mixed audience and were very careful to make their comments broad enough to cover all or to give voice to its diversity. Nonetheless, the program was viewed by some to be skewed toward The Greenleaf Center merely by the use of the word "servant-leadership." Even though most community leadership programs are familiar with the concept of servant-leadership and incorporate it in their programming, some conferees equated any reference to "servant-leadership" as a reference pertaining to The Greenleaf Center per se. On reflection, I'm not sure how we might better have addressed this issue, but it does point out the degree of sensitivity sometimes necessary in demonstrating a balanced collaboration.

Crisis Can Make Collaboration Stronger

One test of the strength of collaboration may be how it responds to crisis. In this case, the collaboration faced a significant test when one of the principal actors—me—resigned a little over a year before the joint conference. In hindsight, it's clear that the collaboration might have collapsed. The foundation of the collaboration was the relationship between Larry Spears and me. Kristin Bakke was relatively new to COMMUNITY LEADERSHIP. The collaboration was not yet widely publicized. There was adequate time to dissolve the collaboration and put on two separate conferences. It would not have seemed imprudent for The Greenleaf Center to view the uncertainty surrounding an executive transition at COMMUNITY LEADERSHIP as a good reason to withdraw or postpone this joint endeavor. Separation of an executive of long standing is stressful for any small organization. Faced with the pressure of finding a new executive while maintaining operations, it would have been perfectly understandable for COMMUNITY LEADERSHIP's board to bow out of any activity that put further stress on limited resources.

To their credit and to the collaboration's, neither organization backed away. There was no wavering of commitment to the joint enterprise. To my knowledge, there was not so much as a discussion about termination of the collaboration by anyone. In an act of servant-leadership, both organizations held the collaboration in trust for the greater good. Having determined that the collaboration made good sense for their organizations, not just the individuals involved, they regarded continuing the collaboration as not really an issue. If anything, the collaboration may have been strengthened by this circumstance. Certainly, the participants expressed a great deal of healing support for one another during this transition period, and that enhanced the atmosphere of trust and caring.

Facilitation Is Important to the Collaborative Process

My changing role in the collaboration following my resignation surfaced an issue that might have been overlooked otherwise. I suspect that the primary motivation for engaging me as a consultant to the project was to maintain continuity. The change, however, resulted in my playing a new and, I believe, highly valuable role for any collaboration, that of facilitator. This is not a role I anticipated. I'm not sure I was even aware of playing this role at the time. I went from representing one party in the collaboration to working for the collaboration itself. I represented neither but was trusted by both. Looking back, I became a shoulder to cry on, sometimes gave structure to discussions, posed questions that kept the decision making on track, injected humor in our discussions, and became more attentive to individual frustrations. Certainly, at times, each of us played the role of facilitator, as is the case in any effectively functioning group. It is also true that the level of commitment to our overarching collaborative purpose held by each individual made for easy facilitation. Nonetheless, an "independent" facilitator could be an asset to any collaboration.

I mentioned that this collaboration was initially undertaken without the level of financial sponsorship the organizations traditionally enjoyed. Thus it represented, at the outset, substantial financial risk. That risk, however, was soon ameliorated by the tremendous philanthropic response this collaboration attracted. Fortunately for us, but unfortunately for our society, collaboration is still unusual and unique enough to attract the attention of foundations. We received tremendous support from the Lilly Endowment, which allowed us much more flexibility in conference planning. Further, we were able to offer sufficient financial aid in the form of partial scholarships to hundreds of individuals and organizations that could not otherwise have participated in the conference. Their support allowed us to get an exciting and improved product to more people. At the same time, local and statewide leadership organizations stepped forward with both financial support and volunteers unsurpassed by past conference hosts. It was the collaborative nature of the conference that attracted this level of support. One need not wait for a grant to undertake serious collaboration.

Build It and They Will Come

Effective collaboration requires an attitude embodied by Robert Greenleaf's test of servant-leadership: "Do those served grow as persons? Do they, while being served, become healthier, wiser, freer, more autonomous, more likely themselves to become servants? And what is the effect on the least privileged in society; will they benefit, or at least not be further deprived?" It is enhanced by empathetic, caring individuals who feel free to "think big thoughts," and are committed to the collaboration's purpose as well as to the personal, professional, and spiritual growth of all who are touched by the collaboration.

As the "proof is in the pudding," this essay should comment on the conference that was the focus of all this collaborative effort. In short, this collaborative conference was a success in all the ways we had hoped. Conferees had the opportunity to experience the best that each organization had to offer. There was a great deal of cross-fertilization between the basic constituencies. Participants experienced great learning and great fun. All in all, high energy and goodwill prevailed. Highlighted by fine and provocative keynote speakers, authors' night activities, and many outstanding sessions featuring the best practices of servant-leadership and community leadership, the conference attracted a combined record number of thirteen hundred extraordinarily diverse people from all fifty states and twelve other nations.

> *The collaboration truly produced synchronicity.*
> *When you decide to do something worthwhile, with a*
> *big dream, and start acting in ways to realize that*
> *dream, good things just happen. Volunteers stepped*
> *forward; big-name speakers responded enthusiasti-*
> *cally to our invitations; Lilly Endowment and others*
> *invested in our dream. Even hotel space theretofore*
> *unavailable to us opened up for us.*
> —Michele Lawrence, conference director, The Greenleaf
> Center for Servant-Leadership

Joe Jaworski, author of *Synchronicity*, opened the conference. He might have been describing this collaboration as he described conditions that are present at times of "synchronicity," when things come together in an almost unbelievable way in our lives: high energy, coherence, a deep sense of satisfaction, distributed leadership, and highly significant results. Speaker Ron Heifetz recommended cultivating two distinct kinds of partners—confidants and allies—and warned us not to confuse their respective roles. This collaboration produced both types of partnerships among its planners and conference participants alike. Margaret Wheatley, author of *Leadership and the New Science*, spoke about the need to learn to come together differently. The servant-leader's first work is "to find people, to really see them; to bring people together; to have more faith in people than they have in themselves; and to create environments where people can be creative, life-affirming, and find health and wholeness." This conference provided just such an environment. Stephen Covey suggested to conferees there are four roles of leadership. The leader must first be a model of credibility, diligence, and the spirit of servant-leadership. The second role of leadership is pathfinding, wherein a vision is discerned. The third role is that of alignment; unless you institutionalize your values, they won't happen. The fourth role is to empower people, actually the fruit of the first three. In their collaboration, COMMUNITY LEADERSHIP and The Greenleaf Center demonstrated all four of the leadership roles very well.

In summary, advice to those who are considering their own collaboration:

- Build relationships at every opportunity. They could result in important collaborations later.

- Allow time for good ideas to emerge.

- Collaboration need not wait on a problem. Do it just because it's the right thing to do.

- Risk is inherent in collaboration. Without it, you can have no reward.

- It is not change people fear; it is loss.

- Meaningful communication is critical. No amount of e-mail, faxes, or memoranda can equal the value of frequent face-to-face meetings.

- Put hard stuff in writing early. Leave everything else as loose as you can. Don't put yourselves in the position of having to say, "We can't do that. It violates our written agreement."

- Differences are as important as similarities. They are the source of creativity, discovery, and change. Invest the necessary time and energy to understand them.

- Crisis can make collaboration stronger.

- Remember the importance of facilitation. If you don't have an independent facilitator, be sure that group members facilitate for one another and the health of the group.

- If in doubt, do it anyway. It will be worth the effort.

Collaboration is not handing out paintbrushes so others can paint your fence. It is not an example of "many hands make light work," nor is it an example of "too many cooks spoil the broth." It is hard work. It is very hard work. It is worthwhile work. It is worthwhile because it makes good things happen.

8

Servant-Leadership Characteristics in Organizational Life

Don DeGraaf, Colin Tilley, Larry Neal

We live in turbulent times! Change is the one constant of our lives. The explosion of knowledge in the last fifty years has produced unprecedented change in the way we live and how we define ourselves. For leaders in a wide range of positions, dealing with change has created a sense of uneasiness in terms of how we serve and lead others in order to produce value for our organizations, our customers, our staff, and ourselves. In response to this balancing act, we often seek to take the easier route of selecting either serving or leading, but not both. The concept of servant-leadership challenges this approach and encourages us to disregard the *either/or* option and instead live in the paradox of *both/and*.

Robert K. Greenleaf first coined the term servant-leadership in 1970 in his essay "The Servant as Leader." From this humble beginning, servant-leadership is now in its third decade as a specific leadership and management theory. Larry C. Spears, in *Reflections on Leadership*, has identified servant-leadership as an approach that "attempts to simultaneously enhance the personal growth of workers and improve the quality and caring of our many institutions

Portions of this manuscript first appeared in a twelve-month series on servant-leadership in the United Kingdom in *Leisure Management* magazine, published by The Leisure Media Company. Contact: +44 1462 431385; www.leisure management.co.uk.

through a combination of teamwork and community, personal involvement in decision-making, and ethical and caring behavior."[1]

Servant-leadership appears to be a contradiction in terms because we see a leader as one who leads and a servant as one who follows. Yet part of the inherent value of the concept of servant-leadership is that both leadership and followership are emphasized. All of us are both leaders and followers in different parts of our lives. One is not better than the other; in the course of our lives we may learn to be good leaders by learning to be good followers, listening to each other and helping one another lead and follow.[2]

The metaphor of servant-leader is a powerful model for today's managers and leaders. Both customers and staff today want leaders who will listen and empower, rather than dominate and tell them what to do. Thus, a servant-leadership approach to delivering products and services encourages partnerships between customers, staff, and leaders and managers.

The power of the servant-leadership model lies in the ability of its ideas to inspire us to collectively be more than the sum of our individual parts. According to Greenleaf, leadership should call us to serve a higher purpose, something beyond ourselves. Thus one of the most important aspects of leadership is helping organizations and staff identify their higher purpose. To Greenleaf, the best test of servant-leadership is this: "Do those served, grow as persons? Do they, while being served, become healthier, wiser, freer, more autonomous, more likely themselves to become servants? And what is the effect on the least privileged in society; will they benefit or at least not be further deprived?"

To achieve this higher purpose of our organizations, we must be passionate about our desire to improve our communities and ourselves. The process of becoming a servant-leader demands that we understand our own strengths and shortcomings. To guide individuals in this process, Spears has identified the following ten characteristics of servant-leadership: listening, empathy, healing, awareness, persuasion, conceptualization, foresight, stewardship, commitment to the growth of people, and building community. The purpose of this chapter is to examine each of these characteristics within the context of servant-leadership and to demonstrate how each characteristic can be applied to management and service delivery. It is important to remember that these characteristics do not create an either/or dichotomy but rather an opportunity to explore how to balance all these characteristics in our lives.

Listening: The Foundation of Servant-Leadership

Listening is the first characteristic of servant-leaders, for it is through listening that many of the other characteristics can be nurtured. When we listen, not just to what others are saying but also to our own internal voice, we create a mindset that fosters such characteristics as empathy, awareness, foresight, and commitment to others.

Consider the sign that hangs in the office of a professor at a large university that states: "MAKE ME UNDERSTAND." This sign is his commitment to listening to whoever walks through that door. Those three little words tell people "I am here to listen, to try to understand your situation." We all should pause and ask, "What kind of messages do I send to people who communicate with me on a daily basis? Do I send the message that I am too busy to talk to them or that I have all the answers? Do I send the message that I am genuinely interested in others and want to hear their views?"

Listening is often the forgotten skill in communication and leading. We acknowledge the importance of communication within our organizations, and we recognize that ineffective communication leads to misunderstandings and mistakes. Yet it is estimated that 45 percent of organizational energy is dissipated because of misunderstanding, and that two out of every three mistakes occur because of miscommunication.

When asked what makes a great communicator, we usually think about being able to speak eloquently and effectively, rather than about listening. But when we listen first, we create the foundation upon which great communication can be established. Think about the benefits when someone listens to us. It builds our self-esteem, shows we have worth, informs us we are not alone, helps us work through our problems, causes us to feel important and respected as a person, and tells us the other person is interested in us. We all need these things, which is why listening is such an important skill to develop and nurture.

For staff that work directly with customers, listening is an especially critical skill, as we try to understand their needs. Through listening and involving a wide range of constituencies in our work, we can create products and experiences that are driven by our constituents' needs.

One way in which we can develop our listening skills is to practice reflective listening. Reflective listening is a skill that enables the listener to understand the content of the message as well as the feelings of the person who is speaking. Reflective listening includes three components:

- *Nonverbal clues:* Learning to be aware of nonverbal communication in oneself and others

- *Understanding the content:* Understanding the speaker's main ideas and checking them out

- *Understanding feelings:* Listening for and being aware of the feelings a person may have when communicating

Reflective listening involves literally reflecting the feelings and content of what is heard by questioning, clarifying, understanding, and summarizing. *Active listening* begins with simple door-openers that communicate to the person talking that you are interested and that you want to hear more. *Door-openers* are responses that do not communicate any of the listener's own ideas or feelings. They include such noncommittal responses as "I see" or "Oh, really" or "You did?"

We can take the idea of door-openers forward by using positive reactors. *Reactors* are phrases that people use in response to suggestions, ideas, and comments from each other. Some reactors are positive and elicit good feelings and good (creative) ideas. Other responses are known as killer phrases, because they tend to stop someone from sharing any additional ideas. For example, here's a selection of positive and negative reactors:

Positive Phrases	Killer Phrases
Keep talking, you're on track.	The problem with that idea. . . .
Keep going.	It's not a bad idea, but. . . .
I'm glad you brought that up.	You haven't considered. . . .
How can we build on that?	We've tried it before.
That's an interesting idea.	You don't understand the problem. . . .
Let's try it.	Has anyone else ever tried it?

As we actively listen and use positive reactors, it is important that we follow up initial comments with clarifying statements that confirm what we are hearing and feeling. Throughout this process, we also need to use appropriate body language that communicates as we are listening. For example, we need to make eye contact and give people our undivided attention.

When we practice active listening, both in what we say and do, we develop the relationships necessary to be successful servant-leaders.

Empathy

We need to go beyond simply listening: we need to be empathic with others. Empathy is the capacity for participation in another's feelings or ideas; it is important in dealing with both staff and customers. Servant-leaders strive to understand and empathize with others. People need to be accepted and recognized for their special and unique spirits. The most successful servant-leaders are those who have become skilled empathic listeners.[3]

In developing empathy for staff, an important first step is knowing the expectations we hold for others, our jobs, and ourselves. This can be difficult, however, as we often don't recognize our expectations in specific situations until those unconscious expectations are not met. The following questions serve to help staff identify expectations connected to themselves and fellow staff members:[4]

Personal Expectations

- How do I expect to stretch myself in my job?

- What can I give to our programs?

- What types of relationships am I hoping to develop?

Professional Expectations

- What professional goals do I want to accomplish?

- What do I expect to learn?

- What do I expect this job to do for me professionally?

Collegial Expectations

- How do I want others to treat me?

- What do I need from my colleagues to be successful?

- What is important to build a sense of community with colleagues?

Supervisory Expectations

- What kind of guidance or autonomy do I expect?

- What do I need from my supervisor to be successful?

- What role do I expect my supervisors to play with the program?

Resource Expectations

- What kind of resource support am I expecting from the organization?

- What do I expect to be available to me at any time?

- How do I expect my resource requests to be handled?

Through responding to these types of questions, supervisors and staff begin to develop a common ground for dealing with one another that makes it easier to handle difficult situations as they surface.

In developing empathy for customers, servant-leaders must not only learn to empathize themselves, they also must help their staff learn to empathize with customers. One specific technique to help servant-leaders build empathy is through mental imagery. Mental imagery provides a unique access to the unfolding of a program or event, and can be used to experience the program from a participant's point of view. Through mental imagery staff can anticipate and solve problems, identify critical moments of interaction with participants, and experience the entire operation of a program or service.[5] For example, in experiencing the entire program or event, mental imagery involves visualizing the event or program, as we would expect it to unfold, and then identifying the necessary steps to making all those elements happen.

Mental imagery and visualization can also be used to improve the quality of programs and events by visualizing all the thousands of specific moments that combine to create the total customer experience. Legendary SAS chief executive Jan Carlzon defines these instances as "moments of truth" in which staff have the opportunity to impact the quality of the experience for participants. These "moments of truth" may be visualized in terms of a cycle of service. According to Albrecht and Zemke, a cycle of service is a repeatable sequence of events in which various people try to meet the customer's needs and expectations at each point.[6] The cycle begins at the very first point of contact between the customer and an organization. It ends, only temporarily, when the customer considers the service complete, and it begins anew when that person decides to come back for more.

By visualizing a cycle of service chart, staff can identify potential moments of truth for the customer. In many ways the chart forces us to see things as the customer sees them, without contaminating our perceptions with our own knowledge of what's supposed to happen behind the scenes. According to Albrecht, this tool works best when we want to focus staff attention on the customer's chain of experience and how the succession of "truth moments" builds to a complete perception of quality by the completion of the cycle.[7] Thus this cycle allows staff to realize that the customer experience is cumulative and should be managed as such.

Healing: Addressing the Spiritual Side of Leadership

We are often reticent to talk about the spiritual side of organizations as well as the spiritual nature of our staff and the customers we serve. Yet the spiritual, or matters of the heart, is important to us all. As many futurists have noted, the desire for the spiritual will be an increasingly important factor shaping everyday life during the next few decades. Godbey also notes that "the necessity of believing in something, connecting with others and to communities, having faith, seems a critical need of humans which is reasserting itself in a post modern era."[8]

Understanding the "matters of the heart" of our organizations can become an increasingly important healing agent in our lives and our communities if we let it. Learning to heal is a powerful force for transformation and integration. The desire to foster the healing process in our organizations comes to us as we listen and empathize with those we serve and those we work with. Fortunately, many leaders today are beginning to recognize the importance of healing within our organizations, as problems and crises are bound to develop. In such times, it is not the problem or crisis but how we respond that demonstrates the true "heart" of the organization.

Consider the events of April 19, 1995, when 168 men, women, and children lost their lives in the senseless bombing of the Murrah Federal Building in Oklahoma City. In the aftermath of this tragic event, the people of Oklahoma City sought to rebuild their lives and find a sense of healing as individuals and as a community. In the years following the bombing, the Oklahoma City National Memorial was an outgrowth of the healing process. The memorial has offered a place of healing for individuals, the community, and the nation. The mission statement of the Oklahoma City National Memorial demonstrates the need for creating a process that allows the healing process to begin. The mission addresses "those who were killed, those who survived and those changed forever." It states, "May all who leave here know the impact of violence. . . . May this memorial offer comfort, strength, peace, hope and serenity." Through the healing process, the heart of Oklahoma City and the nation is revealed, and the process strengthens us all.

The process of creating a healing response to this horrendous event is an example for us all in dealing with problems and crises on any level. In our own lives and organizations, the 1990s were a personal whirlwind from which few emerged unscathed. The management buzzwords and phrases being bandied about by management gurus and business leaders were *downsizing, reengineering,* and *doing more with less.* The result was leaner organizations that had shed layers of middle management, with an emphasis upon youth over experience. Ageism has become a key issue, with evidence emerging that people are now considered over the hill at forty-two and quite likely to remain jobless.

Those left in organizations have been faced with almost constant pressure and change. This period of modern change has been described by Peter Vaill as "permanent whitewater," where we no longer have the luxury of space and time in which to pause, take a breath, and reflect before we are hit by the next wave of change and resultant upheaval.[9] Thus change occurs, and before we can adjust and adapt fully to its requirements, new change supersedes it and further disrupts our lives and the organization.

In the midst of this whitewater, managers have an opportunity to make a difference in either positive or negative ways. William Watson, a co-founder of Holiday Inn, rightly said: "Many executives touch and influence the lives of thousands of people. Their touch can be a blight or a blessing. Their influence can build up a person or tear them down." To be seen as a caring leader is not a sign of weakness. Leaders who take on the responsibility of ensuring that change is tackled sensitively, and who genuinely care about the people in their organization are, in fact, very astute. They demonstrate an understanding of the importance of responding in a healing manner as problems and crises develop. They understand that their key task is to create and maintain a positive environment in which people are motivated to work. This requires a change of emphasis to a more balanced approach to leadership and management, and a greater reliance on the application of the software of management, "human(e) relations."

Awareness: Keeping in Touch with Ourselves and Others

There's an oft-cited English proverb that states "Some men go through a forest and see no firewood." The essence of this quote is echoed by Emily, a young woman in Thornton Wilder's play *Our Town*. Emily dies in childbirth, but is granted a wish to return from death and live one day with her family. Although Emily has high hopes for that one day, she is disappointed, and as she leaves asks, "Do human beings ever realize life while they live it—every minute?" Emily's observation challenges us to live with awareness, reminding us to appreciate all that is going on around us and inside of us, to be in touch with other people and ourselves.

In the ever-changing past decade, the need for managers to be aware of their customers, their staff, and their organizations has been well documented. Yet servant-leaders are asked to take an additional step, to develop self-awareness, "realizing life while we live it—every minute." This entails making time for reflection, to understand the big picture of our organizations and how each of us fits into this picture. This type of general awareness, and especially self-awareness, strengthens the servant-leader. Awareness also aids in understanding issues involving ethics and values. In enables one to view most situations from a more integrated position.

To live so deeply is a special challenge, for it is easy to be superficial. We are so busy: We have so much to do, so many people to see, so many programs to develop, and so many products to sell. We feel that we simply don't have the time to be reflective, to sit back and just think about our jobs, our organizations, and ourselves. Yet finding time to be reflective offers us the opportunity to develop balance in our work lives. It offers us the time to think about the big picture, to understand what we are trying to do through our organizations as well as the values that we are endorsing through our programs and products.

Reflection also offers the opportunity for us to renew the passion that attracted us to our jobs in the first place. The importance of rekindling our own passion as well as the passion of our staff has been documented by McLaughlin, who found that effective youth workers were as diverse as their organizations.[10] The one common denominator they all had was a "fire in their belly." They were passionate about the young people with whom they worked and about the neighborhoods they served. To assess, reflect, and be honest with ourselves is critical if we want to find and sustain our passion in the workplace and in our lives in general.

Covey encourages personal awareness and "beginning with the end in mind" in order to understand the big picture of one's life.[11] Covey points out that each part of your life should be examined in the context of the whole, within the context of what really matters most to you. By keeping that end clearly in mind, you can make certain that whatever you do on any particular day does not violate the criteria you have identified as important to you.

One means by which managers can be purposeful in their reflection is through developing a personal mission statement. Your mission statement can become your constitution, the solid expression of your vision and values. It becomes the criterion by which you measure everything else in your life. As a result, the process becomes as important as the final product in that it encourages us to think through our priorities, to align our behavior with our beliefs, and to think in larger terms than today or tomorrow. This process is not a singular experience; it doesn't end with a personal mission statement. It is, rather, the ongoing process of keeping your vision and values before you and aligning your life to be congruent with the things you value most.

While individual assessment is the building block of our lives, and the basis for team building and shared success in the workplace, it is collective reflection within organizations that can lead to the shared values and missions that motivate staff and create a sense of synergy and accomplishment. One possible result of this type of synergy is the development of values-led organizations. Values-led business, pioneered by such organizations as the Body Shop and Ben and Jerry's Ice Cream, is based on the idea that business has a responsibility to the people and the society that make its existence possible. Values-led business seeks to maximize its impact by integrating socially beneficial actions into as many of its day-to-day activities as possible. The economic and social success of many values-led businesses demonstrates that people are willing to pay to do business with organizations that integrate values into their business practices.

Encouraging personal and organizational awareness is not only the right thing to do, it also makes good business sense. If upper and midlevel managers can model and create mechanisms for reflection within our organizations, we will see better staff, better organizations, and better communities. In the end it will be the customer who benefits as our programs and products help customers to experience life while they live it—every minute.

Persuasion: Beginning with the End in Mind

The appropriate use of power should always be a concern for servant-leaders. Therefore a key characteristic of servant-leadership is reliance upon persuasion rather than positional authority or power in making decisions within an organization. Sadly, the use and abuse of power, especially in the area of people management, is still a major factor in our working lives. Despite considerable weight of evidence, many organizations and managers within them persist with working practices and macho management styles that have a negative impact upon people.

Servant-leadership offers another scenario whereby leaders encourage workers to build consensus around the true purpose of the organization as well as the means of achieving this purpose. Within this type of environment, staff are encouraged to use persuasion rather than coercion in persuading others of their views. For example, if people are convinced of the way of doing something or the need to meet a tight deadline, they are more likely to deliver. Effective organizations are not characterized by impersonal, authoritarian hierarchies that bully people into producing results under pressure, but by leaders who are highly interpersonal in their relationships with people, are effective persuaders, and lead by example. As Anita Roddick of the Body Shop says of her organizational culture, "We communicate with passion and passion persuades."[12]

In building consensus, it is important to remember that persuasion is a two-way process. Effective followers need to use persuasion to good effect when passing views, opinions, information, and intelligence on to their leaders, especially when they see that a decision has the potential to have a detrimental effect upon the organization, its services, or its customers. A bad leadership decision is more likely to be changed by sound and persuasive argument, backed up by objective information, than through confrontation.

The concept of dialogue is an important component in the art of persuasion. In a dialogue, nobody is trying to win. There is no attempt to gain points. Dialogue is based on common participation, in which we are not working against each other but with each other.

Dialogue offers a good context for us to explore the true purpose of an organization—to begin with the end in mind. In order to be in a good position to persuade people about the benefits of your product or service, it is important to understand the concept of benefits-based management (BBM). Today's world demands that leaders understand not only societal changes but also the benefits that people can expect from their products, programs, and services. This knowledge is vital in order to plan and develop programs and services with specific benefits in mind. It is only through an underlying commitment to fostering specific benefits that they will be achieved.

Within the service-based organization, a benefits-based model focuses upon the long-term benefits of participation in the program or service, where benefits are defined as follows:

- The realization of desired and satisfying on-site psychological experience

- Changes that are viewed to be advantageous or improvements in condition (gains) to individuals (psychological and physiological), groups, and society

- The prevention of a worse condition[13]

An example of the application of BBM can be seen in organizations that offer leisure experiences. Within these types of organizations, BBM is turning out to be a major factor in helping dispel the popular myth that leisure provides something of value only as long as the pleasurable experience lasts. BBM moves the leisure profession and industry forward a quantum leap by integrating the concept that value is added to people's lives even after on-site participation in a leisure activity.[14]

The fundamental question raised by a benefits approach for any organization is, Why should a particular product or service be provided? The answer to this question is formulated by clearly defining positive and negative consequences of delivering that service, with the objective being to optimize net benefits or add as much value for customers as possible. To do this, leaders and staff must understand what values their products and services add, articulate those values, and understand how to capture them. Such knowledge would help leaders and staff persuade others of the value of their products or programs.

Conceptualization: Seeing the Big Picture

From an early age, we are taught to deal with complexity by breaking things down into their separate parts. The flip side to this approach is that, in order to see the big picture, or *see things whole*, we need to put the pieces back together. The ability to see things whole is related to the ability to look at a problem or an issue from a conceptual perspective. The problem is that to achieve the ability to see things whole, managers must think beyond the day-to-day realities of the organization that often consume them.

Too often, organizations are bereft of any clear vision, and instead are driven by the need to achieve short-term operational and financial objectives. The key is to achieve the appropriate balance between conceptualization and a day-to-day focus. This is referred to as inductive and deductive reasoning, which relates to the process of large-to-small and small-to-large reasoning. Both are critical, but like the workings of the eye, focus is clearer and leadership more effective with the fluid adaptation of our thought processes.

In our discussion of awareness, we emphasized the need for leaders to make time for self-reflection and to identify their personal values in order to create their personal mission statement. In developing these conceptual skills, leaders can begin to integrate their personal values into the life of the organization. Indeed, only by assessing your personal vision and values first can you begin to create and translate that vision to your management team and throughout the organization. Everyone needs to be clear about what we are trying to be and what we will look like when we get there.

Michele Hunt describes leaders who have these conceptualizing skills as *dream makers*.[15] These people have the necessary insight and foresight to perceive the consequences of their actions. They have the ability to see their actions in relationship to others, and to collaboratively transform themselves and others, putting vision and values to work in their businesses, their communities, and the world in general.

Two critical skills related to conceptual thinking are the ability to be a lifelong learner and the ability to set priorities. In their book *Leaders: The Strategies for Taking Charge*, Bennis and Nanus observe that good leaders never mention the need for charisma or other glib formulae for success.[16] Instead, they talk of persistence, self-knowledge, and a commitment to lifelong learning. Bennis and Nanus also note, "Learning is the essential fuel for the leader, the source of continually sparking new understanding, new ideas and new challenges. Very simply, those who do not learn do not long survive as leaders."

But simply learning is not enough. Leaders must be able to focus this learning into specific priorities. If we have too many priorities, we can be paralyzed rather than empowered. Prioritizing the objectives for an organization demands that we conceptualize where we want to go to be our best. This is a difficult task, as most decisions about priorities are not choices between the good and the bad, but rather between the good and the best. In the words of Stephen Covey, "So often, the enemy of the best is the good."[17]

With this in mind, leaders must begin to conceptualize the dreams of their organizations by addressing such questions as, What business are we in? The answer to this fundamental question will go a long way in determining the *why, what,* and *how* an organization should function. The literature is full of examples of lost opportunities due to lost vision. In the United States, the hotel and railroad industries failed to capitalize on the changing needs of their customers. The hotel business traditionally catered to the upper end of the market and failed to see that as people became more mobile, they needed inexpensive places to stay. The travel market was ripe for a new type of provision, which the hotel sector should have capitalized on, but, in fact, motels arose as almost a separate sector of the industry. The mainstream hotel chains did not pioneer low-cost accommodation. That innovation required a new set of players completely.

Likewise, if railroad executives had seen themselves as being in the transportation business rather than in the railroad business, they would have put the first man on the moon! They failed in two areas. First, they did not anticipate the impact of the commercial airliner on their own business and, as a result, did not get involved in this new form of transportation. Second, they failed to upgrade their technology, services, and equipment to match their customers' changing needs.

To understand how this is relevant for leaders today, consider human service organizations, where the challenge is to respond to issues of the present. Although most human service institutions were a part of the social reform movement that responded to the problems of the Industrial Revolution around the turn of the twentieth century, today's successful organizations have been able to retool and respond to the needs of today. Jane Addams, an early social reformer in Chicago, wrote in 1893, "The one thing to be dreaded in the settlement [house movement] is that it lose its flexibility, its power of quick adaption, its readiness to change its methods as its environment may demand."[18]

Today, we are part of a new era that is coming to terms with a rapid pace of change. Leaders within human service organizations need to develop visions and programs that can meet the needs of the people caught up in the pressures associated with time and resources. We need to be bold; we need to experiment to meet the challenges of the times. We may fail a hundred times, but we need to keep developing services that best serve the needs of people today.

The following words, etched over the entrance to the main post office in St. Louis, seem to sum it up best: "Where there is no vision, the people perish."

Foresight: Plotting the Course

Foresight is important to help leaders understand lessons from the past, the realities of the present, and the likely consequences of a decision for the future. This characteristic is closely related to conceptualization, yet still distinct. Conceptual skills allow us see the big picture, the *where we want to go*. Foresight allows us to map out how we are going to get there by anticipating the various consequences of our actions and then picking the actions that will serve us best.

The importance of the characteristics of both foresight and conceptualization cannot be overstated, as they address perhaps one of the greatest criticisms leveled at servant-leaders. This criticism stems from the view that by waiting and empowering others, servant-leaders abdicate their power and lose the opportunity to truly shape the organization by their own vision of the future. In this way, servant-leadership is not viewed as visionary, but rather as a feel-good approach that makes others like the organization, and in which the servant-leader simply absorbs and carries out the ideas of others.

However, this viewpoint of servant-leadership overemphasizes the idea of the servant, and ignores the power of the creative interface between these two seemingly opposite ideas. Consider the words of the ancient Chinese philosopher, Lao-Tzu: "The wise leader knows how to be creative. In order to lead, the leader learns to follow. In order to prosper, the leader learns to live simply. In both cases, it is the interaction that is creative. All behavior consists of opposites; learn to see things backwards, inside out and upside down."[19]

Throughout this chapter we have examined characteristics that may lend themselves more to either being a servant or a leader. The true power—and the ultimate challenge—of servant-leadership comes from blending the characteristics of being a servant and leader together. Remember, balance isn't *either/or* but *both/and*. In this light, the characteristics of conceptualization and foresight are particularly important if servant-leaders are going to be visionary. This is a tough balancing act for servant-leaders: They must balance the need to empower others with the need to be strong, visionary, transformational leaders. It demands that leaders be aware of their individual situations, that they listen to others, conceptualize the big picture, and persuade and empower others to lend their own talents in fulfilling the mission of the organization.

In this way, servant-leaders are not victims of their organizations and the people they lead: they are the co-creators of the future. They must seek to find ways to create win/win situations, which ensure that all concerned—leader, staff, organization, and customer—survive and thrive.

Foresight and insight enable the servant-leader to adopt three fundamental shifts of the mind. The first is a shift in the way we think about the world. Instead of seeing it as mechanistic, fixed, and determined, we need to begin to see it as open, dynamic, and alive. The second shift occurs when we come to understand that everything is connected to everything else. In the words of the American naturalist John Muir, "When we try to pick out anything by itself, we find it hitched to everything else in the universe," and so it is for leaders.[20] It is usually rare that any decision or strategy can or should be taken in isolation or in ignorance of the potential consequences to stakeholders, customers, or other parts of the organization. The adage that for every action there will be a reaction is a useful principle to work by! The third shift occurs in our understanding of commitment. Commitment doesn't mean doing whatever it takes to make things happen. It means, rather, a willingness to listen, to yield, and to respond to the inner voice that guides us toward our destiny.

Here are three general steps to developing foresight in the way we work and approach life:

- *Understand the past.* As Chief Justice Oliver Wendell Holmes observed, "To understand the todays, to talk about the tomorrows, I spent time in the yesterdays."[21] Leaders who have a sense of history, as well as an accurate picture of their organization, are better placed to engage the future.

- *Engage the future.* Leaders should become more purposeful and aware of the world around them by being informed about trends and issues not just within their own area of interest or sphere of influence, but as widely as possible in order to make connections that foster new ideas.

- *Remove the blinders and develop creativity.* We have a tendency toward blind spots, usually caused by conditioning or prior expectations, which must be recognized and overcome if the skills of foresight and conceptualization are to be developed.

It is only by combining these three key steps that leaders can develop the foresight and awareness needed to make the vital difference that distinguishes their organization from the rest. Unfortunately, all too often, the tendency is for a lack of creativity to result from poor awareness and foresight. Too many people at all levels in organizations operate with their eyes wide shut, missing key signals that foretell pending problems or potential opportunities.

One of the best models of the use of foresight is Richard Branson and his Virgin Group. He very rarely, if ever, develops and launches a new product or service. His approach is one of surveying the marketplace and gauging its performance and direction, researching and anticipating the market potential, and then driving hard into it with his own particular branding and style. He has done this from the outset with his original music business, airlines, and, more recently, with mobile phones, financial services, and now health and fitness clubs.

He personifies what Robert Greenleaf was emphasizing when he defined what distinguishes a superior company from its competitors. Branson says, "It is not the dimensions that usually separate companies, such as superior technology, more astute market analysis, better financial base, etc.; it is unconventional thinking about its dream of what this business wants to be, how its priorities are set and how it organizes to serve. It has a radical philosophy and self-image."

Stewardship: Being Accountable and Sharing Control

In *Leadership by the Book: Tools to Transform Your Workplace*, Ken Blanchard notes that "leaders who are servants first will assume leadership only if they see it as the best way they can serve. They are called to lead, rather than driven, because they naturally want to be helpful. They aren't possessive about their position. They view it as an act of stewardship, rather than ownership."[22]

The origin of the word *steward* can be traced back to ancient Greece. The Greek term for steward is *oiko-nomus*—*oiko* meaning *house* and *nomus* meaning *order*. Thus, the steward can be thought of as the manager of the household. Historically, the word *stewardship* means *to hold something in trust for another*. Stewardship was a means to protect the kingdom while those rightfully in charge were away or, more often, to govern for the sake of an underage king.

In today's society, stewardship is often associated with environmental or financial responsibility, yet it can be so much more if we are willing to be accountable for something larger than just ourselves. Peter Block, in *Stewardship: Choosing Service Over Self-Interest*, defines stewardship as "the willingness to be accountable for the well-being of the larger organization by operating in service, rather than in control, of those around us. Stated simply, it is accountability without control or compliance."[23]

To many, this may sound like a recipe for anarchy! But to Block, stewardship is a powerful concept that promises the means to achieve fundamental change in the way we govern our institutions, as it offers the opportunity to preside over the orderly distribution of power. Stewardship springs from a set of beliefs about reforming organizations that affirms our choice for service over the pursuit of self-interest. In this context, the steward is perceived as having been given a vocation to fulfill and the wherewithal to fulfill it. The responsibility rests within.

Being a steward means choosing service to our customers, our community, as well as the world at large and our work colleagues. In the grand scheme of things, it demands that we enlarge our vision of the world and our responsibility to make it a better place for all. It also demands searching out win/win situations whereby, through our actions, our customers win, the larger community and natural world win, and our organizations and the people within them also win.

In dealing with our customers, stewardship demands constantly addressing two questions: Whom do we serve? And for what purpose? These questions serve as the basis for remembering why we are in business and what we are trying to provide through our collective existence. Being good stewards of our programs also encourages us to foster a sense of responsibility in our customers for their own experiences, as well as for the resources they use to create and enjoy this experience.

The concept of stewardship continually challenges managers and leaders to ask how they can best share power with others in the organization and ensure that they have a meaningful role to play. The key is to build partnerships with staff, and to truly recognize the value they bring to the organization. One of the biggest management clichés of recent times is "Our people are our most valuable resource!" While for some organizations this is truly the case, there are still too many in which only lip service is paid to positive staff policies and relations. As one employee recently said, "Yes, people are the firm's most valuable resource—as long as the firm doesn't have to pay us too much and we keep our mouths shut."

There are signs that this situation is beginning to change and that organizations are really beginning to recognize the tangible benefits of stewardship principles. Research in the United States has shown that staff-friendly policies can make an impact directly upon the bottom lines of small and multinational companies alike. However, the reality is that it will probably take considerably longer for the required cultural shift to occur widely.

In dealing with our communities and our natural world, the concept of stewardship encourages us to remember that we serve more than just our customers. We serve our communities, and we hold our world in trust for those who follow. Thus we must continue to examine how we can act responsibly in our organizations and through our products, services, and programs.

On an individual level, being a good steward demands that we try to make ethical, person-friendly, and earth-friendly decisions in our programs and organizations. The famous American naturalist Aldo Leopold suggested that "each question of man's relationship to his environment be studied in such terms of what is ethically and essentially right as well as what is economically expedient. A thing is right when it tends to preserve the integrity, stability, and beauty of the biotic community. It is wrong when it tends to do otherwise."[24]

Commitment to the Growth of People

Traditional leadership models tend to draw out the distinct differences between leaders and followers. Leaders are distinguished as possessing unique talents, which are central to their successful interaction with followers. Leaders direct while followers respond. Followers, often indistinguishable from one another, are valued for their compliance, not their potential.

Servant-leaders, with their commitment to the growth of individuals (both staff and customers), turn this model on its head. Servant-leaders endeavor to put the needs of their followers first, believing in the power of their products, services, and programs to help both staff and customers grow as individuals. Ken Blanchard, in "Servant-Leadership Revisited," summed it up thus: "With the traditional pyramid, the boss is always responsible and the staff are supposed to be responsive to the boss. When you turn the pyramid upside down, those roles get reversed. Your people become responsible and the job of management is to be responsive to their people. That creates a very different environment for implementation. If you work for your people, then what is the purpose of being a manager? To help them accomplish their goals. Your job is to help them win."[25]

Servant-leadership seeks to respect employees, and thereby meet their personal and professional development needs as well as the needs of the organization. It is not an automatic command-and-control method, but instead uses a consultative, participative, non-hierarchical approach that engages people's hearts and minds as well as their hands. It solicits input from employees and offers benefits that reflect the importance of their well-being to the corporate well-being.

This is clearly, or should be, an issue of concern currently. Leaders in a wide range of service industries highlight the difficulties they have in attracting and retaining people of the right caliber. In service industries, the philosophy of finding and retaining the right people should sit at the heart of every company's strategy. At the moment, you have to ask, where is the young talent? Where are the new recruits to the market who will be leading the industry forward in the next forty years? Who is nurturing and developing them?

All leaders should, ideally, want the people in their organization to have the opportunity to develop their potential to contribute as fully as possible to its success. Ben and Jerry's Ice Cream, for example, has identified three areas to encourage employees to grow and develop: technical skills to achieve excellence in day-to-day work, personal skills to give life and vitality to these aspirations, and business knowledge to understand the implications and importance of what each person does. In essence, the company's leaders try to foster the intellectual curiosity of their staff, believing that the more their staff learn and grow, the better employees they will become.

Many service organizations are in a unique position to take advantage of the intellectual curiosity of their staff. Within organizations, people can create programs that evolve from their interests and passions, as well as directly influence the style of delivery to their customers. By fostering an employee's intellectual curiosity, we may in fact be creating an opportunity to expand our programs and services, which in turn can expand our ability to make a difference in people's lives.

But people will only grow and develop in the work situation if the culture of the organization allows it. It requires a proactive approach to ensure that appropriate resources, which include time and money, are available together with the mechanisms to ensure that real growth occurs. Such mechanisms can be both formal and informal. Formal mechanisms include personal development plans, time off for training, appraisals, mentoring programs, and regular feedback. Informal mechanisms can include frequent observation, showing genuine interest in people's progress, adopting a caring attitude, and adopting an open-door policy whereby staff can seek advice as and when needed. All of these require a genuine commitment to people and their growth, both by the organization and by the leaders within it.

Organizations in the service field are also in a unique position in that they can commit to the growth and development of not only their staff but also their customers through the provision of facilities, services, and programs. For example, if a family joins a health club and makes regular use of the range of available opportunities, they will receive a variety of on-site benefits, such as physical exercise, time with family members, rest, and relaxation. These on-site benefits may, in turn, contribute to a number of longer-term benefits for the family, such as improved physical fitness, increased work performance, positive relationships, and better communications with family members. These longer-term benefits may then lead to a variety of longer-term benefits for society, including reduced health care costs, higher productivity, more stable family life, and a positive economic impact on the community.

By committing to the growth and development of staff and customers, servant-leaders can adopt the benefits-based approach to delivering services and recognizing the inherent power of our programs and services to make a difference. It is important to note that the definition of a benefit, as proposed by Driver, Brown, and Peterson earlier in this chapter,[26] parallels the ultimate test of a servant-leader, as identified by Greenleaf. Do those served grow as persons? Do they, while being served, become healthier, wiser, freer, more autonomous, more likely themselves to become servants (the realization of desired and satisfying on-site psychological experiences)? What is the effect on the least privileged in society; will they benefit (improvements in condition) or at least not be further deprived (prevention of a worse condition)?

When considering the growth of people, whether it be physical, emotional, or spiritual, it is sometimes difficult to identify the short- and long-term effects. However, by committing to the growth of people, organizations can make a statement that they are in for the long haul, that they are building long-term relationships rather than simply looking for short-term gains.

Building Community

Throughout this chapter, we have examined the importance of meeting the needs of individuals and providing customers with quality experiences. Yet this is only half the equation, as we have also encouraged leaders to examine their role in delivering socially responsible products, programs, and services to build a better community. There must be a balance struck between the freedom of individuals to pursue their goals and the responsibility individuals and organizations have to live as members of a common society. Thus for servant-leaders there must be a balance struck between delivering quality products, services, and experiences that maximize freedom for individuals and organizations, and also being socially responsible to both the local and global community.

What makes a good community? Robert Putnam, in his review of the "state of community" in America, writes about improving the sense of community by thinking in terms of developing the physical, human, and social capital of an area.[27] Just as a new facility (physical capital) or an opportunity to gain new knowledge (human capital) can increase the livability of a community, so too do social contacts affect the livability of individuals and communities. *Social capital* refers to connections between individuals, the networks, norms, and trust that enable people to act together to pursue shared objectives. Putnam declares we are losing community and that our collective civic life is weakening. This loss of a sense of community is, in part, due to a decline in social capital. This decline in social capital is an important issue for servant-leaders, as one of the benefits of many programs and services is building social capital within communities. Putnam's work challenges servant-leaders to think intentionally about how we can build social capital, both in our organizations and in the community, through the work of our organization.

What characteristics or virtues must people exhibit to create a good community? A community is a sum of its parts, so a good community must be made up of virtuous citizens. Identifying these virtues has been an ongoing task. For example, communities thrive when people have the ability to listen to all views—even those they dislike—and the skill to work through conflicting approaches to solve a problem. Robert Dahl points out that good citizens exhibit the qualities of moral reasoning.[28] They are open-minded, informed, and empathetic. They also have an understanding of the idea of the public good and a sustained desire to work toward achieving the common good and a common ground. As is evident from the work of Dahl, many of the characteristics of servant-leaders are represented in their thinking, including listening, empathy, awareness, and conceptualization.

A virtuous life is a practiced life. People must have the opportunity and be encouraged to practice these characteristics. This means that we must provide opportunities to develop a variety of virtues, such as empathy, stewardship, patience, humility, awareness, and diligence, within our organizations. Our programs and services should provide the opportunity to practice these types of behavior in a nonthreatening environment. An example of this commitment to practicing virtues is contained in the mission statement of Calvin College's intramural program. The mission states, "The intramural program strives to create positive play/leisure opportunities that contribute to the development of individuals, develops and strengthens a caring community on campus as well as encourages students, faculty and staff to lead healthy lives."

This mission is played out in a number of specific ways, including the following policy: "To encourage a sense of community in intramural sports, no referees will be provided for games. It is our hope that such an environment will encourage teams and individuals to be self-monitoring and responsible for their own behavior. An intramural official will be present to help with the logistics of all activities." Although such a policy clearly would not be appropriate for all organizations, the approach attempts to help individuals practice many of the virtues discussed in this chapter.

What role should individual organizations play in building community? The tension between promoting both individual and organizational freedom on one hand and the responsibility to both customers and staff on the other pervades many aspects of a wide variety of organizations. Balancing this tension in organizations is further complicated by such decisions as who to serve, how to serve, and what to provide. Although the approach may differ according to the organization, one constant remains: the desire to serve both the individual and the community.

Historically, such a service ethic has been associated more with the public and voluntary sectors, as opposed to being driven by the bottom line. Yet in today's changing environment, the traditional lines between the public, voluntary, and commercial sectors are blurring. Public and voluntary organizations are being urged to be more innovative and entrepreneurial, while the commercial sector is being asked to be more socially responsible.

As a result, we are seeing more collaboration and cooperation between all types of organizations to meet the demands of financial and social responsibility. As one chief executive of a Fortune 500 company stated:

> Conventional wisdom is that the highest mission of a corporation is to maximize profits. Maximize return to shareholders. That is a myth. It has never been true. Profit is just money and money is just a medium of exchange. You always trade it for something else. So, profits are not an end. They are a means to an end. My philosophy is this: We don't run our business to earn profits. We earn profits to run our business. Our business has meaning and purpose—a reason to be here. People talk today about business needing to be socially responsible as if this is something new we need to do, on top of everything else we do. But social responsibility is not something that one should do as an extra benefit of the business. The whole essence of the business should be social responsibility. It must live for a purpose. Otherwise, why should it live at all?[29]

Servant-leaders must continually look for ways to enhance the quality of life of customers, communities, and staff. For example, if servant-leaders can build and encourage social capital within their organizations, the end result will be stronger communities. The key for servant-leaders to be successful in balancing the needs of individuals and society is to examine the benefits that people are seeking from programs and services and to find ways of ensuring that they experience them. This is within the context of simultaneously demonstrating a caring attitude toward others as well as the environment. This process includes two key components: listening to and understanding the needs of customers, and assisting participants to understand and take responsibility for their actions.

Summary: Putting the Pieces Together

Throughout this chapter we have tried to introduce the concept of servant-leadership and explore its core characteristics. We believe that servant-leadership provides a framework that people can draw upon to create work environments that empower staff to be more responsive to customers and to the communities in which they live and work.

When considering the ten characteristics of servant-leadership, it is important to look at them in relationship to one another rather than as individual elements. Rather than a ladder or a cyclical process, where characteristics build upon each other or lead one to the other, it is more appropriate to view these characteristics as a weaving, with each strand supporting and shaping the others. As with any good weaving, the servant-leader draws greater strength from the combination of these characteristics than from their application in isolation. Those servant-leaders who are able to combine all ten characteristics in a dynamic process will fulfill the potential of servant-leadership to make a difference in the lives of the people they serve.

In drawing the chapter to a close, we would like to highlight three key themes that run through the ten characteristics and form the foundation on which they are built:

- *Reflection*. To commit to being a servant-leader, you must create time to reflect in order to understand who you are and how you relate to staff, customers, and the larger community. Being reflective also provides the opportunity to step back and understand the big picture of the organization while not forgetting the small integral parts that must come together to help achieve its mission. Self-reflection helps you to rejuvenate and find the inner confidence to move forward in dealing with staff and customers, as well as practice such characteristics as listening, empathy, healing, conceptualization, and foresight.

- *Integrity*. One definition of integrity is completeness, the ability to live out one's values and vision as well as dealing with others in a straightforward manner. By being reflective and thinking before acting, servant-leaders can deal with people and programs with integrity. When leaders are perceived as acting with integrity, they can be a healing force within the organization and persuade others to their point of view. Leaders who are perceived to act with integrity are well on the way to earning the trust and support of staff and customers. Joe Batten, consultant to many blue-chip corporations and author of *Tough-Minded Management*, summed it up thus: "Leadership in every phase of your life can only happen if others like what they see in you, respect you, and want to achieve what you are asking them to be and do."[30]

- *Passion*. We have previously highlighted the importance of passion in making a difference. Passion goes beyond simply being dramatic, powerful, and emotional: It is more accurately characterized as an unfailing dedication to an ideal. Thus intensity and duration often demonstrate passion. Seeing things through over the long haul, whether it be a program or the way a department functions, and not being deflected, requires passion. When servant-leaders can demonstrate their passion for many of the core values of their organization, they reaffirm their organization's commitment to the growth of people and to building social capital within their communities. As a result, we must continue to develop the "inner fire within ourselves," which allows us to continue to deliver programs and services at a high level over the long term, as well as encouraging a passion for services within our staff to meet the needs of customers.

In following through on these themes of reflection, integrity, and passion, servant-leaders can begin to weave many of the characteristics discussed in this chapter into their personal and professional lives. Through this integration process, they can create the blend of compassion and effectiveness that is the mark of a servant-leader. However, it is also important to stress that this model presents no easy answers and that, in the end, the concept of the servant-leader is a paradox. This is the real strength of the concept: Remembering that the process of balancing the concepts of servant and leader is not *either/or* but *both/and*.

Thus the power of the concept remains embedded in one's ability to combine the best of being a leader with the best of being a servant. In the end, being a servant-leader is not something you *do* but rather something you *are*. It is about creating the right environment to get the best out of people and unleash their true potential. Servant-leadership should not be misinterpreted as soft management—some of the most tough-minded leaders today are firm believers in and exponents of servant-leadership. Far from it, it is about effectiveness—and there is clearly a need for that! In our experience, the majority of problems related to staff performance can be traced to ineffective or poor management, especially at the middle management level.

We leave the final word to Stephen Covey, who states, "You may be able to buy someone's hand and back, but you cannot buy their heart, mind and spirit. And in the competitive reality of today's global marketplace, it will only be those organizations whose people not only willingly volunteer their tremendous creative talent, commitment, and loyalty, but whose organizations align their structures, systems, and management style to support the empowerment of their people that will survive and thrive as market leaders."[31]

9

Toward a Theology of Institutions

David L. Specht with Richard R. Broholm

This particular moment in history is both a terribly auspicious and an incredibly exciting moment to be exploring Robert Greenleaf's call for a theology of institutions. The highly publicized failures of corporate leadership at Enron, WorldCom, Tyco, Arthur Andersen, and the Roman Catholic Church in the United States have dramatically harmed the lives of tens of thousands of persons inside and outside these institutions while at the same time deeply shaking the confidence of the public at large in our nation's institutions and those who lead them. While there are innumerable opportunities for leadership to fail, these failures were especially grievous, for in each instance they appeared to reflect a fundamental lack of clarity on the part of those in leadership about what and whom they were holding in trust. Add to these specific events the high level of ambient anxiety that has permeated our public and private lives since the events of September 11, 2001 (the attack on the World Trade Center Towers), the ensuing preoccupation of our government with the war on terrorism, and the impact of the present economic malaise on the lives of families, communities, and organizations, and we are faced with a level of collective dispiritedness and lack of confidence in the commitment and capacity of public and private institutions unmatched since near the end of the Vietnam War.

So it is indeed an auspicious moment to be responding to Greenleaf's call for the development of a theology of institutions. Particularly so, because in several instances those whose betrayal of the trust of leadership has been so well publicized have also been active church members. This has been an especially painful and wounding irony in those cases where the failure of leadership has taken place within religious institutions themselves.

At the same time it is also an exciting and provocative time to explore the lively intersection of human spirit, sacred traditions, leadership, and organizational life. For it was precisely during the social and political ferment of the late 1960s and early 1970s, with its widespread apprehension about the trustworthiness of our institutions and those who led them, that Greenleaf began to speak and write about the idea of servant-leadership and its inextricable link to servant institutions.

The Call

An idea whose time has come frequently emerges simultaneously from more than a single source, as its essential truth is recognized from a variety of vantage points. This was certainly the case in the emergence of the call for the development of a theology of institutions, which, at least as we experienced it, arrived from two voices.

Robert Greenleaf's perspective was shaped primarily by his life as a student of organizations and leadership, first within AT&T, and following that, as a consultant to leaders in universities, businesses, foundations, and religious institutions.

In 1970, Greenleaf wrote his seminal essay profoundly reshaping our understanding of the true nature and purpose of leadership, "The Servant as Leader." Two years later Greenleaf's second essay, "The Institution as Servant," was published:

> This is my thesis: caring for persons, the more able and
> the less able serving each other, is the rock upon which

a good society is built. Whereas, until recently, caring was largely person-to-person, now most of it is mediated through institutions—often large, complex, powerful, impersonal; not always competent; sometimes corrupt. If a better society is to be built, one that is more just and more loving, one that provides opportunity for its people, then the most open course is to raise both the capacity to serve and the performance as servant of existing major institutions by new regenerative forces operating within them.[1]

Robert Greenleaf was not alone in recognizing the necessity of raising the servant-capacity of existing institutions. During that same period, from 1964 to 1974, six Protestant denominations came together at the initiative of American Baptist Church leader Jitsuo Morikawa to form Metropolitan Associates of Philadelphia (MAP), an action research program of the World Council of Churches designed to explore how the church could more effectively relate to men and women who lead and serve in so-called secular organizations within an urban context.

Central to MAP's approach was the recruitment of 125 lay associates—men and women employed in a variety of organizations from six sectors of the city: education and arts, business and industry, social organization, politics and government, health and welfare, and physical development. Six urban agents—clergy salaried by their denominations—were assigned, one to each of these sectors, to support and to offer resources to these associates in identifying key issues shaping the future in their sector of the city. Additionally, there were eight worker ministers, clergy who found employment in a variety of secular occupations in the political, business, social service, and educational sectors of the city.

When asked why the church was becoming involved in secular organizations, Morikawa spoke about institutions in distinctly religious terms:

In order to discern, participate in, and celebrate God's activity in the city. The church today is immersed in talk about mission. But little is being done to test out how laity can participate in mission through the public institutions of the metropolis. If humankind is called to affect history and the reshaping of the world, then men and women in business, political, social, health, educational and physical planning institutions must see themselves under the mandate of calling; a calling to corporate responsibility. This means that every institution is confronted with the pressing question, "To what end?" To what purpose do we produce chemicals, educate children, build highways, elect officials, administer medicine, and provide social services?[2]

During its last five years, MAP focused its energies on trying to better understand the change process within institutions and the way in which local churches might offer support and empowerment for laity committed to holding their communities in trust through serving as change agents within the organizations where they worked. They referred to this strategy as their "wager" on the local congregation, and published a resource called *A Strategy of Hope* offering a guide to formation of support groups within congregations and change agent teams within their places of employment. These words from the introduction to *A Strategy of Hope* describe their vision for local congregations:

While many organizations have broken down or become destructive, they are, on the whole, ordered ways of serving God's people by meeting needs and solving problems. We do need them. . . . But, in that they have been structured in such a way that they do not serve all of God's people, but primarily those who are wealthy, white, male, and western, they must be changed. In that they are

structured in a way which keeps us isolated, alienated, and
frustrated, they must be restructured. They must be made
more human-oriented: they must be humanized. . . . The
objective of lay ministry is to develop within the Christian Church a new ministry through the laity to the
organizations of the secular world. . . . If lay people are
to minister to society they will require clergy who can
act as enablers of lay action. They will also require the
church to provide resources, both human and financial,
as well as guidance, training, and support to lay ministry
groups. In fact, the entire structure of the church must
be open to enabling the ministry of the laity.[3]

A *Strategy of Hope* was warmly received by a handful of congregations around the country, but for the most part the support of
church members as change agents within their workplace institutions was simply not a priority for the institutional church. After
MAP's closing in 1974, Dick Broholm, one of its three codirectors,
returned to his alma mater, Andover Newton Theological School,
for a sabbatical time of reflecting on the learnings emerging from
the MAP years and to explore the seminary's readiness to somehow
pursue this work.

Here he found support and interest among some faculty for a
larger vision of ministry—especially from theologian Gabe Fackre
and the seminary's dean of faculty, the late George Peck. With their
support, the Andover Newton Laity Project was launched, featuring an intensive action-research effort involving six local congregations committed to the intersection of faith and work.
Throughout these five years, the pastor and five lay members of each
congregation met on a monthly basis with five members of the
Andover Newton faculty to reflect on their workplace ministries.
They identified nine variables—enabling or blocking forces—that
functioned within their churches to either positively empower
members in their workplace ministries in secular institutions or

block them in discovering and responding to this call. The learnings from this action-research effort were published in 1979 under the title of *Empowering Laity for Their Full Ministry* and shared broadly with workplace ministry advocates across many denominations.[4]

In the early 1980s the Laity Project, by then institutionalized as the Center for the Ministry of the Laity at Andover Newton, launched several task forces of laity and professional theologians in an attempt to further bridge the gap between the church's theology and people's experience in the workplace. By this point I was working with Dick, serving as staff to a task force focused on exploring the implications of this connection, not abstractly, but in the very specific settings of organizations like Digital Equipment Corporation, the Massachusetts State Foster Care Review Unit, the Boston Mayor's Office, and State Mutual Insurance. Once again it was evident that the daily workplace ministries of men and women participating in the task force were inextricably linked not only to individual persons but to institutions as well. It was clear that in order to think theologically about workplace ministry, we would need to begin to think theologically about institutions as well.

We were primed to rediscover in Robert Greenleaf a conversation partner whose thinking and writing spoke powerfully to our own inquiry.

Though not himself a churchman, Greenleaf felt strongly about the role churches could play in the effort to create a more caring society through supporting persons committed to serving as regenerative agents within institutions. In a letter to encourage the work under way at Andover Newton, he contended that "the fundamental reconstruction of institutions cannot take place without a strong supporting influence from churches. So long as these churches have only a 'theology of persons' they cannot wield the needed influence on institutions and their leaders."[5]

He suggested that the church's theological preoccupation with individuals tended to focus people's thinking on "how to ease the hurt of the system, and not enough on how to build a system that can have a positive, growing, liberating, and humanizing impact on people." Moreover, Greenleaf insisted that critical to the task of building transformed institutions is the faith one must have to risk and move boldly into new and uncharted territories. He wrote, "While science helps calculate the odds on a decision, belief sustains one in the inevitable uncertainties and anxieties which the originator of regenerative action must bear. A theology of institutions could be a vital ingredient informing and shaping a faith which empowers such risk-taking and institution building; it could also be a critical resource in the development, preparation and sustenance of persons who are committed to being regenerative agents within institutions."[6]

Simultaneous to Greenleaf's encouragement, Jitsuo Morikawa was also urging Dick Broholm and his staff to pursue the development of a theology of institutions.

> The church has commendably focused its theological discipline on the welfare of individual persons, throughout most of its long history, as a sign of the preciousness of every life in the sight of God. Therefore the ministry of the church is concerned and practiced largely as ministry to persons. But today, more than in the past, the fate or welfare of human life is powerfully affected by the institutions of society; in fact the future is being largely shaped by these economic, political and social institutions of our culture, so that the role of institutions, the moral and social accountability of institutions, becomes perhaps the number one agenda in our historical enterprise. How to confront these powerful organizations, which are our greatest achievement, before they destroy us on the one hand, and how to evoke and provoke them to a fresh discovery and discernment of their true purpose and calling, is the task of an American, indigenous, evocative theology.[7]

At the urging of both Greenleaf and Morikawa, and with the support of a modest grant from the Religion Division of the Lilly Endowment, we began to work more explicitly on the development of a theology of institutions through a series of efforts that continues to this day.

Two Dimensions of Greenleaf's Call for a Theology of Institutions

I believe that there are two complementary aspects of Greenleaf's call for a theology of institutions, one more pragmatic and strategic, and the other more spiritual. In the first we hear Greenleaf the lifelong student of leadership and organizational life. In the second, we hear Greenleaf the spiritual seeker. This dimension of his journey came to fuller and more visible expression through his writings during the later years of his life. Both perspectives are suggested in these three sentences from his essay "The Need for a Theology of Institutions."

> I do not believe that the urgently needed fundamental reconstruction of our vast and pervasive structure of institutions can take place, prudently and effectively, without a strong supporting influence from the churches. And I doubt that churches as they now stand, with only a theology of persons to guide them, can wield the needed influence. I deem it imperative that a new and compelling theology of institutions come into being.[8]

A Strategic Vision for Churches and Seminaries

Beginning with his premise that the best way to raise a society that is more just and loving is to *raise the capacity to service and the performance as servant of existing institutions*, Greenleaf wrestled with the important question of how best to hold institutions in trust in such a way as to awaken this kind of servant spirit. He came to believe that foundations and religious institutions together could play important strategic roles in helping to realize this possibility.

While elements of his thinking about how this might occur are expressed in several of his writings of the late 1970s and early 1980s, nowhere is his vision for this possibility more fully articulated than in an essay titled "A Fable."[9] In it Greenleaf imagines representatives of several foundations noting in conversation together that the essential "machinery" to build a healthier society—seminaries, churches, individuals, and operating institutions—was in place but not functioning. They wondered what might be done to enable seminaries and churches to come alive to the critical role they might play in awakening within these religious institutions a servant spirit. Eventually they undertook a campaign: (1) calling seminaries to their roles as trustees of the larger society through (2) training church leadership capable of helping to inspire and equip church members, and (3) to serve as regenerative forces capable of transforming society's institutions.

Greenleaf's vision for seminaries and churches was not rooted in undue optimism for either. Indeed, while his writings reflect a deep respect for the servant-leadership quality of individual religious leaders (Abraham Heschel, Pope John XXIII, and John Woolman), they also in other places suggest a sobered regard for church institutions as suffering from self-preoccupation and general ineffectiveness in addressing the needs of the larger society.[10] Nevertheless, the combination of his own pragmatism and, I suspect, the influence of persons like Gordon Cosby (pastor of Church of the Savior in Washington, D.C.) and Robert Lynn (then head of the Religion Division of the Lilly Endowment) led him to imagine and then advocate for an enlargement of the strategic role of seminaries and churches in raising the quality of life in the world around them.

In reflecting on the process of thinking toward the desirability of this kind of enlarged role for seminaries and churches, Greenleaf wrote, "Out of my probings, the idea of a *hierarchy of institutions*

evolved. In this hierarchy, I see, at the top, seminaries and foundations. Foundations are in that oversight position because they
have the resources and the opportunity to gain perspective that
enables them to provide conceptual leadership to colleges and
universities. . . . Seminaries are in a strategic position to give similar
support to churches, whose needs are also urgent. In turn, both
churches and universities are well placed to give nurture and guidance
to individuals and to the whole range of operating institutions."[11]

Greenleaf's vision for churches and seminaries resonated powerfully with our own earlier efforts to engage a seminary and local
church congregations in an exploration of what factors in the life
of a congregation function to either enable or frustrate their capacity to support their members in this way. Following the closing of
the Center for the Ministry of the Laity at Andover Newton Theological School, this work with congregations lay fallow for more
than a decade. More recently, research into how to strengthen the
capacity of local congregations to support their members in drawing upon their faith as a resource to their holding in trust their
workplace and community institutions has become the centerpiece
of an exciting initiative at Luther Seminary in St. Paul. Through
its extensive reach as sponsored by the nation's largest Lutheran
theological school, Luther's *Centered~Work* initiative is planning to
engage thousands of congregations in this vision of local churches'
becoming better able to support their members in linking their faith
to their everyday workplace settings within society's organizations.[12]

A Practical Theology Capable of Undergirding
Those Seeking to Hold Institutions in Trust

Greenleaf was convinced that it would be difficult if not impossible
for churches and seminaries to wield the kind of institution-renewing
influence he envisioned so long as their theology was largely individually and interpersonally focused, a focus he deemed important
but inadequate to the task of orienting us toward the pressing
challenge of holding institutions in trust. In his essay "The Need

for a Theology of Institutions," he worried about the absence of such a theology:

> Those who draw their spiritual sustenance from churches and are concerned for preparing people who will care and serve in our complex, tension-torn world have largely extrapolated from the available theology of persons and seem not to have explicitly faced the question of what a committed person does—one who is capable of being a strong quality-building force within our institutions. As a consequence, too much of the effort to care and serve is directed to easing the hurt of the "system" that is grinding people down faster than the most valiant rescue effort can help them; and too little caring effort is going into building a "system" [a set of institutions] that will have a positive growing effect on people. . . . How can a contemporary theology of institutions be brought into being, one that will encourage, prepare, and support committed people to make careers inside institutions as initiators of regenerative quality-building action?[13]

It is this second dimension of Greenleaf's call for a theology of institutions—the task of developing a theological understanding of institutions capable of undergirding the commitment and informing the perspective of those who would hold institutions in trust—that became the focus of our own efforts.

One Effort to Develop a Practical Theology of Institutions

Our approach to this undertaking was informed by a simple premise and a difficult problem. Our premise was that any genuinely useful theology of institutions would necessarily emerge from the collaborative engagement between those whose center of gravity is primarily within the religious tradition (mostly seminary faculty and church leaders) and those who spend the great majority of their time preoccupied with the life and performance of the organizations where they work. An adequate theology of institutions can emerge only from an exploration that engages both these worlds—the theological tradition and the world of organizations—with genuine care and respect.

The difficult problem is to pull this off. Our experience of the engagement of these two worlds with one another was that it was exceedingly difficult to achieve the desired balance. Too often, in engaging the world of secular institutions, the church tends to either blandly and uncritically affirm organizations and their leaders or, on the other hand, to err in the opposite direction of regarding and addressing institutions with an indiscriminately critical and unforgiving eye.

These unfortunate alternatives reflect a broader societal tendency noted by John Gardner when he wrote about institutions as being trapped between those persons (often on the inside) who are comfortable, complacent, and unwilling to see the institution change, and those prophets (usually on the outside) who insist that the institution must change or else they will burn it down. He described this as the battle between "the uncritical lovers" and the "unloving critics" suggesting that "love without criticism brings stagnation, but criticism without love brings destruction."[14]

Perhaps because of an awareness of these two equally undesirable tendencies, in our experience, the thoughtful engagement of clergy and organizational leaders (particularly business leaders) tended to not happen at all. Business leaders tended to shy away from the conversation, suspecting that their organizational world was of no real interest to their pastors, or more problematically, regarded by clergy with suspicion as being fundamentally unworthy of their respect. For their part, clergy, while curious, did not pursue this engagement, in part because they felt ill prepared for the engagement, uncertain what they might bring of value to conversations about complex and frequently high-stakes dilemmas facing the women and men who sat in worship on Sunday.[15]

We were convinced, then, that a theology of institutions capable of undergirding the church's commitment to hold institutions in trust must emerge from a different kind of engagement between church leaders and lay people with operational responsibility within secular organizations. It must emerge from a conversation in which organizational leaders experience their messy worlds and the consequential decisions they face in these settings as being held in trust through an engagement marked both by respect and rigorous engagement.

We were also clear that an essential test of the adequacy of any theology of institutions that emerged from this engagement would be the extent to which it offered a basis for the development and support of "loving critics" capable of holding institutions in trust. One may hold an organization in trust either as a regenerative agent who works from within or as one who accompanies these organizations in a trustee role. Either way, the work of holding an institution in trust demands that one bring a larger sense of one's role and purpose in the world and, similarly, a larger vision for the role and purpose of the institution in the greater scheme of things. A theology of institutions must help us make this essential connection between what is of pressing and immediate concern and what, on the other hand, is of ultimate importance.

Given these clarities, we determined that our approach toward developing a practical theology of institutions should meet the twin criteria of being *tangibly grounded in organizational life* and *clearly informed by theological perspective*.

To ensure that the effort was tangibly grounded in organizational life and experience we took the following steps:

1. Held our meetings on-site at the workplace settings of participating organizations

2. Focused our reflection on consequential and unresolved real-time issues presented by participating organizations

3. Oriented our engagement toward the goal of holding one another's organizations in trust around their well-being and their impacts on constituents both within and outside the organization

4. Worked to ensure that the majority of those participating in our meetings had ongoing operational or trustee responsibility for real organizations

5. Adopted as a key ground rule for our meetings an agreement to maintain the confidentiality of our conversations in order to permit frank engagement with issues of importance

To ensure that our effort was clearly informed by theological perspective we took the following steps:

1. Sought to identify theological conversation partners from seminary and church settings capable of bringing

    Commitment to this exploration of the interface of theological tradition and organizational life

    Curiosity, good listening skills, and an attitude of fundamental respect to their encounter with the complex world of organizational life and its dilemmas

    Insight into and knowledge of the theological tradition and the capacity to make it accessible

2. Worked with theologians to identify relevant concepts or premises within our particular theological tradition capable of reshaping our understanding of organizational life and its purposes

3. Developed a theological model of organizational life, translated it into secular language for use within organizations as a framework for seeing things whole, and worked with organizations to promote its integration and use

4. Developed a process for enabling men and women to gather around an organization and its leaders for the purpose of holding the organization in trust around a difficult challenge facing it

What follows is a brief description of what this effort has yielded to date and how it has come to expression in the life of a particular organization.

Four Theological Premises for Those Who Would Hold Organizations in Trust

We have come to identify several theological premises that shape the way we regard institutions and consequently how we engage them. These premises form the basis of a *practical theology of institutions*, constituting a theology capable of informing our practice. In speaking with others, we have found that the essential truth of some of these premises resonate with similar truths emerging from other religious traditions. It bears acknowledging, however, that our articulation of these premises does in fact derive from a particular religious perspective—the Reformed Protestant Christian tradition—one which we do not regard as normative or authoritative for people whose religious persuasions are different from our own.

Having acknowledged this, here are four premises (some perhaps provocative) that we believe are important elements of a practical theology of institutions.

Premise #1: Institutions Are Part of God's Order

Walter Wink, a biblical scholar whose writings on the *powers and principalities* have powerfully shaped our theological understanding, writes of institutions: "These Powers are the necessary social structures of human life, and it is not a matter of indifference to God that they exist. God made them. For this reason . . . the account of creation in Genesis does not end in chapter 2, with the creation of the world, but in chapter 10, with the creation of the nations. . . . The meaning is clear," he concludes. "Humanity is not possible apart from its social institutions."[16]

Premise #2: God Loves Institutions

As part of God's world, institutions are the object of God's love. However, it is not enough to say God loves institutions in an abstract or general sense. Our tradition understands God's love to be not only a universal attribute of the divine, but also the essence of God's intimate concern for each of us as individuals. Believing that God's love is both universal and particular, we are compelled to declare not only that God loves institutions in general, but that God loves each institution in all its messy particularity.

From my perspective, the implications of this assertion are stunning! They begin to become apparent when you try out the premise by completing the statement, "God loves . . ." with the name of a particular institution.

God loves the New York Fire Department. God loves Johns Hopkins Hospital. God loves the AARP, the NAACP, and NASA. God loves TDIndustries. So far, so good.

What goes on for you, however, when you make the same affirmation for other, perhaps less likely, institutions? God loves Enron, WorldCom, or Tyco? If you are anything like me, this latter assertion may leave you a little edgy. Nevertheless, I believe it is true, and that rooting ourselves in this conviction offers an important basis for the kind of compassionate regard for organizations that is capable of enabling us to hold them in trust as critical lovers.

Premise #3: Institutions Are Living Systems

The affirmation that institutions are living systems links two important assertions, both fundamental to seeing institutions whole. The first is that *institutions are alive*. To say this is to recognize that the "being-ness" of institutions comprises not only their more tangible outward and physical reality (facilities, people, formal organizational and information systems, technology and equipment), but along with this a less tangible interiority or animating spirit whose energy is reflected through a combination of historical memory, shared convictions and dreams, proud successes, and bitter disappointments. This animating spirit (spoken of by others as an organization's DNA or culture) is enduring, a red thread persevering through the institution's story line over time, and must be well understood by those who would seek to hold the organization in trust.

The other assertion of this premise is that *institutions are systems*. As such they are wholly interdependent with the entire evolving world around them, both impacting and affected by everything that takes place throughout the constantly emerging reality of the existing order. A fundamental mindfulness discipline of healthy organizations is maintaining a consistent awareness of these twin dimensions of the institution's utter interdependence with the world around it: both its fundamental dependence upon that world and the inevitable intended and unintended consequences of its decisions and actions upon that same world.

Of course, the recognition of institutions as systems also has significant implications for the way we understand the internal life of organizations—as a whole composed of a constant and dynamic interdependence of countless elements exercising conspicuous or invisible influence on one another.[17] The threefold model organizational life developed by Seeing Things Whole and presented later in this chapter is a theological recognition of the systemic nature of organizations.

It is around this awareness of organizations as systems (and as existing within systems) that we find particularly relevant both Greenleaf's reminder that the root meaning of the word religion (*religio*) is *re-bind*, and his recognition of the importance of seeing things whole as the basis for this.

Premise #4: Institutions Are Called and Gifted, They Are Fallen, and They Are Capable of Being Redeemed

Here we have three important theological assertions about the nature of organizations embedded in a single statement. While each is essential in its own right, they are presented here together for an important reason.

Institutions are called and gifted. As expressions of God's dynamic and unfolding order, institutions are here for a reason. They are intended to be instruments of God's healing and reconciling purposes, and are both gifted and called to serve the common good in particular ways. They exist for good purposes; they are capable of good things; and good things are expected of them.

Institutions are fallen. As members of God's order, institutions are prone to inflating themselves, forgetting their membership in the larger community of God's creation, and to acting in ways that neglect or harm the common good. In this sense, they are much like each of us, capable both of great good and immeasurable harm.

Institutions are capable of being redeemed. Unlike the first two dimensions of this assertion, which to many may appear self-evident, this third is clearly a statement of faith. No matter how unlikely, how apparently fallen or broken, institutions are capable of reawakening to their own best possibilities. Part of holding an organization in trust is reminding it of its own best possibilities, and calling it back toward a recommitment to this potential. This is particularly difficult when the institution's collective sensibilities have become anesthetized by the gratification of their narrower self-interests, paralyzed by fear or anger, or burdened by the shame of past failures.

Fundamental to holding an organization in trust, particularly around its brokenness, is the recognition that all three of these realities—that the institution is gifted and called, that it is fallen, and that it is capable of being reawakened to its best possibilities—all three of these exist in every institution. Moreover, they exist not as mutually exclusive truths, but rather they coexist simultaneously as possibilities within the life of each institution, each present in some measure at any given moment in the organization's life.[18]

A Theological Framework for Seeing Things Whole in Organizational Life

A theology of institutions should do more than offer us a basis for reflecting from the perspective of religious faith on the nature and purpose of organizations while looking in on them from the outside. Ideally it should be capable also of informing the perspective and decision making of those who would serve as regenerative agents operating within.

Here, of course, we begin to reckon with an important truth about our organizations. Namely, that their spiritual and religious orientation is far from homogeneous. Instead, those who work within our organizations comprise an exceedingly rich mosaic of religious traditions, spiritual practices, and secular philosophical and values-based orientations. From the perspective of the organizational leaders with whom we were working, while organizational decision making and performance consistent with their own sacred ideals was highly desirable, they were committed to pursuing this in a way that did not impose their personal religious belief system on their coworkers. "What we need," they said, "is a nonreligious way of gaining theological perspective together on the challenges and decisions we face."

Our approach to this was to discover a theological model of organizational life that could then be translated into secular language for use within organizations as a framework for seeing things whole. We found that framework in the theological notion of the *Threefold Office of Christ*. The Threefold Office of Christ, attributed to theologian John Calvin, identifies the roles of Prophet, Priest, and King as three essential dimensions of the life and ministry of Jesus. These same roles are prominent in Hebrew scripture, each representing a unique expression of power and a way of mediating

God's relationship with Israel and the surrounding world. In early conversations searching for a theological framework for understanding institutions, Andover Newton theologian Gabriel Fackre proposed the Threefold Office as one possibility,[19] in part because it was one of the early ways the Christian Church described its own institutional life (the Body image is another). It also gained currency because it resonated strongly with institutional leaders, who found it aptly describing normative dimensions of organizational life.

In consultation with Fackre, we developed nonreligious language describing these three dimensions in organizational life while still reflecting the theological tradition. Each of the dimensions represents a cluster of preoccupations, associated stakeholders, core values, and ways of exercising power that are characteristic in organizational life. There are predictable and legitimate tensions among these three areas, and at times these tensions can operate destructively within the life of the organization. In a healthy organization, these dimensions function not as separate fiefdoms within the institution but rather as a commonwealth of collaborative service. When any one area loses sight of this fundamental interdependence with the other dimensions, it is prone to a more destructive expression of its concerns. The three dimensions are Identity, Purpose, and Stewardship.

The Identity (Priestly) Dimension of Organizational Life

Theologically, Identity represents an understanding of Jesus as high priest who, having experienced the vulnerability of the human condition, offers his life as a sacrifice capable of restoring to wholeness the brokenness in the divine-human relationship. This dimension is primarily concerned with healing, wholeness, and well-being of the gathered life of the organization. The primary stakeholders associated with this dimension are those who work for the organization. Its preoccupations include a concern for how the organization structures the character and quality of its gathered life, how it creates an environment that reflects its core values, and how it draws members of its workforce toward their fullest potential. This includes how the organization designs its work spaces; how it recruits, hires, evaluates, rewards, and dismisses its employees; how it disseminates information; how it distributes power and assigns accountability; and how it models investment in and commitment to the values it professes. Marks of faithfulness in this dimension include explicit acknowledgment of the values and principles guiding the life of the organization; personal resonance between those who work for the organization and these values; private and public life congruent with these values; and the capacity for honest self-reflection, including recognition of instances when the organization has, to some measure, failed to uphold its values.

The Purpose (Prophetic) Dimension of Organizational Life

Theologically, Purpose represents an understanding of Jesus as the prophet who bears witness to an alternative order, or witness that includes both the articulation of a compelling vision and a critique that recognizes the dissonance between things as they are and what ought to be. Unlike the Identity dimension's inward focus, the Purpose dimension is focused outward, on the organization's interface with and impact on the world around it. The primary stakeholders associated with this dimension are its customers or clients, its suppliers, its competitors, and the natural and human communities whose lives are in some way affected by the organization. Its preoccupations include a concern for the clarity of the organization's vision and mission, how it structures the processes for producing a "good" that is needed and valued by others, how it markets or sells this good, and how it serves the client and the wider world—in short, how the organization justifies its existence to the larger world around it. Marks of faithfulness in this dimension include a mission that offers a serious response to real needs in the world around it, accountability to the world around it for the exercise of its mission, an understanding of service that leaves those served better informed, less dependent, and more empowered in the exercise of their own capacities.

The Stewardship (Royal) Dimension of Organizational Life

Theologically, Stewardship represents an understanding of Jesus as ruler. Other kings had most often used their power to make things happen in a coercive way, bending persons and institutions to their will. Instead, Jesus modeled a fundamentally different understanding of leadership in which serving, empowering, facilitating, and persuading are primary tools. In organizational life the primary stakeholders associated with this dimension include management, owners, and trustees. Its preoccupations include a concern for how the organization secures and applies its resources (human, financial, and material) to sustain its viability while balancing the legitimate needs of each of its stakeholders and the wider community. Marks of faithfulness in this dimension include decision making and actions that express confidence in the long-term sustainable future of all stakeholders, governance marked by inclusivity, and structures and systems that constantly evolve to sustain the capacity of the organization to employ its unique gifts in service to the world around it.[20]

It was our work with the threefold model that led us to posit a fifth theological premise relating to the nature of faithfulness in organizational life and performance.

Premise #5: Faithfulness in Institutional Life Is Predicated on the Recognition and Management of Multiple Bottom Lines

Success in organizational life cannot be measured by performance related to a single bottom line. Seeing things whole in organizational life necessitates recognition of multiple dimensions of institutional life and performance. Each of these dimensions represents fundamental accountabilities, multiple bottom lines in an ongoing dynamic relationship that is inevitably characterized by some degree of tension.

The challenge of balancing the legitimate concerns associated with these multiple bottom lines came into focus in a dramatic way at Engineered Products.[21] We had worked with this company in using the threefold framework as a tool for seeing things whole concerning important organizational decisions.

"I remember at one point we were bidding for a major contract," Ed, the GM of Engineered Products, recalls. He says, "This was not a new contract. It was a product we had already been producing for one of the Big Three auto manufacturers. We were competing to retain the contract to produce this component. The stakes were high for us, because not only had we engineered it, we had, of course, heavily invested in the machinery for producing it. Moreover, this product represented more than 15 percent of our business. We felt we couldn't afford to lose this contract. Our customer, on the other hand, was committed to maximizing their own bottom line by pressing for the lowest possible bid on the product, so the competition between our company and our competitor—a company we respect a lot—was fierce. They had structured the bidding process to encourage a race to the bottom—every time they would receive a bid from one of us, they would turn around and show it to the competitor and invite them to try to beat it.

"Because of this, the bidding got ridiculously low—so much so that we had pretty much cut our profit margin out of the proposal in an effort to get our numbers down. Nevertheless, our competitor came back with another bid that was even lower than ours. You have to understand that at this point, our adrenaline was flowing. Our team went into a marathon session to make our proposal irresistible. Because we had already given up our profit margin on the product, the only way we could sweeten our proposal was to offer cost reductions on other product lines we provided for this manufacturer. We were so bent on winning, however, that we didn't hesitate to do even this. It was a momentum thing.

"It wasn't until a few hours later, after we had faxed out this final proposal, that the full impact of what we had just done came home to us. To win the business, we had given away the earnings margin which supports our research and new product development and our employees' gain-sharing compensation plan—the very things that help to make us so competitive. We looked at each other and said, 'What have we just done!?' And at that point, we knew there was only one thing we could do. We called our customer and withdrew our proposal.

"Our competitor won the contract and we're glad they did. They have taken a beating with it. We're fortunate that we came to our senses in time. That's when it became clear to us that in order for our company to stay healthy, we have to pay attention to more than just one bottom line."

A Process for Holding Institutions in Trust

During the past ten years, a network of colleagues from across the United States has developed around this exploration of the intersection of religious belief and organizational life. Those involved include organizational leaders, theologians, and organizational development practitioners. They have come together twice a year during this time for the purpose of sharing ideas and experimenting with different approaches for gaining theological perspective on organizational life. Their consistent priority in these gatherings, however, has been the goal of holding one another's organizations in trust.[22]

Their gatherings take place over a two- or three-day period. Participants come together at the facility of the host organization over a light supper on the evening of the first day, usually a Friday, some having traveled considerable distance for the sole purpose of serving someone else's organization. Old friends greet one another, and typically a few new friends are welcomed into the circle for the first time.

Following supper, representatives of the host organization guide a walking tour through their facility, allowing participants to soak in the organization's atmosphere and perhaps in some way catch glimmers of its spirit through the arrangement of its work spaces, from the photos on walls, and expressions on the faces of nearby employees. Participants then regather for a time of orientation in preparation for their work of the next day.

They are reminded by the facilitator that they have been called to gather as a circle of temporary trustees, whose purpose for the next twenty-four hours is to hold a member organization in trust around a difficult challenge it is facing. As temporary trustees their role is not to "solve the problem" by offering expert advice about the dilemma facing the organization. Rather they are to draw upon their own lived experience and the sacred ideals and lore of their faith traditions for wisdom and perspective and inspiration, which may be a source of encouragement and guidance to the leadership team of the focus organization as they wrestle with the challenge that will be described.

They are reminded of the importance of listening deeply with ears and hearts, and of maintaining a discipline of confidentiality. They are invited to be mindful that they have, by virtue of the intentions they bring and the trust they are about to assume, entered together into sacred time and sacred space.

And then, for the remainder of that evening, they continue the process begun earlier through the walking tour of meeting the focus organization as its leadership team shares stories of the organization's beginning (For what reason did it originally come into existence?), its purpose (Who does it serve, and how?), its employees (Who does the work, and what is it like for them to work here?), as well as critical or defining moments in the organization's history and, ultimately, the challenge that currently faces it as an organization.

The rhythms of these trustee gatherings are familiar. The participants are weary from the fullness of their own workweeks and their travel to be here on a Friday evening. And yet, to a person, they lean forward in their chairs, eyes alive, as they drink in these stories, attuning themselves to the unique character of this particular organization, its journey, and the challenge before it.

On this particular weekend, we were gathered to hold Engineered Products in trust. Ed, the general manager, began his evening presentation by referring to our walking tour earlier that evening through their manufacturing plant. "Do you know the last line we stopped at? The one where you met some of the folks assembling our product? Eight months from now, these folks will no longer have jobs here at this plant. We're moving these lines to Mexico. We've got to in order to meet the price-downs demanded by our customer. We simply can't squeeze any more cost savings out of this line without reducing the direct labor costs associated with it. We've struggled to gain every efficiency we can, and simply don't have any options left. And it's killing us. These are our people. They're good at what they do, and some of them have been with us for a long time. And you want to hear something really scary? We don't know how long we'll be able to stay in Mexico either. Because everything is already migrating to China, where the additional savings on labor are impossible to ignore."

Ed went on to remind participants of the recent history of Engineered Products, a firm that develops high-tech components for the transportation industry. The great majority of the firm's business had been with Big Three U.S. auto manufacturers. It had gained a reputation for producing a technically superior product, and had done well despite increasing pressures related to industry changes.

"Things began to change dramatically six or seven years ago as the Big Three, in response to the competitive pressures they were experiencing from particularly the Japanese auto industry, began to aggressively seek savings from their suppliers—companies like us. Initially, we were able to respond to the price-downs our customers were demanding by tightening up our manufacturing process. This was actually a good thing for us and our customers had a right to expect it. We're really proud of the quality and efficiency of our manufacturing operation. This has not been enough for our customers, however. The pressures were enormous, and it hasn't always been easy to keep our head."

By the time of this gathering, the relationship between Engineered Products and its customers had undergone a complete metamorphosis, moving from a mutually beneficial collaboration between customer and supplier to one that felt more like the wary relationship between predator and prey. "Our customers began to demand access to our books so as to determine what additional cost savings we might be able to achieve. They were demanding a 'down payment' of $300,000 or $400,000 or more on the cost savings we would deliver over the life of the contract, with the regular stipulation being that we would guarantee between 5–10 percent additional cost savings for each year of the product. Many of our competitors were going out of business, and we were focusing nearly all our engineering resources toward our manufacturing process. This was at the expense of research and new product development, something we've always been known for and taken pride in. This inability to better protect our R&D has come back to haunt us."

"Have you considered simply not complying with your customer's demand for a price-down?" one trustee inquired.

"Yes," Ed responded. "In fact, as a leadership team we had determined that the next time we were asked to deliver a price-down that was impossible to achieve without damaging the company, we would refuse. We didn't have to wait long."

"What happened?"

"When we received the product order, the customer had simply written in a 5 percent cost reduction that they had not negotiated with us. We responded indicating that we could continue to provide the product at the existing price."

"And what did they do?"

"They gave the contract to a competitor. We didn't blink, and we lost. This is why we can't see any option to relocating this product line to Mexico. We simply can't afford to lose it, and there's no other way of achieving the price-down they're demanding."

"Do you have any new product launches that can replace the line that's leaving?"

"No. That's what I mean about our inability to better protect our R&D. In the past, we've been able to replace departing products in our North American facility with new product launches, and in that way have been able to keep our people working. This time, we don't have anything ready to go."

The leadership of Engineered Products had come to describe their organization in terms of three dimensions—a model of organizational life with theological roots. The three dimensions—Identity (the character and gathered life of the organization), Purpose (how the organization serves the world around it), and Stewardship (how the organization relates to its resources and governs itself)—each represent a cluster of legitimate concerns that frequently exist in some measure of tension with one another. These three bottom lines must be held in creative balance by those who would hold organizations in trust. Each of these dimensions also represents clusters of typical stakeholders (Identity: employees, their families, and communities; Purpose: customers, suppliers, and competitors; Stewardship: owners, managers, stockholders) whose needs and interests are similarly in tension.

At this point, the thirty men and women who had gathered to hold Engineered Products in trust moved into three working groups, each focused on one of these three dimensions of Engineered Products' life. Each group was accompanied by a member of Engineered Products' leadership team, present to answer questions and provide additional information. They were asked to reflect on three questions, and to report back on any insights that emerged for them.

The questions were:

- Who are the primary stakeholders associated with your area?

- What do they care most about?

- What might it mean to faithfully engage them around the related challenges of

    The job loss related to the movement of the product line?

    The continued pressures toward price-downs and competing as a global company?

As you might imagine, the meeting of each of these working groups was unique, focused as they were by the different stakeholder groups whose needs were quite different from one another. The meeting focused on the Identity dimension of Engineered Products was particularly dynamic, as participants joined Engineered Products leadership in worrying about the implications for those whose jobs would be lost as the result of relocating the product line. One of the tangible decisions facing EP's leadership was the question of when to tell employees working on these product lines that their jobs would be moving to Mexico.

This conversation took a surprising turn when one of the participants, with some hesitation, offered this reflection. "Your dilemma got me thinking about something Robert Greenleaf wrote in his initial essay, 'The Servant as Leader.' I want to preface it, though, by letting you know of the enormous respect I have for your management team and for the obvious integrity and great skill you are bringing to your leadership in a very difficult situation. I have some appreciation of the kind of very difficult market pressures you are dealing with here. We are also facing them in our own industry, but my sense is that they are not as acute as those you have been wrestling with in the auto industry. We are proud to be associated with you.

"At one point in his essay, Greenleaf observed that a central ethic of leadership is that of foresight, and said something to the effect that if you find as a leader that you are facing a dilemma with no good options to choose from, then it is almost certain that at some point earlier on you stood in a crossroads—maybe not recognizing it at the time—where your decision or lack of decision somehow contributed to getting you where you are now. Assuming that may be true, I wonder how it would be at some point for you as a leadership team to reflect on when those moments of decision making might have occurred. With the benefit of hindsight, do you recognize now decisions that you were faced with then that, had you made them differently, things might have—*might* have, not *would* have—unfolded in a way that left you with better options to choose from in this moment? The point in doing this is not to beat your-selves up, but rather to lay any burdens down that you might uncon-sciously be carrying around and to harvest any learnings you can, because I don't think these market dynamics are going to change anytime soon."

———

Early the next week, Ed and his leadership team met together to reflect on the insights and questions emerging from the conversa-tions of the past weekend. Several days later, they gathered their employees for one of their occasional brown-bag luncheon meet-ings. After offering a general update on overall market conditions, Ed told the employees that he knew that many of them were anx-ious about the possibility of their jobs disappearing with the antic-ipated movement of product lines to their plant in Mexico, and he wanted to give them as much information as possible to help them plan for the transitions that some of them would be facing. He shared with all of the employees the rough schedule for the staged movement of these lines over the next ten months. He acknowl-edged that the next scheduled product launches were far enough away to prevent any smooth transition, and that consequently most of these jobs would be lost for the foreseeable future. He then out-lined preparations the company was making to help those losing jobs to find new employment. Already, as a result of conversations with other local industries, they had identified a need for thirty employees with similar skill-sets.

Ed then went on to say, "Obviously, this is painful, and we hoped it would never come to this point. We worked hard to prevent it, and while there are a lot of good decisions we have made over the last several years, we have not been perfect. In looking back, there are a couple of decisions that, had we made them differently, may have helped us to avoid this." After describing a few of those deci-sions, Ed concluded, saying, "Again, while in looking back we found a lot to feel good about, those particular decisions I just described are ones we wish we had made differently."

When I asked Ed what kind of response he received from the employees, he said, "At the end of the meeting, one of the folks who's scheduled to lose her job stood up and said, 'This is why we like working here. You've always been up-front with us.' When you go out on the floor, spirits seem remarkably good."

"You know," Ed continued, "the group coming together to hold us in trust that weekend was incredibly important. Part of it is that it is a great group of folks, who bring so much wisdom and insight to bear on our situation. But a lot of things we talked about, we'd already been thinking about before the gathering. This time, though, we were talking about our situation in the midst of a community. In hearing ourselves describe our situation to you all, we somehow felt the impact more powerfully, and we felt accountable to a wider community for doing everything we possibly could about it."

Some Next Steps

While the learnings continue to emerge from these initial efforts to develop a practical theology of institutions, it is clear that there is much work yet to be done. From our perspective, several fronts feel particularly important and deserving of our attention. They represent a recognition of the importance of both deepening and broadening the conversation.

Language and Sacred Ideals

From the outset our conversations within organizations have been framed with the nonreligious language of ethics, purpose, and values. This reflects a conscious decision, arrived at in conversation with our organizational partners, to cast the conversation as inclusively as possible, to enable broad participation from employees throughout organizations, regardless of personal religious or spiritual persuasions. For this reason, the Threefold Model of Organizational Life—at its root a theological framework—has been translated into nonreligious language, and used as a framework for eliciting and organizing the core values of a given organization.

Leaders within some of the organizations with whom we have been working have expressed the belief that this threefold framework is more universal than might first appear, given its theological roots in the Reformed Christian tradition. It also seems to connect, using a different language of interpretation, to the religious traditions of Judaism and Islam. The challenge that confronts us is how to explore these possible connections without trivializing the depth and profundity of each tradition, on one hand, and by discovering a way to learn from the rich uniqueness of each, on the other.

The first challenge might be met by having Jewish and Islamic scholars examine the threefold model from their religious traditions to determine its usefulness and relevance. The second challenge, of discovering ways to learn from the rich uniqueness of one another's traditions, especially within the context of the organizational environment where people work together, is more daunting.

Our colleagues have expressed their hope (as well as their ambivalence) that we might deepen the conversation about organizational faithfulness within a given organization by discovering ways of inviting employees to draw upon their own religious and spiritual traditions as a wisdom resource to critical organizational decisions. Their ambivalence (and our own) reflects an awareness of how easy it is for such conversations to become divisive, particularly when participants share their own religious perspective in ways that suggest that it ought to be authoritative for others in the organization.

One promising resource for supporting such a conversation resides in the work and research of Dr. Douglas Schoeninger and his colleagues, who have been developing "rules of dialogue." These rules are grounded in his belief that each person, whether acknowledging this or not, is a child of God and, as such, has a unique contribution to make and a truth to share that can enrich the whole. Therefore, it is important for individuals both to feel free to speak their own truth and to provide hospitable space for others to speak their truth. The rules Schoeninger has been developing, when agreed to by participants in the dialogue, help create a safe space where people can risk sharing ideas that are not fully formed, in the understanding that one's truth is never finished.

We believe the best place to begin experimenting with these rules is an ongoing work group within the same organization where people have already established a trust level and respect for one another's contribution to decision making. In accepting and using the rules, we believe participants would establish a structure for safe dialogue that might enable them to consciously draw on their unique sacred beliefs and traditions and discover what they share in common, as well as new ideas to deepen their common and individual journeys.

Forming Religious Congregations That Empower Servant-Leaders and Enable Servant Institutions

As noted earlier, in Bob Greenleaf's vision of servant-leaders serving as regenerative agents in developing servant institutions, he saw an essential role for religious congregations. In his essay "The Need for a Theology of Institutions," he wrote, "I do not believe that the urgently needed fundamental reconstruction of our vast and pervasive structure of institutions can take place, prudently and effectively, without a strong supporting influence from the churches."

The reality, however, is that very few congregations of any religious tradition are committed to and structured for the equipping of their members for service in their day-to-day workplaces. Even fewer congregations recognize and affirm the critically important role their members can play in serving as regenerative agents in building servant institutions. As Greenleaf recognized, this failure is in large part due to the absence of a theology of institutions. It also reflects the orientation and training provided by seminaries, where clergy are prepared for their leadership roles in congregations. And finally it is a function of the way most congregations are structured so that their principal focus is on their interior life and the needs of the congregation as institution.

In collaboration with Luther Seminary's Center for Life-Long Learning in a new initiative called Centered Life-Centered Work, Seeing Things Whole has shared the fruit of its research and the emerging model for how temporary trustees can hold an organization in trust. This model is now being tested in the East and Midwest to determine its relevance for both secular organizations and religious congregations that are open to becoming centers of support and empowerment for their lay members in their role as institutional servant-leaders.

In addition, Faith At Work, a national organization of clergy and laity, has undertaken a three-year research project with seven congregations to explore how the congregation can restructure itself to become the kind of empowering model envisioned by Bob Greenleaf. These findings will be shared over the next several years in *Faith@Work* magazine, as well as with the leadership at Luther Seminary in St. Paul.

We have a long way to go to realize Bob Greenleaf's vision for religious institutions and the way they can serve to support and inspire a society of servant-leaders and servant institutions. But his vision is a compelling one and his insights continue to lend depth and urgency to our efforts. Someday, in the not-too-distant future, we trust we will see the emerging realization of his dream, as expressed in "The Need for a Theology of Institutions": "The movement I hope to see is when all institutions will become more serving of all persons they touch, to the end that those being served will grow as persons: while being served they will become healthier, wiser, freer, more autonomous, more likely themselves to become servants."[23]

10

Foresight as the Central Ethic
of Leadership

Daniel H. Kim

Rereading Robert Greenleaf's essay "The Servant as Leader" is always an exercise in humility for me. His writings are a constant reminder of the high personal standards a leader must set to be worthy of people's full commitment. Of all the things that Greenleaf wrote about in his essay, I have found the following passage to be the most striking and most humbling to live up to:

> The failure (or refusal) of a leader to foresee may be viewed as an ethical failure; because a serious ethical compromise today (when the usual judgment on ethical inadequacy is made) is sometimes the result of a failure to make the effort at an earlier date to foresee today's events and take the right actions when there was freedom for initiative to act. The action which society labels "unethical" in the present moment is often really one of no choice. By this standard, a lot of guilty people are walking around with an air of innocence that they would not have if society were able always to pin a label "unethical" on the failure to foresee and the conscious failure to act constructively when there was freedom to act.[1]

I have never heard anybody say it in that way. Others may admonish us for not having exercised better foresight or for incorrectly anticipating the future and call it a failure of planning or an error in judgment. But to call it an *ethical failure* is such a strong stance that it compelled me to take a deeper look at the issue so that I could come to a better understanding of why he stated it in such a provocative manner.

Another reason I have been drawn to his point about foresight is that my own professional path has led me to the field of system dynamics, which in many ways is about developing foresight through a deeper understanding of the underlying systemic structures that produce our reality. The fact that he refers to it as "the central ethic of leadership" makes it all the more intriguing to explore. Why is it an ethical failure rather than some other kind of failure? This is the question I want to take some time to explore.

Foresight in the Face of Complexity

I once subscribed to a financial newsletter that focused on investing in a basket of eight stocks selected from the companies that make up the Dow 30. At first glance, this might seem like a very limited investment strategy: After all, how many options do you have for picking eight stocks out of a universe of only thirty stocks? When I pose that question to people, most people would readily agree and when asked for a numerical guess, most guesses fall somewhere in the hundreds and a few in the thousands. A few who are familiar with the odds of winning a lottery realize that this is a very similar situation and make a guess that is in the millions. The correct answer is that there are slightly over 5.7 million different combinations of eight companies that you can select out of a universe of just thirty stocks.

For most of us, that is a mind-boggling number to come out of such small numbers as eight and thirty. But it's even worse than that when we consider the number of possible combinations with human groupings inside an organization. Even in a small organization with thirty employees, you can create many more millions of different combinations (teams) of various sizes. In addition, unlike a static grouping of companies that do not interact with one another, the human groupings are capable of relating to each other in continually different ways, making the possible number of combinations virtually infinite. Add to that the dynamic forces of the external environment that are continually impacting the organization, and you find yourself facing a situation in which there appears to be no hope of exercising foresight.

Forecasting Versus Predicting

It would seem then that the enormous complexity of our modern organizations leaves us incapable of exercising foresight, thereby sentencing us to be ethical failures as leaders. This would be true if we equated foresight with making accurate forecasts about the future (which is impossible to do). Fortunately for us, foresight is about being able to perceive *the significance and nature of events* before they have occurred (which is achievable).

In his scenario-planning work at Royal Dutch Shell, Arie de Geus and his colleagues were careful to draw the distinction between making forecasts and making predictions about the future. They realized very early on that there was no reliable way to accurately forecast the future with numerical calculations about what the oil price might be at a specific date. However, what they were able to do was develop a deep understanding of the geopolitical realities of the various countries in which they operated and combine it with their knowledge of the oil industry as a way to develop scenarios that helped their managers predict future directional consequences of current events. In a word, their scenario-planning efforts gave them the capability of exercising foresight that guided them even during times of turbulent change.

To understand the difference between forecasts and predictions, de Geus offers the following illustration: If it rains in the foothills of the Himalayas, we cannot forecast exactly when the rivers will swell and flood the valleys, but we can predict with certainty that the flooding will occur. The better we know the structure of the terrain, the greater knowledge we have about the flooding to follow. An ethical responsibility of all leaders is to know the underlying structures within their domain of responsibility and be able to make predictions that can guide their people to a better future.

Helping Versus Meddling

Whenever I ask managers whether they think they are helping or meddling when they take actions in their organizations, their answer is a unanimous "helping" chorus. When I follow up with "How do you know you are helping?" the answers are a quieter "because we intend to be helpful." When I push a little harder on the question, most will admit they really do not know whether they are helping or meddling. My question then is, "If I really don't know whether my actions are helpful or harmful, shouldn't I be investing some effort into finding out how I might be able to know the difference?" Failure to know whether I am helping or meddling is another aspect of the ethical failure because I lack the foresight to know the future consequences of my own (and my people's) actions.

Dr. W. Edwards Deming, a pioneer in the quality improvement movement, often illustrated the difference between helping and meddling (or tampering) with a marble-dropping experiment that goes something like this:

Let's say we mark an "X" on a tabletop. We then hold a marble in our fingers about two feet above the table and we aim for the X. Our goal is to have the marble land exactly on the X. So, we drop the marble and we find that the marble strays a little bit to the left. We mark the spot where it finally comes to rest, and then we pick up the marble and try again. In this first round of the experiment, each time we pick up the marble, we will keep aiming for that X and then mark the final resting position of the marble after it lands. After 40 trials, we will have a random pattern of dots surrounding the X around which we draw a circle that encompasses all the dots. Now, we proceed to the second part of the experiment where we follow a different strategy. Each time we pick up the marble, instead of aiming for the same spot on the table (the X), we change our aim to compensate for where the marble ended up in the previous round. For example, if the marble ended up an inch to the right of the X, the next time we will aim it an inch to the left of the X. If we dropped the marble 40 more times following that strategy, the question is "would the pattern of dots form a circle that is smaller, same, or larger than the circle drawn in the first round and why?"

You might take a moment to formulate your own answer before you continue reading.

Now, I have done this thought experiment dozens of times with hundreds of managers, and I generally get all three answers—smaller, same, and larger—but there is only one right answer in this case. What is interesting about people's answers to the question isn't whether they got the "right" answer or not, but rather the reasons people give for why they think it is the answer they gave.

Those who say that the circle is smaller explain that because we are compensating for the directional deviations from the previous round, we are reducing the error that was produced. On the face of it, this seems like a plausible answer. After all, if you shoot a gun at a target and your first shot goes a little to the left, you will make an adjustment the next time by shooting a little to the right. In that case, the shoot, compensate, and shoot again strategy does work and you are able to zero in on your target. So, why isn't this the right answer for the marble experiment? This is because the strategy only works if the aiming is the primary source of the variation. Unlike shooting a gun, the major source of variation for where the marble comes to rest does not come from the aim.

Then there are those who guess that the circle would be the same size precisely because they know the cause of the variation does not come from the aim. They know that changing the aim is not going to improve the results, therefore they conclude that it will not make a difference to the pattern of dots. This would be true if the changes we made to our aim were so minor in comparison to the other sources of variation that its effects were negligible. However, in our experiment, the changes to our aim were in direct proportion to the underlying variation we experienced, so its impact is quite significant.

The correct answer is that the circle gets larger. Even though some people are able to give the right answer, not everyone can provide the correct explanation of why it is true. This fact is important, because getting the right answer or the right results is not good enough; we must also know the reasons why it is so. Otherwise, it may just be a lucky guess that we cannot count on the next time, or an intuition that we are unable to pass on to someone else. The reason the circle gets larger is that we are introducing more variation by constantly changing the aim. The primary source of variation in the first round was due to the surface of the table interacting with the marble. Since we did nothing to reduce that variation, any other variation we introduce simply adds to the variation of the system.

So, if we were really interested in tightening the circle of dots, what should we do to be of help? We need to focus on reducing the primary source of variation. We can accomplish this by a number of different actions. We could make the table surface softer by covering it with layers of felt cloth so that the marble is less likely to bounce and roll. In addition, we could glue some Velcro on the marble so that it would stick to the cloth where it landed. These actions are *helping* actions because they are changing the underlying structures that determine the capability of the system.

Special Versus Common Causes: Understanding System Capability

The ability to discern between whether one is taking helping or meddling actions is what has allowed us to improve the quality of virtually all manufactured products. This is because we now have a much deeper understanding about the sources of variation in a manufacturing process and can work systematically to reduce those variations. Through the application of statistical process control (SPC) techniques, we are now able to quantify what the capability of a system is in terms of its variability.

Prior to the application of SPC, when a machine was producing a piece that was outside specifications, the operator would adjust the machine to compensate for the error. This was analogous to our marble experiment and would produce the same results. The very actions to correct the problem would actually exacerbate it. Unlike the marble experiment, however, the impact of the adjustment action did not produce clear and immediate negative results. In the short run, the adjustments often seemed to improve the results but then deteriorated over time. There seemed to be little rhyme or reason as to why the adjustment worked at times, and why it didn't work at other times. Therefore, it was not possible to produce consistent results.

What SPC did was provide a way to determine what is the system capability of a manufacturing process. Through the application of statistical theory, one could calculate the range of variability that was normal to the system. For example, a drill press that is supposed to drill a 10 mm hole will not be able to drill a hole that is exactly 10.000 mm every single time. Because of various factors (irregularities in the drill bit, minute movements in the drill linkages, the effects of vibration, variability in the piece being drilled), the holes that get drilled may fall somewhere between 10.000 mm and 10.009 mm. If we determine that this range is the system capability of this drill press, then any variations that fall between these two limits are considered to be *common* to the system and the correct action to take is to do nothing. If a variation exceeds these limits, however, that is considered to be a *special* cause, and other corrective actions must be taken because something other than the normal operating of the system caused the higher variation. This capacity to distinguish between special and common causes (and between helping and meddling actions) revolutionized all manufacturing processes and led to dramatic increases in the quality of virtually all manufactured goods. Unfortunately, the ability to make such distinctions has not been translated very well in domains beyond manufacturing.

There is an important link between understanding the underlying capability of a system and having the capacity to exercise foresight. Through the marble experiment we saw that although we cannot *forecast* where each individual drop of the marble will end up, we can *predict* with absolute certainty that the pattern of drops will get bigger over time. Therefore, we know that the act of changing our aim is actually *meddling*, not helping. Taking actions (or causing actions to be taken) that are actually worsening the state of affairs constitutes an ethical failure of leadership because we are taking actions under the guise of "helping" when, in fact, the underlying justification for our actions is illegitimate.

Foresight and the Role of Vision

In addressing this issue of an ethical failure, Greenleaf's writing has another aspect that also needs to be explored. It has to do with his thoughts on awareness and perception. He writes:

> The opening of awareness stocks both the conscious and unconscious minds with the richness of resources for future need. But it does more than that: it is value building and value clarifying and it armors one to meet the stress of life by helping build serenity in the face of stress and uncertainty. Awareness is not a giver of solace. It is just the opposite. It is a disturber and an awakener. Able leaders are usually sharply awake and reasonably disturbed. They are not seekers after solace. They have their own inner serenity.[2]

If we are to exercise foresight, we need to continually expand our awareness and perception, to take in more than what we might if we kept the focus of our attention too narrow and strictly logical. We must go beyond the limitations of our own direct experiences and cultivate a capacity to see things yet unseen, to see the unseeable. And when we begin to see things that nobody yet sees, we must have the capacity to stay centered even if that awareness is not well received by others or makes us feel uncomfortable. We must develop our capacity for insight—the capacity to grasp the inner or hidden nature of things.

Seeing and Acting at Multiple Levels of Perspective

One way of expanding our awareness and perception is to broaden the ways in which we see the world. Although there are multiple levels of perspective from which we can see and understand the world (see Figure 10.1), most of us tend to inhabit only one or two levels. The framework that I refer to as "Levels of Perspective" is based on a classic insight in the field of system dynamics that posits that structure drives behavior. So if you want a different behavior from the one you are getting, you must figure out a way to change the structures that are producing the behavior, rather than trying to change the behavior directly.

Figure 10.1. Levels of Perspective.

Levels	*Action Modes*
Vision	Generative
↑↓	
Mental Models	Reflective
↑↓	
Systemic Structures	Creative
↑↓	
Patterns over Time	Adaptive
↑↓	
Events	Reactive

In recent years, the structure level was split into systemic structures and mental models to differentiate between the outer structures of the physical world and the inner structures of the psychological world. I added the vision level to highlight the fact that the visions we hold have a powerful impact on the mental models that we believe in. For each level, there is an appropriate action mode that provides the highest leverage. To help you understand this framework better, I will walk through level by level by starting from the bottom and working up.

Events Level and the Reactive Action Mode

If you listen to the way most people go through their day, you might conclude that they live at the level of events. Life is composed of a series of events, starting with the alarm clock's ring in the morning, followed by showering, shaving, dressing, eating breakfast, driving to work, and so on. When something happens to us at the event level, we must respond to it by taking *reactive* actions (for example, a car in front of us brakes suddenly, we must react fast and apply our own brakes). Although we may often bemoan the fact that we are too reactive, it is an important survival capability to have. If, for example, we find ourselves in the path of a runaway bus, it is definitely not the time to become reflective about one's situation and ask, "How did I get to be in this dangerous situation?" The highest-leverage action you can take is to jump out of the way of that specific bus in that particular moment. Any other action mode at the Events level would be of lower leverage (to say the least!). Living only at the events level is quite limiting, however, because at this level, all we can do is react to things as they happen to us.

Patterns Level and the Adaptive Action Mode

By moving up to the patterns over time level, we are able to increase our leverage in creating our future because we can take adaptive actions. The use of *adaptive* here is quite literal in that you take actions to adapt to the pattern that you have identified. For example, if you see sales exhibiting a seasonal cycle, you adapt to it by staffing to match the up-and-down pattern of sales. In other words, you take the pattern as given and do not attempt to change it. Taking adaptive actions is an improvement over just taking reactive actions. If we were stuck at the events level and only taking reactive actions, each week as we experienced a growth in demand we would be saying, "Oh my, this week we're short sales staff," and then scramble to get more people on the sales floor. Then, the following week, we would be reacting again to another shortfall and scrambling to get more people at the last minute. Each occurrence remains as a surprise requiring last-minute scurrying and is quite disruptive. At the patterns level, we notice the pattern of rising sales and adapt to the pattern by scheduling more salespeople for the subsequent weeks. This adaptive action is an improvement because it reduces the last-minute scramble and disruptions to people's schedules. But here again we are still responding to what is happening to us rather than creating our future, foreseeing the future we are actually trying to create.

Systemic Structures Level and the Creative Action Mode

When we move up to the level of systemic structures, we are seeing the world from the source of the patterns and events we have been dealing with at the lower levels. This is where we can identify the various systems, structures, processes, and policies that are producing the events and patterns. If we want to change the patterns, we must take *creative* actions to add new structures or modify the existing structures. So if we notice a pattern of defects on the production line, we must determine the system capability of the machines involved. If we discover that the defects are due to the inability of a machine to produce the specified tolerances, a creative action might require upgrading the machine to one that is capable of producing lower variability. Hence, changes to the systemic structures will produce changes to the pattern of behavior and the events. However, it usually is not as simple as that. Even if one identifies the right parts of the systems to change, getting others to agree to making the systemic structure changes may not be easy. And even if you do get the changes approved and implemented, that is no guarantee that the new systems will produce the desired results. This is because the effectiveness of our systemic structures is dependent on the extent to which people's mental models (deep beliefs) are aligned with the changes in the systemic structures. The Achilles heel of most change efforts (studies have shown that over two-thirds fail to produce the desired results) is that they do not move beyond this level to engage the organization at the level of mental models.

Mental Models Level and the Reflective Action Mode

If we are truly interested in effecting systemic change, we must work at the mental model level to ensure that such models are in alignment with the changes we are wanting to implement at the systemic structure level. Mental models are our deep beliefs about how the world works and how things ought to be. They represent our *theories* for explaining why the world works the way it does. Mental model work is usually not necessary for small, routine, incremental changes, the kind that do not challenge our prevailing beliefs about the way the world works. However, when changes in systemic structures (such as activity-based cost accounting) require us to abandon one way of looking at our world (allocating costs following generally accepted practices) and adopt a whole different way of seeing things (allocating costs based on the direct activity level associated with a given part), the successful adoption of the new system is likely to be very elusive unless we engage people at the mental models level.

To engage at this level means that we must take reflective actions—actions that require us to surface, suspend, and test our deepest beliefs or theories about the world. The territory of mental models is very much linked to foresight and our ability to see. It's not just about seeing the future; it has to do with our ability to see, *period.* How do we come to know the world? How do we come to see the world? How do we know what we know? It is important to note that "to change" is not included as a reflective action, because the minute we try to change someone else's mental model, we have dropped to a reactive action mode, and we have lost the leverage of taking reflective actions.

Vision Level and the Generative Action Mode

Working at the mental model level is tough, which may explain why so few organizations make a serious attempt to work at that level. So why would anybody work at that level? This is where the level of vision is so critical. Unless we are deeply connected to a vision that we care about bringing into reality, we are not likely to take on the difficult work of surfacing our collective mental models and suspending and testing them. By moving up to the vision level and taking generative actions that reconnect us to our sense of purpose and to visions we deeply care about, we have the desire and the impetus to resolve differences in our mental models. So when we begin to surface some of our beliefs that may not be giving us the result we want, it's a time to question and re-vision what it is we really care about. It is about exercising our generative capacities— our human dignity, spirit, and ingenuity—the wellspring with which we create visions of the future that we truly care about. Once we develop the common ground of a shared vision, it allows us to shift away from a stance of trying to determine whether a mental model is right or wrong, to one of seeking to understand which ones will be most useful in achieving our vision. And when we are clear about which mental models will serve us, they function as the guiding specifications (or principles) for the kinds of systemic structures we need to have in place to produce the patterns and events that we want to create.

Leading from Higher Levels of Leverage

So we can expand our awareness and perception by becoming more conscious of the five levels of perspective and developing our capacity to see from multiple levels and act in the appropriate mode. This means that we must rise above our tendency to stay at the patterns and events levels and simply adapt or react to things that happen to us. As leaders, we must climb higher and see the world from the higher levels and have the skills and capabilities to act in a creative, reflective, and generative mode. But what happens to most of us? We may get the concept of these levels intellectually, but then we come face-to-face with the day-to-day urgency of events and we get caught up in lots of reactive firefighting actions. We excuse ourselves by saying, "We're so busy, we don't have time for this."

When we excuse ourselves from operating at the higher levels of perspective, we are abdicating our responsibility as leaders to ensure that our people have a vision to guide them. This does not mean that the leader has to be the author of the vision, but the leader does have the responsibility for making sure that a vision exists for the organization. Exercising foresight is about creating compelling visions of the future that will tap into the latent aspirations of our people so that they can rise to the greatness within them. That is exactly what John F. Kennedy did for the United States when he articulated, not his personal vision, but the vision of the American people to put a man on the moon and bring him back safely before the end of the decade. The vision united Americans in a common goal and inspired them to rise to the challenge and accomplish something that was literally impossible to do at the time the vision was articulated.

There is a biblical proverb that states "where there is no vision, the people perish." I believe this is true because without vision, our people suffer death by a thousand paper-cuts. They are driven to their graves through an endless stream of meaningless activity performed at the event level, reacting to one thing after another. They become the walking dead in the passionless halls of our hyperactive organizations. So the failure to lead with foresight is an ethical failure because where there is no vision, our people really do perish.

Will the Real Vision Please Stand Up?

Unfortunately, *vision* has become such an overused word that it has lost its meaning in many organizations. It has become jargon that everyone recognizes, but most don't quite seem to know what it means. When people talk about vision, they are often talking about its close cousins—idle dreams, vision statements, and corporate objectives. These distinctions are more than just a difference in semantics; each one represents a very different approach for guiding people's actions, and they are related to each other in a particular way (see Figure 10.2).

Some people talk about visions as if they were idle dreams. These people do not see any practical significance to visions because they consider them to be pie-in-the-sky dreams that will never become reality. They tend to view all visionaries as idle dreamers because vision is always about the future (rather than the present) and the visions themselves often seem fantastically impossible to achieve. For these people, anything that is not rooted in the here and now is discounted as being "airy-fairy" or impractical. But visions are not the same thing as idle dreams. Idle dreams are meant to remain idle—that's what provides them with their magic and generative power. When we relieve ourselves of the need to produce, produce, produce and simply dream, dream, dream, our imagination lights up with all kinds of possibilities. As leaders, we should encourage all our people to devote some of their time to daydreams because this is the fertile soil from which visions are likely to sprout.

Figure 10.2. The Four Faces of Vision.

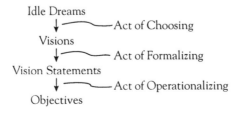

Other people mistake vision statements for a real vision and think their job is done when they have gone on a visioning retreat and crafted a vision statement. They see the process of sharing the vision as one of simply "rolling out" whatever it is that the senior management has created via vision cards, posters, videos, speeches, and other forms of one-way communications that tell everyone the vision that they now share. These efforts almost always lead to a cynical organization that does not value the vision because people in it do not experience the vision as being valued by the senior executives, nor do they feel valued themselves in the process. Those who mistake vision statements for vision do not realize that the drafting of a vision statement marks the beginning, not the end, of a visioning process that is continuous and ongoing in the organization. In a sense, they are committing an error that is analogous to mistaking a photograph for the real person because that is what a vision statement is (a static snapshot) relative to a true vision (a living energy in the organization).

Then there are those who equate vision with corporate objectives. This is a particularly dangerous confusion because it has such great appeal for those who want to keep everything grounded and pragmatic. Proclamations like "Our vision is to hit 20 percent ROI this year" resonate with people who are interested in driving people to perform to measurable yardsticks. The issue here isn't whether setting numerical objectives is good or bad (there are arguments for both), it is what happens to the power of vision when we turn it into a specific objective that is then translated into individual performance objectives. When I ask managers what kinds of objectives they will agree to if they are going to appear on their performance evaluation, the universal answer I get is "achievable ones." And therein lies the problem. When reduced to objectives that we know we will be measured against, everyone comes up with what is doable, not what is desirable.

So what qualifies as real vision? Visions are clear and compelling pictures of the future that people truly care about bringing into reality. Vision does not need to pass a reality test because whether we think it is achievable or not is a distant matter relative to the primary consideration of whether we care enough about it to commit ourselves to bring it into reality. There may appear to be no difference between a vision and an idle dream because sometimes the only thing that separates the two is the fact that we have made a choice to commit to bring the vision into reality. Once we have made such a commitment, then vision statements can be useful. Just as photographs of loved ones are useful to carry around, a vision statement allows us to share our vision with people who do not have a firsthand relationship with it. With regard to objectives, of course we will need to set many objectives along the way, but that is quite different from making the objectives themselves the vision. Compelling visions provide us with the energy and desire to set and meet numerous objectives, including ones we would never have accepted if they were set before us in isolation. In short, visions are powerful because of the simple fact that we care about them. When our *emotions* are engaged, we are moved to action.

Foresight and the Power of Choice

As noted, choice plays an important role in vision. If we never exercise choice, we will forever stay in a state of wanting things without ever taking steps toward attaining them. It is the conscious choice to bring something into reality that transforms an idle dream into a vision that has the power to tap people's energy and commitment. Making a choice is a powerful act.

Hierarchy of Choices

In *The Path of Least Resistance*, Robert Fritz differentiates between making Fundamental, Primary, and Secondary Choices (I've added the rest to fill out the picture for organizational relevance).[3] Fritz points out that it is very difficult to make choices at one level if we have not yet made a choice at the level below it. In the case of vision, Fritz refers to that choice as one where we are making a primary choice—choosing a clear picture of a result we want to create. Given that there are literally an infinite number of possible choices we can make about what vision to pursue, what will provide a meaningful context within which we can make such a choice? Or, more pragmatically speaking, what will help us narrow the possibilities? The answer lies in making the fundamental choice first (see Figure 10.3).

The fundamental choice addresses the big question "why?" and serves to clarify one's purpose in life, one's *raison d'être*. The ability to be clear about one's own life purpose is critical for establishing a strong foundation on which all future choices will rest. This requires deep self-knowledge and high personal mastery for leaders to be clear about *who* they are, which in turn, requires a deep awareness of the core values that define each person. Understanding core values is a matter of identity, both at an individual level and at an organizational level. Knowing who we are is an absolute requirement for being able to articulate our reason for being. In my experience, core values and purpose are so intimately interrelated that they collectively form the basis of identity. That is to say, the values we deeply believe in and our sense of purpose define who we are as individuals and as organizations.

The reason I find the hierarchy of choices so important is that I encounter many people in organizations who are struggling with making choices at the level of strategy and tactics and finding it very difficult. Without the clarity of primary choices to guide them, they have no common basis for making the secondary choices. When they get stuck, rather than going down a level and clarifying, the tendency is to move up a level and try to make tertiary choices (which may come easier because the stakes are lower). As they make these tactical choices, they then work backward to see how their tactical choices may help them to decide on choices of strategy. In the end, the people in the organization are all very busily engaged in executing numerous activities (and making a lot of choices), but very few have any idea how their activities are connected to a broad strategy or a common vision, let alone a sense of purpose.

Figure 10.3. Hierarchy of Choices.

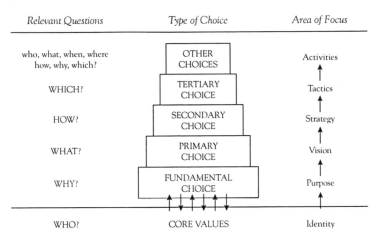

Relevant Questions	Type of Choice	Area of Focus
who, what, when, where how, why, which?	OTHER CHOICES	Activities
WHICH?	TERTIARY CHOICE	Tactics
HOW?	SECONDARY CHOICE	Strategy
WHAT?	PRIMARY CHOICE	Vision
WHY?	FUNDAMENTAL CHOICE	Purpose
WHO?	CORE VALUES	Identity

Source: Adapted and expanded from Fritz, *Path of Least Resistance,* 1989.

Order from Chaos Without Control

What does all this have to do with having foresight? Well, imagine that you are the leader of a large product development team, several hundred people strong. Everyone is busily engaged in all kinds of activities, presumably in support of developing the next generation of your product. My question is, How do you know that your people are working as hard as they can to produce the kind of product they are supposed to produce? One approach would be to go down the path of tightly controlling as much of the process as possible. This would require an army of inspectors, a sophisticated monitoring system for checking up on people's progress, and so on. In an attempt to police that everyone is making the right choices at each step of the way and that they will make choices that we can count on, we opt to control as much of the process as we possibly can. Such exercises in overcontrol, however, often do not produce the desired results.

There is an alternative to the control approach. Instead of operating on the assumption that chaos will reign unless we carefully control everything, the science of chaos teaches us that order can emerge out of a seemingly chaotic system if we understand the underlying principles that can produce that order. For example, scientists have learned that long-term predictions of the weather are virtually impossible because minute changes in one part of the earth could lead to large changes in another part thousands of miles away. Point forecasts were not possible (as we have already discussed). However, when they plotted the data over a long period of time, a curious thing happened. Although you could not predict the short-term changes in the weather, when plotted over a long period of time, *all* the data confined itself within a certain boundary. They called these plots *strange attractors*. Linking this back to our example of the product development team, what would be the equivalent of these strange attractors that would provide us with that long-term predictability of operating within certain boundaries, even as the day-to-day point activities would be unpredictable and seemingly chaotic? What would allow us to trust and foresee our desired results without the need for enforcing tight control systems?

My belief is that an organization's core values, purpose, and vision can serve as the strange attractors that will allow us to create order out of seeming chaos without the need for tight control systems. When every member of a team (or organization) has internalized the core value and purpose of the team and has a clear picture of the result they are all striving for, they will be guided every step of the way by the clarity of these choices at the foundational levels. Their individual choices at the secondary and tertiary levels, and beyond, will all naturally conform within a certain boundary set by the organization's own strange attractors.

There is a scene from the movie *A Few Good Men* that I believe illustrates rather well what I am talking about. In this movie, a colonel at a U.S. Marine base had ordered an illegal "code red" to be conducted, which resulted in the accidental death of the targeted cadet. There is apparently a cover-up where the colonel has denied ever giving an order and the two corporals involved are accused of having taken the actions on their own. The two have been charged with homicide and a lawyer has been assigned to them. The scene begins with their lawyer coming in to share some good news. He presents them with the government's deal: If they agree to a plea of involuntary manslaughter, they'll be out of jail in six months.

The two corporals turn down the deal. They did nothing wrong and they refuse to accept the dishonorable discharge that will probably come with the deal. One of the corporals says he believes he did his job and won't sign a piece of paper that says he didn't. He chooses to hold firm to the code of honor he embraced when he joined the marines, even if it means the possibility of being judged guilty by the court, even if it means losing his freedom. To do anything less would be to deny his honor, his unit's honor, and the honor of the corps itself.

What I like about this scene is how clearly and powerfully the hierarchy of choices are portrayed in action. The corporal makes it very clear that he has made a fundamental choice to join the marines because that resonated with his core values and sense of purpose. With that as his solid foundation, the primary choice was very clear to him—an end result that would preserve not only his honor, but his unit's and the service's honor as well. It did not matter to him that the alternative might be life in prison because it was clear to him that that result (or vision) would be preferable to being discharged without honor. That then leads to making a different choice at the level of strategy—to plead "not guilty" instead of going the plea-bargaining route that his lawyer was recommending. What if we as servant-leaders helped create organizations in which all our people were that clear about their purpose and core values? What kind of a future would we be able to create?

There is a different kind of foresight that comes from having such clarity at the levels of purpose and core values. The clarity guides the organization and produces predictable outcomes that we can foresee even before they happen and without knowing much of the details.

Stewards of Our Children's Future

Having said all this, why do we care about exercising foresight in the first place? When Greenleaf talks about it as an ethical failure, who is suffering from our failures? For whose sake must we live up to his challenge of developing our capacity for foresight? To answer these questions, I would like to share a humorous story:

> Sherlock Holmes and Dr. Watson went on a camping trip. As they lay down for the night, Holmes said, "Watson, look up at the sky and tell me what you see."
>
> And Watson said, "I see millions and millions of stars."
>
> Holmes said, "And what does that tell you?"
>
> And Watson replied, "Astronomically, it tells me that there are millions of galaxies and potentially billions of planets. Theologically, it tells me that God is great and that we are small. Meteorologically, it tells me that we will have a beautiful day tomorrow. What does it tell you?
>
> Sherlock says, "Watson, you fool. Somebody stole our tent!"

This is a great reminder about how we are all susceptible to waxing philosophical about the challenges we face or getting so wrapped up in our own intellectual prowess that we can miss the obvious as well as the not so obvious. In the end, foresight is about being able to see all things that are important to our future. Otherwise, one day sometime in the future, people are going to look back and say to us, "You fool, somebody stole our children's future!" because we did not have the foresight to understand our organizational complexity, to articulate a compelling vision, and to make the foundational choices to guide our people.

Answering the Call to Service

As I said at the outset, answering the call of servant-leadership is a humbling experience. My hope is that each of us remembers who we are and that we will be ever vigilant in continually developing our foresight so that we stand ready and able to answer the call to be true stewards of our children's future. Answering the call will require us to rediscover who we are as individuals and connect with the highest aspirations in ourselves and in our organizations. Answering the call requires us to ask the deeper question "Who am I?" and answer it repeatedly until we have stripped the layers and layers of varnish we have applied over ourselves and revealed the beauty of the natural wood that is our true self. Only then, from a place of authenticity, may we answer the call to serve. I close with a poem I wrote about answering the call to be my authentic self.

Calling

You call my name
long after it has been forgotten
by all who say they love me.
You touch me
at the core of my being
while others have left,
believing there is nothing there.
You breathe love
into the vessel of my heart
and fill it with warmth and tenderness,
even as others take from me,
my last gasping breath.
You hold me
in a sacred space
honoring me for who I am

while others honor me
for who they want me to be.
You call my name
and I am moved to tears,
because I too had forgotten.

—*Daniel H. Kim*

When the call of service calls your name, how will you respond?

11

Servant-Leadership, Forgiveness, and Social Justice

Shann R. Ferch

One of the defining characteristics of human nature is the ability to discern one's own faults, to be broken as the result of such faults, and in response, to seek a meaningful change. Socially, both forgiveness and the disciplined process of reconciliation draw us into a crucible from which we can emerge more refined, more willing to see the heart of another, and more able to create just and lasting relationships. Such relationships—robust, durable, enjoyable, courageous—form what is best in people, in families, and in the workplace. The will to seek forgiveness, the will to forgive, and the will to pursue reconciliation may be a significant part of developing the kind of wisdom, health, autonomy, and freedom espoused by Robert Greenleaf in his idea of the servant-leader, an idea whose time has arrived, an idea that is destined to remain on the vanguard of leadership theory, research, and practice.

In reflecting on the uncommon and profound depth of Greenleaf's theory, I am reminded of the hollow existence experienced by so many, a thought captured by Thoreau's societal indictment—the observation that most people "lead lives of quiet desperation." It is a difficult truth, one that runs subtly beneath the surface of our lives, our organizations, and our communities. More specifically, I am reminded of my grandfather. Upon his death from alcoholism some years ago I remembered feeling disappointed in the lack of time I'd had with him, a lack of good time spent in conversation, of good experiences shared. He died having lost the basic respect of others, a man without an honored leadership position in his own family, a person no one went to for wisdom or sanctuary. In his later years, filled with despondency and self-pity, he was largely alone. Though he had once been strong and vital, few family members were close to him when he died. At one time he had been a true Montanan, of unique joy and individual strength, a man who loved to walk the hills after the spring runoff in search of arrowheads with his family. But in his condition before death his joy for life was eclipsed. He had become morose and often very depressed—a depression that hailed from the sanctions the family had placed on him disallowing him to obtain alcohol for the last years of his life. In the end, it seemed he had given up.

"What happened to him?" I asked my father.

"He stopped dreaming his dreams."

In making this statement my father echoed a truth put forward by Greenleaf in 1977: "For something great to happen, there must be a great dream. Behind every great achievement is a dreamer of great dreams."[1]

Servant-Leadership

The idea of the leader as servant is rooted in the far-reaching ideal that people have inherent worth, a dignity not only to be strived for, but beneath this striving a dignity irrevocably connected to the reality of being human. Philosophically, if one believes in the dignity of the person, the ideas of servant-leadership and the experience of leading or being led from a servant perspective not only make sense, they contain the elegance, precision, and will-power necessary for human development.

The nature of change in the contemporary climate is both complex and swift. Notably, the intensity of such movement has brought with it the exposure of major character flaws in local, national, and international leadership personas, thus increasing the urgency for a more purposeful, more lasting response in society. Presently, leaders who are able to build community without sacrificing productivity, and who are able to embrace diverse potential rather than adhering to traditional, more hierarchical approaches, are inspiring a growing movement in business, the social services, education, and religion.[2]

The more traditional model of leadership, often based heavily on hierarchical structure and a designated chain of command geared toward increased efficiency, has resulted not only in the moral decline of the relational environment but a pervasive malaise common to the psyche of the contemporary working person. The practices of servant-leadership foster a deeper, more personal sense of vision and inclusiveness, and they produce answers to the failures of leadership found in traditional models. On the rise in scholarly literature, studies in forgiveness and restorative justice form one expression of the present need for answers regarding failures of leadership. Such studies validate the capacity for moral fortitude, point to greater efficiency and productivity, and maintain a healthy sense of hope and meaning in organizations.

Seeking Answers to the Failures of Contemporary Leadership

A common experience of being led from the traditional model is one of dominance or control, while the experience of being servant-led is one of freedom. In the words of Greenleaf, those who are servant-led become "healthier, wiser, freer, more autonomous" and "more likely themselves to become servants."[3] A true sense of forgiveness, not a false forgiveness that overlooks the harm caused by others but a true forgiveness inherently bound to the ideas of integrity and justice, can move us toward the kind of robust and resilient relationships that build the foundation of legitimate power, both personally and professionally. It is in legitimate power, a form of power Greenleaf expressed from a servant-first mentality, that we experience the human capacity for love and greatness.

Throughout society, in the culture of families, groups, communities, and corporations, the call for effective leadership is increasing.[4] The old leadership model in which leaders directed others toward increased productivity at the expense of personal meaning often concentrated on correcting problems and maintaining the status quo.[5] Change itself is at such a rapid pace that people often find themselves caught in a storm of stress.[6] Moving forward, taking the wisdom of past models, moving beyond the industrial mindset to the relational, we face the increasing need for leaders who inspire through integrity to a higher vision of what it means to be human.[7] In response to this, Greenleaf proposed we need leaders who understand the nature of humanity and who can foster a deep sense of community.[8] Such leaders embrace diversity rather than insisting on uniformity. They understand what it means to develop the freedom, health, wisdom, and autonomy of others. They understand forgiveness and are able to develop just restoration, rather than push for legality and retribution.[9] The ideas of servant-leadership, uniquely positioned in contemporary leadership theory and practice, can be seen in movements that have brought dead organizations to new life, and reconciliation and healing to nations deeply wounded by human atrocities.[10]

My first recollections of trying to understand servant-leadership have to do with my connection to significant others who gave me a vision of the dignity of life. Often these were people who stepped out of their world into mine and drew me into the larger concept of living to which they had attuned their lives. This concept, something central to their own identity, inevitably had to do with internal, relational, and societal movements that have noticeably transformed humanity—movements such as quietness, discernment, courage, forgiveness, and love. Even without an intentional understanding of Greenleaf's ideas, each of the people who influenced me, women and men, were servant-leaders. In each person was a sense of fearlessness regarding self-discovery, accompanied by a disciplined, creative approach to relational meaning that became an antidote to the terrifying emptiness that is too often our collective experience of one another.[11]

Before being influenced toward a greater understanding of what it might mean to be a servant and a leader, early on I was almost entirely given to images of bravery or ambition. I lived consumed by hopes of advancement and adulation. Much of my early professional development was spent envisioning others adoring me, me as the sports champion, me on top of the world, the big money maker, the professional man, the leader of mighty corporations. And before this, as a high school student athlete, I lived needy for the praise of others, often carrying about a vague wish that by some chance others would suddenly devote themselves to telling stories of my excellence. Conveniently, in the world I'd conceived, my faults were protected; I didn't want anyone to notice my faults or point them out, and I spent most of my energy trying to please others so they would have nothing to be disappointed in concerning me, even as I lived a life that was both unaware and unconcerned with the personal well-being of others. If someone poked a hole in my facade, as did happen on occasion, my deflation was immediate and complete and people discovered that inside I was defensive and rigid, a fragile person. I had little idea what it might mean to be true to myself or someone else.

I grew up in Montana, where basketball was a thing as strong as family or work, and Jonathan Takes Enemy, a Crow Indian who played for Hardin High School, was the best basketball player in the state. He led a school with years of losing tradition into the state spotlight, carrying the team and the community on his shoulders all the way to the state tournament, where he averaged forty-one points per game. He created legends that twenty years later are still spoken of in state basketball circles, and he did so with a fierceness that made me both fear and respect him. On the court, nothing was outside the realm of his skill: the jumpshot, the drive, the sweeping left-handed finger roll, the deep fade-away jumper. He could deliver what we all dreamed of, and with a venom that said *don't get in my way*.

I was a year younger than he was, playing for an all-white school in Livingston. When our teams met in the divisional tournament, he and the Hardin Bulldogs delivered us a crushing seventeen-point defeat. At the close of the third quarter with the clock winding down and his team with a comfortable lead, Takes Enemy pulled up from one step in front of half-court and shot a straight, clean jump-shot. Though the range of it was more than twenty feet beyond the three-point line, his form remained pure. The audacity and power of it, the exquisite beauty, hushed the crowd. A common knowl-edge came to everyone: Few people can even throw a basketball that far with any accuracy, let alone take a legitimate shot with good form. Takes Enemy landed and as the ball was in flight he turned, no longer watching the flight of the ball, and began to walk back toward his team bench. The buzzer sounded, he put his fist in the air, the shot swished into the net. The crowd erupted.

In his will to even take such a shot, let alone make it, I was reminded of the surety and brilliance of so many Native American heroes in Montana who had painted the basketball landscape of my boyhood. Stanford Rides Horse, Juneau Plenty Hawk, and Paul Deputy of St. Labre. Elvis Old Bull of Lodge Grass. Marty Round-face, Tim Falls Down, and Marc Spotted Bear of Plenty Coups. Joe Pretty Paint and Jonathan Takes Enemy himself of Hardin. Many of these young men died due to the violence that surrounded the alcohol and drug traffic on the reservations, but their image on the court inspired me toward the kind of boldness that gives artistry and freedom to any endeavor. Such boldness is akin to passion. For these young men, and for myself at that time, our passion was basketball.

But rather than creating in me my own intrepid nature, seeing Takes Enemy only emphasized how little I knew of courage, not just on the basketball court but in life. Takes Enemy breathed a confidence I lacked, a leadership potential that lived and moved.

Greenleaf said, "A mark of leaders, an attribute that puts them in a position to show the way for others, is that they are better than most at pointing the direction."[12] Takes Enemy was the embodiment of this. He and his team seemed to work as one, and he and they were able to play with fluidity and joy and breathtaking abandon. I began to look for this leadership style as an athlete and as a person. The search led me toward people who led not through dominance but through freedom of movement, and such people led me toward the experience of humility, forgiveness, and relational justice. One of the most potent experiences of this came from the mentoring I received from my future wife's father.

Jennifer and I were in our twenties, not yet married. I was at the dinner table with her and her family when Jennifer's father said something short, a sharp-edged comment, to her mother. At the time her father was the president of a large multinational corporation based in Washington state. Thinking back, I hardly noticed the comment, probably because of the nature and intensity of the ways I had previously experienced conflict. For me most conflicts revealed a simmering anger or a resentment that went underground, plaguing the relationship, taking a long time to disperse. I didn't give her father's comment a second thought until some time after the meal when he approached me as I relaxed on the couch. He had just finished speaking with his wife over to one side of the kitchen when he approached.

"I want to ask your forgiveness for being rude to my wife," he said.

I could not imagine what he was talking about. I felt uncomfortable, and I tried to get him and me out of this awkward conversation as soon as I could.

"You don't have to ask me," I said.

But from there, the tension only increased for me. I had not often been in such situations in which things were handled in an equitable way. My work experience had been that the person in power (typically, but not always, the male) dominated the conflict so that the external power remained in the dominant one's hands, while internally everyone else (those not in power) suffered bitterness, disappointment, and a despairing, nearly hopeless feeling regarding the good of the relationship. Later in my family and work relationships I found that when I lived from my own inordinate sense of power, I, too, like those I had overpowered, would have a sick feeling internally for having won my position through coercion or force rather than through the work of a just and mutual resolution. In any case, in the situation with Jennifer's father, I felt tense and wanted to quickly end the moment by saving face for both of us. "You don't have to ask me," I said.

"I don't ask forgiveness for your benefit," he answered. "I ask in order to honor the relationship I share with my wife. In our family if one person hurts another, we not only ask forgiveness of the person who has been hurt, but also of anyone else who was present in order to restore the dignity of the one we've hurt." Later I found the same practice was common in the culture he had created in the corporation he led.

From a relatively brief experience, I gained respect for myself and began to see the possibilities of a family and work culture free of perpetual binds and rifts, and free of the entrenched criticalness that usually accompanies such relationships. My own life was like a fortress compared to the open lifestyle Jennifer's father espoused. I began to understand that much of my protectedness, defensiveness, and unwillingness to reveal myself might continue to serve as a fortification when in future conflicts, but would not lead me to more whole ways of experiencing the world. I also began to see that the work of a servant-leader requires the ability to humble oneself and the desire to honor relationships with others as sacred. In Greenleaf's work, this takes the form of listening and understanding, and only the one who is a servant is able to approach people first by listening and trying to understand, rather than by trying to problem-solve or lead. Just as "true listening builds strength in other people,"[13] it follows that a lack of listening weakens people. In the following section a story by Tolstoy illumines this idea.

Tolstoy on the Essence of Listening and Understanding

Traditional leadership models often create an environment in which leaders take action without accountability to the emotional or spiritual well-being of themselves or those they lead. This can result in an elitist mentality in which leaders carry a false sense of direction. In the following paraphrase of the Tolstoy story "The Three Hermits," the bishop is such a leader, a person with good intentions but blind to the dignity latent in those he seeks to lead. In this way, even well-meaning leaders who do not make themselves accountable to the deeper issues of leadership end up diminishing themselves and others by approaching the work environment as leader first rather than servant first.

A bishop was traveling on a merchant ship when he overheard a man speaking of three hermits who had lived for years on a nearby island, devoting themselves to prayer. Crew members didn't believe the man, saying it's just a legend, an old wives' tale. But the man persisted. He related how some years before, he had been shipwrecked off the island in question, taken in by the hermits, and sheltered and fed by them while they rebuilt his boat. He told the crew the hermits were devout men of prayer, the most saintly men he'd ever met.

Overhearing this, the bishop demanded that the captain take him to the isle. It was out of the way, and the captain was reluctant, but the bishop was determined and he offered to pay the captain for his trouble. The captain relented and in the early morning, while the ship anchored off shore, the bishop was let off on the hermits' island. The hermits emerged walking slowly toward the visitor. They were old and of grizzled appearance, with long beards. Having been so long from civilization, they spoke little and appeared meek or afraid. The bishop asked them how they'd been praying. The tallest one seemed to be the spokesman.

"Very simply, my lord," he said. "Three are we. Three are Thee. Have mercy on us."

"I must teach you how to pray then," said the bishop.

"Thank you, my lord," the three hermits replied, and the bishop proceeded to require them to memorize the Lord's Prayer. It was long, hard work; the hermits were out of practice. Throughout the day they fretted at how difficult it was for them to memorize it, and they feared they were disappointing the bishop. In fact, night had nearly fallen before the three could recite back to the bishop the prayer he'd taught them, but finally the last of them had it and the bishop flagged the small boat to take him back to the ship. He felt he had served his purpose that day, served God, and enlightened the three men.

When the ship set sail he was on deck, high up in the fore of the ship, near the captain, looking back at the ship's wake and the path of the moon. They'd been moving for some time now but he didn't feel like sleeping. He felt satisfied. The work had been hard work, but good work, and necessary. Just then he saw a silver sphere far back on the dark of the water moving toward the ship at a tremendous pace. The bishop was afraid. The entire crew was on deck now watching it, trying to make out what it might be. At last the sphere seemed to split off into three. Then he saw clearly, three lights, three men, long beards flowing in the wind—it was the hermits, moving over the water with great speed. They approached the ship and floated up to where the bishop was seated, stopping in front of him just beyond the railing. They had pained looks on their faces.

"What is it?" cried the bishop.

"Father, Father," pleaded the taller one, "forgive us. We've forgotten the prayer you taught us. Please teach us again."

Hearing this the bishop immediately fell on his face. "Go your way," he said. "Pray as you have prayed. God is with you. Have mercy on me."

Servant-Leadership, Forgiveness, and Social Justice

Gadamer in philosophy and Freire in education speak of the importance of dialogue in understanding the world and initiating change across broad human science, societal, and interpersonal levels.[14]

Greenleaf speaks of the absolute necessity of trust, a form of love in which people are free of rejection. Greenleaf stated: "The servant always accepts and empathizes, never rejects. The servant as leader always empathizes, always accepts the person, but sometimes refuses to accept some of the person's effort or performance as good enough."[15] In meaningful dialogue the servant as leader submits to a higher perspective, one that can be pivotal to the development of the self in relation to others. Greenleaf addressed this when he stated that the real motive for healing is for one's own healing, not in order to change others, implying the true motive to serve is for one's own service, one's own betterment. In this light a person seeks to heal or seeks to serve not necessarily for others but for greater personal good and, by extension, the greater good of the community. Such healing may take place best in a community that initiates and sustains meaningful dialogue.

Meaningful dialogue gives rise to the forces that unhinge the way we harm each other, opening us toward a more accepting and empathic understanding of one another. Greenleaf, in forwarding an ideal of love in community, places servant-leadership firmly in the contemporary landscape of the family, the workplace, and the global pursuit of social justice. In this landscape, the retributive justice represented by the legal system in mediating familial and professional conflicts is replaced by the idea of a community of forgivers, people with the foresight and vision to build a just and lasting reconciliation, people interested in the deeper restoration that is the result of a disciplined and unflinching look at the wrongs we do to one another.

Forgiveness studies in the social sciences have gathered an immense following in the last two decades through research that is beginning to connect the will to forgive with lowered depression, lowered anger, fewer heart problems, and lower immunodeficiency levels.[16] New bridges are being formed from the social sciences to the study of leadership, pointing organizations toward the acceptance and empathy Greenleaf envisioned. This involves the development of leaders who are able to understand the way people diminish one another, leaders who are able to invigorate in the organization a culture of acceptance, empathy, and relational justice. From this perspective the servant-leader creates an environment in which forgiveness can be asked and granted, and the servant-leader creates this by example. Two people who come together to reconcile, who choose to forgive and be forgiven, can experience a cleansing in which embittered rigidity becomes transformative openness.[17] The leader exemplifies this process, and in settings of strong relational trust, the process becomes embedded in the life of the organization. An early look at forgiveness in leadership settings was published in the *Journal of Leadership Studies*, detailing an intentional, specific approach to forgiveness work.[18]

Globally, in the contemporary landscape the traditional route of retributive justice is shown in the response to World War I and World War II, and reaches its apex in the international spectacle of the Nuremburg trials. Though retributive justice seeks a just answer to wrongs committed, it usually does so through punitive or violent means (imprisonment or death, for example). Retributive justice, especially in its most undisciplined or wanton forms, tends to beget greater alienation between people, continued oppression, greater atrocities, and greater spiritual poverty. Restorative justice, promoted by leaders such as Martin Luther King Jr. during the civil rights movement, and Nelson Mandela and Archbishop Desmond Tutu in response to the atrocities of apartheid in South Africa, has sought a different answer to the harms of humanity.

Martin Luther King Jr., an exquisite servant-leader on the international scene, stated that the oppressor will never willingly give up power—a statement of clarity, which often draws us toward either violence in an attempt to overthrow the oppressor or silence in an attempt to escape the oppression: the fight-or-flight response. King, a pupil of Gandhi, advocated neither violence nor silence. He furthered his discernment regarding the unwillingness of the oppressor with the following revolutionary idea, an idea akin to Greenleaf's concept of the servant-leader's response to injustice: King proposed that rather than hate or distance ourselves from the oppressor, we should love the oppressor.[19] He believed that when we love the oppressor we bring about not only our own salvation but the salvation of the one who harms us.

The first democratically elected president of South Africa was Nelson Mandela, another extraordinary contemporary servant-leader. From a country of bloodshed and hate, he and those around him effectively built a country of hope. He held to a vision of South Africa involving reconciliation, where black and white Africans could live and rule together without retribution or violence. He spent more than twenty-seven years as a political prisoner, eighteen imprisoned at Robben Island, yet Mandela refused to be vengeful either personally or politically. Notably, upon his release he refused to gain power through suppression of dissent. Finally, his refusal to deny the humanity of those who imprisoned him or those who confessed to the most heinous of human rights abuses drew the people of his country toward the monumental task of forgiving in the face of grave injustices, forgiving even with regard to atrocities that had demonstrated the brutality of the human condition at its worst levels.[20]

Mandela, Tutu, and other democratically elected officials designed the Truth in Reconciliation Commission in response to the atrocities committed during the apartheid years. They felt that retribution, either legal or punitive, would only result in widespread violence, a violence that had plagued many African countries in their emergence from colonialization. The commission set a specific and drastic vision, and due to the deep respect the majority of South Africans felt for these leaders, the country implemented a plan of forgiveness and reconciliation, of restorative justice, unlike any the global political community had ever known. Rather than seek out those who committed crimes against humanity to bring them to justice and punish them, the commission asked for honesty. The commission asked people to honestly admit what they had done, where and when and how they had harmed, abducted, tortured, and killed others. The result of telling the truth was that the perpetrators would receive amnesty; they would go free. At the same time, the commission asked the people of South Africa to make a forgiveness response. The commission made this vision of truth and reconciliation an Act of Law, hoping it would give people a chance to hear word of lost and dead family members, friends, and loved ones, and a chance to truly grieve the harms the nation had experienced.

Tutu, chairman of the Truth and Reconciliation Commission of South Africa, stated it clearly,

> The Act says that the thing you're striving after should be "ubuntu" rather than revenge. It comes from the root [of a Zulu-Xhosa word], which means "a person." So it is the essence of being a person. And in our experience, in our understanding, a person is a person through other persons. You can't be a solitary human being. We're all linked. We have this communal sense, and because of this deep sense of community, the harmony of the group is a prime attribute.[21]

South Africa, now some years after the Truth and Reconciliation Commission hearings, remains largely free of bloodshed. The country's legacy, unique to the political, governmental, and military communities of the world, has begun to be defined by forgiveness and reconciliation rather than by force, retribution, or violence.

I do not think it far afield to say that most Americans have not read the works of Martin Luther King Jr., one of our own, let alone the works of leaders such as Mandela and Tutu. Often we generate an egocentrism that insulates us, even from the kind of international servant-leadership ideas that are presently changing the world. In an unrelated but poignantly fitting statement made by Greenleaf while attending an international symposium in 1976, he stated: "Our African friend has said that we Americans are arrogant. It hurts—but I accept the charge."[22] In acceptance, empathy; in empathy, listening; and in listening, understanding. Such understanding may turn our self-absorption toward real care for others and in turn make us wiser, more healthy, and better able ourselves to become servants, better able ourselves to lead.

Conclusion

The hope of forgiveness and reconciliation is not without its critics. We shed our naïveté when we realize human evil exists despite our best efforts to forgive and reconcile. The echo of King's words remains—the oppressor will never willingly give up power. Even so, the deeper echo of King's words rings higher, stronger: when we love the oppressor, we bring about not only our own salvation but the salvation of the oppressor. In these words we find solace regarding our own failures, the inequities and injustices, the character flaws, the great harms. Members of our own families can live with an enduring sense of loving and being loved. Women and men in our communities can be true women, and true men, not displaced, not diminished. And in our workplace we can work with joy, a sense of calling, and the personal meaning that accompanies good work. These things are possible, for it is in the servant-leader, in the movement toward healing the self, toward truly serving, that an answer to the failures of leadership emerges. On the horizon of this landscape, a landscape that is as personal and spiritual as it is political and global, we see ourselves free of what binds us, and we walk in such a way that others are drawn forward so that they too, may be free.

12

The Servant-Leader

From Hero to Host

An Interview with Margaret J. Wheatley

On November 15, 2001, Larry Spears, president and CEO of The Greenleaf Center for Servant-Leadership in Indianapolis, and John Noble, director of the Greenleaf Centre-United Kingdom, met with Margaret J. Wheatley in Indianapolis, Indiana. What follows is a record of the conversation that took place.

LARRY SPEARS: *Do you recall when you first encountered Robert Greenleaf's writings? Do you have any remembrances of your initial impressions?*

MARGARET WHEATLEY: I've been trying to remember. I think it was through Max DePree. What I enjoy most about Greenleaf's work is realizing that every time I go back, I read something that feels completely new and relevant. And each time I'll read a paragraph or an article it suddenly feels completely contemporary and relevant and it's different from what I noticed last time. In that way his work stays very contemporary and exceedingly relevant. I think that's the mark of a great thinker. It's not just that he was a visionary and saw the need for the servant as leader. It's truly great concepts and ideas that are timeless and fundamental. That's what I enjoy most. Every time I pick up anything of his to read I realize that I'm going to be surprised again. It's not the same old thing.

LARRY SPEARS: *Is there any particular thought or idea about servant-leadership that has struck you as a source of wisdom or importance?*

MARGARET WHEATLEY: I was recently struck by Greenleaf's admonition to "do no harm." I've been saying to a number of colleagues that doing no harm is becoming exceedingly difficult. It's not just about doing good, it's actually avoiding harm. We don't see the consequences of our actions. America is in the midst of a huge wake-up call about what is the cost to the rest of the world for us to be living the life we are living. It isn't about terrorist activity; it's about noticing that we put an extraordinary demand on the rest of the world for resources and energy, and that our way of life does not work well for most other people because of the demands we put on them. So that's what I've been feeling about "doing no harm"—we don't even know what we're doing that's causing harm. I know Greenleaf wrote that in a much simpler time, but I was really struck by that this time through.

LARRY SPEARS: *In light of the events of September 11, have you any thoughts as to what servant-leadership has to offer to the world today that might be useful, and what we who are involved in this work may be thinking positively about?*

MARGARET WHEATLEY: That's a very important question. I have been asking: "What is the leadership the world needs now and what are we learning about leadership from actually being followers?" By this I mean some of us who have been leaders are now followers, watching our government and our military trying to lead us. What are we learning about all this? I think the questions are writ large. "What are you learning now that you are a follower? What makes for effective leadership?"

Now more than ever, we have to fundamentally shift our ideas of what makes an effective leader. We have to shift them away from this secretive, command-and-control, "We know what's best." We have to leave all that behind, even though it may be effective in the moment. I'm certainly learning that there are different needs at different times when you are a leader. Different styles, different modalities. But what I find in servant-leadership that I still find missing in the world is this fundamental respect for what it means to be human. And I think that right now the greatest need is to have faith in people. That is the single most courageous act of a leader. Give people resources, give them a sense of direction, give them a sense of their own power and just have tremendous faith that they'll figure it out.

We need to move from the leader as hero to the leader as host. Can we be as welcoming, congenial, and invitational to the people who work with us as we would be if they were our guests at a party? Can we think of the leader as a convenor of people? I am realizing that we can't do that if we don't have a fundamental and unshakable faith in people. You can't turn over power to people who don't trust. It just doesn't happen. So what I think I'm learning from September 11 is that it's possible that people really are motivated by altruism, not by profit, and that when our hearts open to each other we become wonderful. The level of compassion and gentleness that became available, taking a little more time with each other, all of that, I think, has shown me the things that I have treasured for a long time in people. But I think it's very clear, and so we have an opportunity to notice how good we are. If you don't have faith in people, you can't be a servant. I mean, what are you serving? If you're not serving human goodness, you can't be a servant. For me it's just that simple. There is no greater act on the part of the leader than to find ways to express that great faith in people.

The other part about the timelessness of servant-leadership is, what do you do if you can't control events? There is no longer any room for leaders to be heroes. I think one really needs to understand that we have no control, and that things that we have no control over can absolutely change our lives. I think it will take a little while for Americans to really accept that there is no control possible in this greater interconnected world. There are lots of things we can do to prepare, but there is no control. One of the great ironies right now is that no matter how good you were as a business before September 11 and no matter how skilled you were at planning, and no matter how skilled you were at budgeting, everything has shifted. The only way to lead when you don't have control is you lead through the power of your relationships. You can deal with the unknown only if you have enormous levels of trust, and if you're working together and bringing out the best in people. I don't know of any other model that can truly work in the world right now except servant-leadership.

Even within the military, *command and control* is not what's making it work right now, and it hasn't for a long time. I was just reading about a huge fiasco with the Delta Force as they went into Afghanistan at the start of our military action there in October 2001. Instead of their normal procedure, which is to operate as small teams, and work in quiet and stealth, they were parachuted in—a hundred of them—because that's how central command decided they should be used. And they were furious, absolutely furious! They nearly got killed, they got out by the skin of their teeth, and they had several casualties. They exclaimed, "You can't do this to us! We know how to fight. You can't create these huge theatrical events and you can't have centralized control and expect us to do our job." So even under the facade of command and control, one of the things I've always noticed in the military is that it works on the basis of deep relationships, long-term training, and relying on every individual soldier—especially in special operations. I can't think of any other model than servant-leadership that works in times of uncertainty. Our time is now!

JOHN NOBLE: *What were the markers in your life, the people and events that have shaped your thinking and helped to get you to where you are now?*

MARGARET WHEATLEY: The list of people changes depending on where I am right now in my life. But I do believe that there were seminal events, there were a few moments that I will always remember. And the reason I don't want to go for people is that the list keeps changing. Just now, the people who inform me most are the earlier historians, like Otto Spengler and Arnold Toynbee, who had an organic theory of civilizations as living beings, which is quite similar to how I'm feeling about this time in history. It's one of decline, the winter of Western civilization.

In terms of events I think that the one that is still really pertinent to me was when I realized that as consultants, no matter what we did, we really didn't succeed. I was working as consultant to a large consultancy firm and asked them to recall a successful engagement and what made it work. I realized that people couldn't, and if they did, it was one little event in a long stream of work. I've had the same experience of feeling completely frustrated and I wrote about this in *Leadership and the New Science*.[1] I think it was that realization that opened me to asking if there might be another way of looking at all of this. That's when I really started looking back to my former discipline, science. I feel very grateful to have studied what I studied so that at one point I could bring it all together. I was comfortable reading science and loved the scientific imagination and also had the historical imagination and love of literature, and loved to be in philosophical questioning. And all of those weren't connected for me until I grew to notice that they could be connected. What I'm doing now is not anything I actually created. It really does feel like the work I've been prepared to do.

JOHN NOBLE: *Over the last few years we have increasingly heard the phrase "spirituality in the workplace." What does that phrase mean to you and where have you seen spirituality in the workplace particularly epitomized?*

MARGARET WHEATLEY: For a long time I was terrified by the phrase, the combination of spirituality and the workplace. I was afraid of how we might use spirituality rather than simply honoring the fact that people are spiritual beings, people have spirit. This is not even a religious viewpoint. There is such a thing as the human spirit. It's an awareness that people have something beyond the instrumental or the utilitarian. People have deep yearnings, a quest for meaning, and an ability to wonder. This is a nonreligious view of what spirituality might mean.

When did we forget this, about being human? When did human beings become so instrumentally viewed, and when did we start to see ourselves as objects, just to be filled with information and sent to work? When did we lose that awareness? It's just mind-boggling if you think about it. I feel the same sort of puzzlement at the whole focus on emotional intelligence now. When did we forget this? It really shows you the bizarre side of our Western civilization, that we have to relearn what is so obvious in other cultures.

When spirituality became connected with the workplace in the 1990s it was initially just another way to motivate people. There were many of us saying, "Be careful here." Because, if the only reason a boss is going to acknowledge that someone has a spiritual life is to figure out how to get more work out of them, and if they don't get more work out of them, are they then going to forget the fact that we all have spirit?

Then we had a nice shift to the idea that if you don't acknowledge that people have spirit, you really can't have a productive workplace. It wasn't using spirit for productivity; instead, it was acknowledging who the person is, who the whole person is. Now I see our spirit in the questions we're asking. People are questioning the meaning of life. The meaninglessness of just working harder, consuming more, becoming disconnected from your children, these large questions have started to well up in people. *We do all have spirits.*

In terms of organizations, I look to see those organizations that describe back to me a real understanding of what is a human being. They don't have to use the words *soul* or *spirit*, but I get from them that they have a deep appreciation of fundamental creativity and caring, that they really rely on the wholeness of the people who work there. I haven't seen it in a lot of large corporations recently. Even those that had those strong values, they've been whipped around in the past year. But I consistently hear this from smaller manufacturing companies. I've had some wonderful conversations with those folks because they really understand and rely on the people who work there. They do all sorts of innovative things without consciously talking about spirituality in the workplace. What they talk about is human beings. That's more than enough for me! You know, if we can just understand what it means to be human then that brings in our spirits.

JOHN NOBLE: *It's a Wonderful Life has been a favorite film of mine for as long as I can remember, and George Bailey a personal hero. How did you make the connection with servant-leadership and how did you set about making that wonderful video?*[2]

MARGARET WHEATLEY: Well, I have to give credit to the producer, who didn't know a lot about servant-leadership and just said to me "I think this movie is about servant-leadership." I just said, "Please let me write this." It was interesting for me knowing the lens they were going to use to go into that movie, which I hadn't really watched *carefully*—it's always on at Christmas. I think it came at the right time because I was into my own developing awareness of how confining it was to believe we knew what our life purpose was, and I had just written about that in what was a sort of spiritual autobiography.

I got into the film having already had that awakening in my own consciousness, that you really need to stay available to life and to what life wants you to do. When I looked at the movie, it was just such a great teacher for me, personally, about what it's like to be present and respond to the needs of people as they come to you. To be able to see that at the end of your life there was direction, there was guidance, but the only way you were aware of the guidance was to just surrender. And, of course, that's the highest spiritual practice.

LARRY SPEARS: *Can you elaborate a little on some of the qualities that George Bailey has as a servant-leader?*

MARGARET WHEATLEY: What's interesting about George Bailey is his unintentional servant-leadership, which is also spontaneous and from the heart. I think it's an interesting question for any of us if we just felt free to go where our hearts led us in the moment. How do we respond to someone instead of hiding behind a role or some old rule—this is something that I think Jim Autry's poetry really captures. If, in a workplace, someone comes to you with a deep need and you can only respond with, "Well, this is the policy." Or, "I'm sorry. I'd love to make an exception, but if I make an exception for you I'd have to make an exception for everybody." It's just one of the most crippling phrases and thoughts we have in our society. You know, we just can't seem to respond at the level of the individual. We think that if we do, everyone else will be angry at us or want the same thing, yet it's not how life is at all. It is about what George Bailey did, that individual response, in the moment where he let his heart open and lead him. And when you do that you don't actually feel that you are sacrificing something. It's really interesting that when you are responding as your heart leads you, you are actually deeply satisfied even though, as in the case of George Bailey, it led him to an entirely different life. It didn't lead him away from Bedford Falls, and it didn't lead him out into the world. His heart just kept him responding to current crises at home. But I don't think in those moments that we experience it as sacrifice. We experience it as very fulfilling always to just respond to a person who needs something.

What I see in organizations are the boxes of our understandings of who we can be for each other. And those boxes in our organizations, which are also boxes of the psyche, really make it impossible for most people to act spontaneously the way George Bailey did, to just help when help is needed. When there's a crisis of any kind, whether it's a crisis like in that movie, or in real life like the crisis we've recently gone through, we don't see people hesitating to figure out how to serve. People don't hesitate; they just hope that what they're doing at a very instantaneous and spontaneous level will help somebody else.

What I think about crisis is that it's an easy opportunity to see how good we are, spontaneously. But if you look at life in organizations, it's amazing how fear-based they are, so that we are afraid of spontaneity. We are afraid of people's spirits, actually. We are afraid that if we give people any room they'll go off on some crazy direction with the work. I encounter this all the time. A manager will say, "We can't just give people choice here, we can't give people enough room to define meaningful work for themselves because God knows what they'll do." We always assume that they'll take the organization in a completely different direction. We are so afraid of each other that we want to box it into a plan, to a job description. And the loss of that, what we lose with that fear of each other, is extraordinary.

I am frequently struck by the great tragedy of how we have constructed work, the great loss. We've made it so hard to be in good relationships, we've made it so hard for people to contribute, we've made it so difficult for people to think well of themselves and then we say, "As a leader I'll come and I'll pump you up and I'll give you my vision, I'll make you feel we can do it." But it's not based on a deep love of who people are, a deep respect. As a leader, how do you pump up what has been killed?

I actually had an experience of this on a symbolic level. I was with a group of nuns in a chapel and one of them fainted, and before the medics came (apparently this was not unusual, because she had some sort of condition) nobody panicked. They called 911, but before help got there we just sat there in prayer for this person as other sisters went up and held her—it was all very gentle. And then the medics rushed in and they had oxygen and they had defibrillators, all sorts of high-tech equipment, and they surrounded this woman and just started clamping machines on to her body and then pumping in oxygen. I thought they were blowing up a balloon!

The symbology of it for me is that we are in our organizations and we've actually created a lot of death and destruction and a complete loss of people's confidence in themselves. Leaders don't have confidence in people. And then we rush in with this high-tech machinery, and just try and pump up people and motivate them with a new initiative or a new computer system or a new leadership vision. But what goes on in organizations is often not based on people being human. It's based on people being objects to be used for the accomplishment of goals of a very utilitarian kind.

"Whom do we serve as leaders?" I've asked that question of a lot of people. Whom do we serve? We are serving human beings. That is a radical shift in this culture at this time. But we are serving human beings, and the best way to know who another human being is, is to notice yourself fully, what you need, what's meaningful to you, what gives you heart in your work. If we could just notice our own humanness it would be a very big step forward to being able to relate to other people. If we are a leader, especially if we notice our own humanness, we notice that we have spirit, we notice that we have questions of meaning. I think all of the work that is done in helping leaders to wake up to their own humanity and their own spirituality is very essential work. It also keeps us away from using servant-leadership as the next instrument of control.

LARRY SPEARS: *There's one more theme in* It's a Wonderful Life *that strikes me. There is a Quaker phrase, "Speaking Truth to Power." Have you found ways in your work to encourage people to lovingly confront the people in power when things are not right and need to be addressed, but in a way that also honors those in power as human beings?*

MARGARET WHEATLEY: I have. In the past I have relied on processes that would allow people to listen to each other, and I haven't relied on what I would rely on now, which is personal courage. I was just reading a survey of fifty thousand workers in which half of them said they'd never dream of speaking up at work. And we are dealing with many, many years now of people having tried to give voice to their concerns and then being met with rebuff or ridicule or being told, "It's not your job!" And so we have had now for a long time an incredibly dependent workforce that is quite hostile. So we get *Dilbert*! *Dilbert* is the best representative of our deep cynicism for all those years of disrespect and maltreatment. People say to themselves, "Well, I'm not going to tell them anything, because they don't listen and they're a bunch of idiots, and I tried and it didn't work." We have our own internal conversation that keeps us from stepping forward. But then as employees we just get angrier and angrier and sometimes that erupts at meetings. This sometimes happens if there's a leader who says, "Well, I really want to find out what the pulse of the organization is. I'm going to start doing breakfast meetings." And then all they get is grief from people. I think it's one of the worst things you can advise a leader to do, especially if you know there's all that pent-up anger.

What I found works is if I can shift the content of the conversation and the dynamic, so as to move it from cynicism and anger to something more helpful. To do this, I change who is in the conversation. If the organization is struggling with something, and it's stayed within a certain level of employees and the boss, or we are trying to think through an issue but it's just our small little team; whenever we're stuck, then is the time to invite people in who aren't normally included.

It's the simplest solution but it's so powerful. It's actually a biological principle, which is when a living system is suffering and in ill health, the way to create more health is to connect it to more of itself. You create feedback loops from different parts of the system. It works at the level of our own bodies as a living system in that if we're suffering from some disease it doesn't help to just treat the symptom, we have to look at our whole life and look for information from other parts of our system. What are our sleeping patterns, what is our anxiety level, what's our exercise level? It doesn't work to look at just the one problem. We need information from our whole system.

This same activity also works brilliantly in organizations, to bring in customers, to bring in students, to bring in congregants, to bring in the people we think we don't need to hear from. Usually we fear hearing from them, because we believe we'll only hear complaints and anger. But in fact when you create more diversity, more plurality in the conversation, people step forward and demonstrate that they too care about the organization. As a process I rely on this now to an extraordinary degree. If we are in a certain pattern, if we are angry with each other, if we can't figure out how to solve the problem, bring in new voices. And then all the dynamics shift and you get really useful information that helps you then to see the problem differently.

I have a great belief in the power of whole systems, getting the whole system in the room. And it changes us from being angry and rigid: It changes us as individuals to realize, "Wow, I never thought of that!" "Gee, do you really see it that way?" We're going through that at a national level right now. I mean, there are new voices in the room. We're learning a lot about Islam, we're learning a lot about oil and Arab-U.S. relations, we're learning a lot about globalization. We have available now a lot more information that can really help us change our minds, as long as we are willing to be in that conversation.

If you want to change the conversation, you change who's in it. That doesn't mean that you have to coach people on how to be empathic presenters to a leader. You don't have to coach a leader on how not to get angry if someone's giving terrible feedback. You just get out of those intensely personal and confrontational moments because you have a lot of new voices in the room. And people really do get interested as soon as they realize there is a fundamentally different perspective available. Most people actually get interested in that. I have been in hierarchical situations where the voice that shocked everyone with its perspective was a young woman. A new employee, female, who suddenly said something and everyone went "Wow!" I've also seen it happen in faculties when we listen to students for the first time, or we listen to the people who hired our graduates. You never know where these comments are going to come from. They're usually so shocking that people are humbled and climb down off their soapboxes.

I want very much to say something about personal courage. One of the things that is sorely lacking in our lives is a necessary level of courage to stand up against the things we know are wrong, and for the things we know are right. There has been a kind of complacency—it feels more fear-based to me—where people, especially in organizations, are too afraid to speak up and we have become, I believe, moral cowards in a way. We give all sorts of reasons why we can't speak up. There are so many grievances in organizations that I think people have developed a sense of helplessness about it, and I understand that feeling of helplessness and saying, "I would never speak up." But I also live with an awareness that if we don't start speaking up we are going down a road that will only lead to increased devastation and destruction. Edmund Burke said *"The only thing necessary for the triumph of evil is for good men to do nothing."* Julian of Norwich said, *"We must speak with a million voices: it is the silence that kills."*

I think we're in that place right now, and what I find personally so uncomfortable is that as much as I want to raise my own voice on behalf of several different issues, I notice that I feel more powerless than at any time in my life. I think that's part of the tension of this time, realizing that we have to lift our voices for the things that we believe in, whether it's inside an organization, or as a nation or as a planetary community. We feel that there are serious things that require our voice, and yet we also feel that it may not make a difference. That's the place I'm in every day right now. The other forces at work are exceedingly more powerful. I wonder whether we can rally ourselves as people around the things we care about, and really make the change. The essence of my work right now is based on that belief that we can get active in time, but I also realize that this is a time when there are exceedingly strong countervailing forces from our leaders. For example, leaders pursuing aggression as the solution, or business still wanting to maintain its hegemony in the world without assuming responsibility for broader needs, or America still believing it can act in isolation; can we raise our voices on behalf of a different form of capitalism, a different form of compassion in our foreign policy, a different form of leadership in our organizations? I know if we don't raise our voices I can predict the future, and it's very dark. If we *do* raise them, well, it has worked in the past. I am hopeful that it will work now, but I'm not nearly as certain as I'd like to be.

JOHN NOBLE: *In* Leadership and the New Science *you said that vision could no longer be the prerogative of the leader or CEO and increasingly vision would have to be the shared vision of everyone in an organization. From your experience are you seeing that happening?*

MARGARET WHEATLEY: The deeper theory under those statements was that vision was a field and that fields are those invisible forces that shape behavior. I find a lot more credence is being given to the understanding that there are fields we can't see, invisible influences that affect behavior. People would have called that far-out thinking before, but I find that people are much more open to that today than ten years ago. Creative vision is a powerful influence in shaping our behavior and you don't need to specify a lot of controls or roles if you have vision. People can do what they think is right and it can lead to a very coherent organization that is moving in concert toward achieving its vision. I have certainly come across a number of organizations that are working that way now, but I've also experienced in the last year or two that we've been in an enormous leap *backward* organizationally since times started to get uncertain. And now we'll just have to wait and see whether this level of uncertainty leads us forward into new ways of leading or even further backward into command and control.

One of the possibilities is that try as we might we will realize that command and control just doesn't work because you can't control! We might be learning that. But recently, I have seen an enormously retrogressive movement in organizations based on fear, based on a weakening economy, based on what I think is a normal human reaction that when you get scared, you go backward; you default to what didn't work in the past! The power of vision to rally people or to give people a reason to live, to work hard and to sacrifice, we are seeing that at the national level right now. I don't necessarily think we're seeing it in its best form. It's true that in human experience, "if there is no vision the people perish," and whether there's a scientific explanation for that, or a spiritual explanation—I'd be just as happy these days with the spiritual definition—which is that a vision gives us a sense of possibility, a vision gives us a sense of working for something outside our narrow, self-focused efforts and therefore it rallies us at our deep human level to be greater than we are.

I'm happier with that explanation than field theory, and the reason I'm happier with it is that it is much more focused on what are the capacities in being human and how we can bring these forth. Science helps people be comfortable with that, and feel a little more trusting that you can create order through having a clear vision. But the next part of that is just as important. Once you have a clear vision you have to free people up. This is where autonomy comes in. People need to be free to make sense of the vision according to their own understandings and their own sensitivity to what's needed. If you combine the sense of great purpose and human freedom, if you can combine a vision that brings out the best of who we are and then gives us the freedom in how we're going to express that, that is how things work, in my experience.

JOHN NOBLE: *I previously worked for an organization where I once suggested that the leaders should begin to stand aside and ask the next generation of leaders for their vision and then begin to work with that in order to create a new future. My thought was that the current leaders could assume the role of stewards, supporters, servants. It didn't happen. Have you come across an organization that has worked in this way?*

MARGARET WHEATLEY: Yes. It was the U.S. Army, under General Gordon R. Sullivan. I am in absolute support of what you were trying to do. When General Sullivan was Chief of Staff, which was in the early to mid-1990s, he said he spent 50 percent of his time thinking about the future and how to create an army for the world that was not yet known. He did simulations, he did think tanks, he did all sorts of scenario planning on what would the world be like and how could you create the army and technology to defend it. He had to think fifteen years ahead, minimally. He was really pushing out as far as he could see, using very good minds. So I did find that kind of thinking in the armed services. Then the marines got into it seriously, and the air force did, too. But I think it's the only place I've seen it.

What I see in common contrast to that is organizations where to even *ask* younger people what their vision is feels like a breach of cultural norms like "They should be respecting *us!*" "Who are they? They don't know anything!" This is what I run into when I ask educators to involve students. We don't look to our younger generations as a source of any kind of wisdom, and partly I think that's because, as a culture, we so fear dying and we so fear aging. You created the role of elder there, and you were asking the senior people to become wise people who would be acting in service to the next generation. That's really countercultural in the West. You could have found support for that in most other cultures, but not in the West where we have so feared aging. As one of my African friends says, "You call your elders elderly, and that's part of the problem!" To actually ask leaders to think of themselves as elders and stewards for the future is a radical proposition. I think it's very important work and I'm not surprised it didn't go anywhere because of the weight of the culture.

One of the things I've been quite intrigued by is the number of younger leaders I have encountered who are college age, who are now intent on training high school kids to be leaders. They're not even looking to us anymore! They'd love it if we talked to them, but they acutely feel the need to steward younger people. I find that quite remarkable. I'll tell you why it's so difficult, I think, in the corporate arena. Maybe our short-term focus is shifting now, and one of at least the temporary consequences of September 11 is the realization that you just can't spin these organizations for the short term, because you don't even know what the short term is. When General Sullivan retired from the army and went to serve on corporate boards, he was dismayed that nobody was thinking about the future. He said they'd spend hours figuring how to get the stock price up by half a penny, yet nobody was talking about how to develop the next generation of leaders.

I think it's for us to develop intergenerational collaboration. You were suggesting something much stronger than that. But just to call in the voices of the future into our present deliberations is not happening enough, and yet it is one of the most powerful things. Once you get people into these intergenerational conversations it is so inspiring for everyone to be talking with each other. It's the right work, but very difficult to do.

LARRY SPEARS: *In* Leadership and the New Science *you wrote, "Love in organizations is the most potent source of power we have available." What do you think that servant-leaders inside our many organizations can do to unleash love in the workplace?*

MARGARET WHEATLEY: It's simple: *just be loving!* Why has expressing love become such a problem when it's a fundamental human characteristic? This is where I think we have overanalyzed and overcomplexified something that is known to everyone alive. Babies know how to unleash love. It's all about our relationships and being available as a human, rather than as a role. It's about being present and being vulnerable and showing what you're feeling. You know, we don't want to reveal who we are. Even the best of leaders try to be objective rather than relational, and that's supposedly adding value to our work lives if we treat each other objectively. But it's again one of those huge things we get wrong. You can't have love if you can't have relationships, and you can't have relationships with one another if you have this curse of something called *being objective*, or *one size fits all*, as a policy, or having to go by the manual. I can feel the fear that so many of us have that, "Well, if it's not objective, we couldn't possibly live in the messiness and the intimacy that would come about by treating each human being as their own unique self." But I think that objectivity makes it impossible to be loving. Objectivity doesn't allow love, because love takes you to intimacy and uniqueness and very personal territory. We need to get away from the belief that you can run an organization using what are called *objective measures* or *objective processes*, which are actually just completely dehumanized. The fear of love in organizations is that it makes your life as a leader far more complex. But it also makes you much more effective.

I was just listening a few days ago to a woman who had recently retired as the chief of the Calgary police force, and she talked about what it took to be personally available and present for each of those officers, so that she was always embodying the values, finding ways for them to embody the values, and believe in the values and become the kind of police officers they wanted to be. She worked from a very clear perspective that it's not the corporate values that count, it's whether people can enact their personal values inside the corporation. I thought that was a brilliant rethinking of that. She would work with everyone on what they were trying to accomplish and the values they were trying to bring forth. And from those, of course, you get a wonderful corporate culture and very strong values. But she kept saying that this was enormously time-consuming and was very difficult work that required her to be there all the time. And so I understand why leaders don't want to go down this *love* path or the *relationship* path, because it requires so much. But that's where I think you have to want to believe in people. I believe on September 11 there were numerous corporate leaders who suddenly realized that people really were the most important thing to them, even though an hour before they'd been working a system that ignored human concerns. But then they got the wake-up call of their life. When I said that you have to want to believe, you really have to want to have relationship, and there are an awful lot of people in our workplaces, not just leaders but whole professions, who have never wanted relationships. They've wanted the work, and hopefully we are now realizing, most of us, how important relationships are.

LARRY SPEARS: *For many, serving others is inextricably tied to their own sense of spirituality. Are there practices you have found useful in terms of how we can better develop our own servant's heart?*

MARGARET WHEATLEY: Well, I think first I would just underline where you're focused, which is we do need practices to develop this, and I would say the "this" we need practices for is to open our hearts. For most people it's not something you can rely on as spontaneously occurring. For some it is, but, especially if you're in the workplace, your heart gets pretty hardened. You shut down, or you just find that you can't express your love and compassion and so you take it elsewhere. So even if you start out with a naturally open heart and a generous spirit toward others, there are many, many structures and processes in modern work and modern life that actually close us down. So we do need a practice to maintain an open heart.

I am a strong believer in meditation personally, but I think any process by which you withdraw from the world and focus on your own inner grounding is useful. For some people, that's running; for some people, it's playing tennis. I can get very similar grounding when I ride horseback, because you can't lose your attention for too long without losing your seat! For some people it's walking, or flower arranging. Whatever it is, it's just to notice what it is that revives your sense of feeling grounded, present, and peaceful. I have often felt that I need to leave my room peaceful in the morning because I don't expect it to get any more peaceful while I'm out doing work. So that's the first discipline—practicing what gives you your grounding and your peace, and to not let it slip away. The world just keeps pulling at you and I find that every so often I have to say, "Okay, Meg. Just notice you're spending less time cultivating your peacefulness and let's get back to serious practice." People of any religious order know the value of a routine to one's practice, whether it's a daily liturgy or a daily practice. Whatever it is, it's the routinization that really helps over time. So it's not just episodic, or only when you feel like it. Your whole being benefits from knowing every morning you're going to pray or run or whatever. So I find it needs to be routinized.

Once I decided that the work was really how to keep my heart open, that led me to a number of practices beyond my own meditation, although some of the meditations I work with now are traditional practices to keep your heart open. One of the ones I've loved the most is to realize that when I am suffering, whatever it is—whether it's anger, fear, feeling discounted or treated rudely or whatever—I remember that the experience I've just had is an experience that millions of people around the world have, just by virtue of being human. If I'm sitting in a hotel room one night feeling lonely, just for a moment I might reflect that, "Just like me, there are millions of people around the world feeling lonely at this very moment." This practice has been an extraordinary gift, of going from your personal experience outward to the human experience. Your own private experience is being felt by countless other human beings, and somehow this changes the experience from personal pain and anxiety to your heart opening to many others. And then when I see someone else I think, "You're feeling just the way I do." That practice has opened my heart more than any other single practice and has made me feel part of the human experience and the human family.

LARRY SPEARS: *What do you find most compelling about Buddhist practices?*

MARGARET WHEATLEY: What I find to be enormously helpful about a Buddhist perspective on life is that it really isn't a religion. It is actually just a way to live your life. I have my own very eclectic theology. I was raised Christian and Jewish, so I started out with that eclecticism, and Buddhism has really introduced me to the day-to-day practices that I feel have really opened my heart and made me far more understanding and gentle. And, what is more important to me, it has made me far less likely to condemn quickly and far more willing to be in the presence of suffering and not to run from it. And to bear witness, to just be with whatever's going on and not to be afraid of it. All of that is not a theology, it's a practice. In my book *Turning to One Another*,[3] there's this very strong influence about the practice, and I have a whole section on bearing witness—of just being with another person's experience and not having to fix it, or counsel someone away from their grief. It's actually very fulfilling, and it takes the stress off when you stop feeling that you have to fix people's human experience. You just have to be there. These are capacities I didn't have, but now have, since I started doing these practices.

I have found that many Buddhist practices have helped me be with people differently and have changed my expectations of what needs to happen if I'm just with someone. Just being with someone has become really important rather than saying the right phrase or the right word that will fix it. Now, the irony of this is that I'm still a public speaker who gets up on stage allegedly to say things that will fix things, and yet what I'm finding—and I've heard this from other speakers as well—is we are realizing it's who we are when we *are* up there, and not what we're *saying*. And so I very much want to be the presence of peace and possibility for people. I feel that is something I can be, and have been, and in order to be that, I need to experience peace fairly regularly from this much deeper place that is available to me through my different practices.

I think that the central work of our time is how to be together differently. Can we live together with our hearts open, with our awareness that we can't stop suffering, that we can certainly be with it differently? Can we notice where we are causing harm and try at least to do no harm? And can we be together without fear of what it's like to be together, to really just not be afraid to be with other people? That would be a huge step forward for a lot of us. And we're all crying for it, we're all crying to be together in more loving ways because this is what it is to be human. So many of us were overwhelmed by the experiences of September 11, but we saw people being together without the divisions that had separated them moments before. Buddhism is a series of practices that keep my heart open and keep me being present, rather than fleeing from what is day-to-day life. In that way I think it has also saved my life.

JOHN NOBLE: *In many organizations the word* change *has become a noun rather than a verb and all too often people use phrases such as "You are afraid of change" to hurt each other. When you have encountered this in organizations how have you addressed the problem?*

MARGARET WHEATLEY: There's a wonderful quote from a contemporary Buddhist who said, "Change is just the way it is!" I've worked a lot and written quite a bit on how we are actually responsible for creating resistance to change. I don't know who said it first, but "We don't resist change; we resist being changed." Most organizations fail to involve people in the design of change, in the redesign of organizations, or they don't involve people soon enough or substantially enough. What we get is something that is predictable in everything that is alive, from bacteria on up. When you do something to another living being, that being has the freedom to decide whether it's even going to notice what just happened or what somebody has done. So the first freedom is you *choose whether you notice or not*. And the second freedom is you are then completely free to *choose your reaction to it*.

You can't impose change on anything alive. It will always react, it will never obey. This is one of the principles I've embraced for many years. Life doesn't ever obey, and yet we still think in organizations that we'll find the perfect means, the perfect vision, the perfect writing, the perfect PowerPoint presentation to get people to say, "Great! This is just perfect!" And instead, what people do is change the plan, file it away and never look at it again, or modify it. We look at all that and we say they are resisting change, but they're not. They're responding like all life does—they are reacting. And they're actually being quite creative. I've asked people to just look at that dynamic, which is so fundamental.

We get in organizations and we forget about that dynamic we all know so well and we say, "I'll tell you what to do and you'll do it." And it doesn't happen. I must have asked this of tens of thousands of people, "Can you think of a time in your experience when you gave another human being a set of directions and they followed them perfectly?" And in the few cases where people have followed the directions perfectly I've asked, "Did you actually like that person?" Because those people are robots, those people aren't there. We've destroyed their spirits. If they do just what we say we have killed the spirit. And we don't like being around those people. We have a profound disrespect for people who act like automatons, even though, if you look at most managers, they still think they want an automatic obedient response. So, if life doesn't obey but it always reacts, then the other principle from that is that if you want people to support something, they have to be involved in its creation. This has been a very old maxim in the field of organizational behavior, that people support what they create. I say that people *only* support what they create.

What this means for any organizational change process, most of which have been appallingly disruptive and have failed (we now know that almost 80 percent of them fail), is that they should make sure that they only use participative processes. That doesn't mean having everyone involved in every decision, but to be thoughtful and creative about how we are going to bring along everybody and involve people at different points so that this truly is owned by everyone, because it's their creation. It's a no-brainer; these things work! I find when I speak about participation, people still think that I mean everybody in the room doing all the work at the same time. But it's not that.

I've worked with small teams of employees and charged them with, *how are you going to involve everyone in your network, everyone in your department?* And they are much more creative! They'll do TV shows, they'll actually create simulations to put people through the same experience that they have just had. They're enormously creative. I've also found, over time, that when you've charged a small group of employees with making sure that everyone knew about it, that the whole organization seemed to pay attention, and then it was very easy for people to know about it. I also work with the principle that participation is not a choice. If you don't get people involved, you're just breeding resistance and sabotage that you'll then spend months or years trying to overcome.

LARRY SPEARS: Leadership and the New Science *is generally considered to be one of the most important books on leadership to be published. Did you have a sense when you were writing it that you were on to something?*

MARGARET WHEATLEY: I didn't have a sense of what I was on to. I didn't really understand that I was presenting an entirely different worldview. I thought it would be easier to convince people of the shifts that would need to take place because I didn't know it was about changing a worldview, and changing a worldview takes a long, long time. The original 1992 edition had a lot of questions, but as far as I can remember I hadn't the faintest idea what this work would mean. I just wrote it because it felt like the work I was supposed to be doing. I can't remember now who I was while I was writing it. I can remember some of the fear and hesitation, experimenting with a new voice as a writer, and all of that, but I don't remember what I thought.

LARRY SPEARS: *Was your move to Utah significant in the writing of* Leadership and the New Science?

MARGARET WHEATLEY: It was absolutely tied to that book coming forth. I told my friends in Massachusetts that had I stayed there I'd have written deep, introspective works in the tradition of some writers there, and I realized, retrospectively, that I needed the open space. The West for me is freedom, and the wilderness is for me the deepest experience of harmony. I live in the wilderness—or it's at my back. I had no idea why I was moving to Utah at the time. I think it was just to be liberated into life, really, into the experience of what is space and wilderness and sky. And also just the incredible beauty of Utah. The red rocks of Utah are still my most sacred place to go. Again, I had no idea of why I was going—it felt really weird—but now it feels like, "Of course! That was it!"

JOHN NOBLE: *Your recent book is titled* Turning to One Another: Simple Conversations to Restore Hope for the Future. *What led you to choose the subject of conversation?*

MARGARET WHEATLEY: Actually, I didn't choose the subject of conversation. I chose the action of *turning to one another*, and conversation is the simplest way to do that. To actually be willing to listen and talk to other human beings is the way throughout time that we have thought together and dreamed together. The simple act of conversation seems so far removed from our daily lives now, and yet we all have a vague memory of what it was like. Since September 11, we have been profoundly different conversationalists and felt the need to talk to each other and to be together. So I rely on the ancientness and primalness of human beings being together, and being together through this act of listening and talking as a way for us to surface, or to develop, greater awareness of how we are reacting to what's going on in the world. Therefore, hopefully, from that greater awareness of what we care about, what we're talking about or struggling with at a very personal level, we will become more activist. We will become more intelligent actors to change the things we think need changing.

That idea is based on a more recent tradition in Paulo Freire's work called *critical education*, which is that you create the conditions for change by educating people to the forces and dynamics that are causing their life. You can start that work through conversation (or through literacy training, as Freire did). In conversation, people can become more aware of what their life is, whether they're happy, what they might do to change it. Then people do become activists, because it's their lives and their children's lives that are affected. Those are the deeper underlying threads that led me to write the book, which is different from anything I've written before. It's not written just for leaders or people in organizations. I wrote it for the world. I don't mean that to sound pretentious, it's just that the people I work with now are in so many different countries, all ages, and I just kept them in my imagination when I was writing, and I wanted to make sure that it didn't assume anything except our common humanity and our common desires for a world that does truly work for all of us. A world that is based on our common human desires for love and meaning from work and a chance to contribute.

The other piece that truly informed this was my experience with the Truth and Reconciliation Commission in South Africa, which was life-changing for me. I only attended it once but followed the proceedings every time I was in South Africa during its three-year history. And the one day that I went was unbelievably impactful. It was when the parents of a young American Fulbright scholar who had been murdered, Amy Biel, were present. Their daughter had been slain in one of the townships after driving into a very angry crowd. Her parents were there listening to the description of her death by her killer, and they were sitting next to the mother of the killer, sitting two rows in front of us. It was an experience you don't normally have in your life, one of such forgiveness, and violence, and repentance. The primary thing I learned in observing the Truth and Reconciliation Commission hearings was that the power of speaking your experience is what heals you. The power of feeling we are heard is what heals us. It made bearing witness a much easier act. *I don't have to fix the person—I just have to really listen.*

And from that experience I started to see it in so many different settings how, when we truly listen to people, they can heal themselves. My trust in conversation is that it also allows that level of listening, and there are other people who have written specifically about conversation. I am using the process to restore hope to the future; that was the underlying theme. I wrote it in March 2001, and I had no idea of what was to come on September 11. But I could already see that the future was looking pretty hopeless, and I had a lot of people saying, "What does this mean, restore hope to the future?" And now we all know.

LARRY SPEARS: *Do you have any closing words of hope or advice for servant-leaders around the world?*

MARGARET WHEATLEY: A few phrases come to mind from a wonderful gospel song, "We are the ones we've been waiting for." This is the time for which we have been preparing, and so there is a deep sense of call. Servant-leadership is not just an interesting idea but something fundamental and vital for the world, something the world truly does need. The concept of servant-leadership must move from an interesting idea in the public imagination toward the realization that *this is the only way we can go forward*. I personally experience that sense of right-timeliness to this body of work called servant-leadership. I feel that for more and more of us we need to realize that it will take even more courage to move it forward, but that the necessity of moving it forward is clear. It moves from being a body of work to being a movement—literally a movement—how we are going to move this into the world. I think that will require more acts of courage, more clarity, more saying *this has to change now*. I am hoping that it *will* change now.

Endnotes

Chapter Three

1. R. K. Greenleaf, "Trustees as Servants" (Indianapolis: The Greenleaf Center, 1990), p. 19.

2. Greenleaf, "Trustees as Servants," p. 28.

3. R. K. Greenleaf, "The Institution as Servant" (Indianapolis: The Greenleaf Center, 1976), p. 16.

4. Greenleaf, "Trustees as Servants," p. 25.

5. Greenleaf, "Trustees as Servants," p. 31.

Chapter Five

1. "Servant Responsibility in a Bureaucratic Society," in R. K. Greenleaf, *Servant Leadership*, 25th Anniversary ed. (Mahwah, N.J.: Paulist Press, 2002), p. 313.

2. R. K. Greenleaf, "Trustees as Servants" (Indianapolis: The Greenleaf Center, 1990), p. 40.

3. R. K. Greenleaf, "The Servant as Leader" (Indianapolis: The Greenleaf Center, 1991), p. 12, italics in the original.

4. Ivan Illich, *Medical Nemesis* (New York: Random House, 1976).

5. "Servant Leadership in Foundations," in Greenleaf, *Servant Leadership*, 25th Anniversary ed., p. 218.

6. T. Parsons, "Introduction." In M. Weber, *The Theory of Social and Economic Organization*, edited by T. Parsons (New York: Free Press, 1947), pp. 56–77.

7. M. Weber, "The Sociology of Charismatic Authority." Republished in translation in H. H. Gerth and C. W. Mills, (trans. and eds.), *Max Weber: Essays in Sociology* (New York: Oxford University Press, 1946), pp. 245–252.

8. Greenleaf, "The Servant as Leader," p. 30.

9. "The Requirements of Responsibility," in R. K. Greenleaf, *On Becoming a Servant Leader* (San Francisco: Jossey-Bass, 1996), p. 44.

Chapter Seven

1. R. Moxley, "Leadership as Partnership." *Leadership in Action* 19, no. 3 (1999): 9–11.

2. For example, see A. Bergstrom and others, *Collaboration Framework . . . Addressing Community Capacity* (Fargo, N.D.: National Network for Collaboration, 1996); P. Mattessich and B. Monsey, *Collaboration: What Makes It Work, A Review of Research Literature on Factors Influencing Successful Collaboration* (St. Paul, Minn.: Amherst H. Wilder Foundation, 1992); and K. Ray and M. Winer, *Collaboration Handbook: Creating, Sustaining, and Enjoying the Journey* (St. Paul, Minn.: Amherst H. Wilder Foundation, 1994).

3. D. Crislip and C. Larson, *Collaborative Leadership: How Citizens Can Make a Difference* (San Francisco: Jossey-Bass, 1994).

Chapter Eight

1. L. C. Spears (ed.), *Reflections on Leadership: How Robert K. Greenleaf's Theory of Servant-Leadership Influenced Today's Top Management Thinkers* (New York: Wiley, 1995), p. 2.

2. D. DeGraaf, D. Jordan, and K. DeGraaf, *Programming for Parks, Recreation and Leisure Services: A Servant-Leadership Approach* (State College, Pa.: Venture, 1999).

3. Spears, *Reflections on Leadership*.

4. D. Jordan and D. DeGraaf, "Developing Summer Superstars." Presentation at Wisconsin Park and Recreation Association annual meeting, Fond du Lac, Wisconsin, February 28–29, 1996.

5. R. Rossman, "The Use of Mental Imagery in Leisure Program Design." Presentation at the World Leisure and Recreation Association, 4th International Congress, Cardiff, Wales, United Kingdom, July 17, 1996.

6. K. Albrecht and R. Zemke, *Service America* (Homewood, Ill.: Dow Jones-Irwin, 1985).

7. K. Albrecht, *The Only Thing That Matters* (New York: Harper Business, 1992).

8. G. Godbey, *Leisure and Leisure Services in the 21st Century* (State College, Pa.: Venture, 1997), p. 86.

9. J. Sturnick, "Healing Leadership." In L. C. Spears (ed.), *Insights on Leadership* (New York: Wiley, 1998), p. 191.

10. M. McLaughlin, *Urban Sanctuaries: Neighborhood Organizations in the Lives and Futures of Inner-City Youth* (San Francisco: Jossey-Bass, 1994).

11. S. Covey, *The Seven Habits of Highly Effective People* (Provo, Utah: Covey Leadership Center, 1990).

12. Cited in J. Kouzes, "Finding Your Voice" (Spears, *Insights on Leadership*, p. 324).

13. B. Driver, P. Brown, and G. Peterson, *Benefits of Leisure* (State College, Pa.: Venture, 1991).

14. DeGraaf, Jordan, and DeGraaf, *Programming for Parks, Recreation and Leisure Services*.

15. M. Hunt, *Dream Makers: Putting Vision and Values to Work* (Palo Alto, Calif.: Davies-Black, 1998).

16. W. Bennis and B. Nanus, *Leaders: The Strategies for Taking Charge* (New York: HarperCollins, 1985).

17. Covey, *The Seven Habits of Highly Effective People*, p. 157.

18. J. Addams, "The Subjective Necessity for Social Settlements: A New Impulse to an Old Gospel." In T. Y. Crowell (ed.), *Philanthropy and Social Progress*. New York: Crowell, 1893.

19. C. Thompson, *What a Great Idea* (New York: HarperPerennial, 1992), p. 89.

20. "Sierra Club Centennial," *Sierra* 77, no. 3 (1992), 52–73; quote from p. 73.

21. Holmes as cited by C. Edginton, D. Jordan, D. DeGraaf, and S. Edginton, *Leisure and Life Satisfaction: Foundational Perspectives* (New York: McGraw-Hill, 2002).

22. K. Blanchard, *Leadership by the Book: Tools to Transform Your Workplace* (New York: Random House, 1999), p. 42.

23. P. Block, *Stewardship: Choosing Service over Self-Interest* (San Francisco: Berrett-Koehler, 1996), p. 6.

24. A. Leopold, *A Sand County Almanac* (St. Paul, Minn.: Highbridge, 2000), pp. 224–225.

25. K. Blanchard, "Servant-Leadership Revisited." In Spears, *Insights on Leadership*, p. 25.

26. Driver, Brown, and Peterson, *Benefits of Leisure*.

27. R. Putnam, *Bowling Alone: The Collapse and Revival of American Community* (New York: Simon & Schuster, 2000).

28. Dahl, R. "Participation and the Problem of Civic Understanding," in A. Etzioni (ed.), *Rights and the Common Good: The Communitarian Perspective*. Belmont, Calif.: Wadsworth, 1995.

29. T. Kiuchi, "What I Learned from the Rainforest." Keynote Speech from World Future Society meeting, San Francisco, July 16, 1997.

30. J. Batten, *Tough-Minded Management* (New York: AMACOM, 1989).

31. S. Covey, "Servant-Leadership from the Inside Out." In Spears, *Insights on Leadership*; quote on p. xii.

Chapter Nine

1. Robert K. Greenleaf, "The Institution as Servant," written in 1972 and republished in R. K. Greenleaf, *Servant Leadership*, 25th Anniversary ed. (Mahwah, N.J.: Paulist Press, 2002), p. 62.

2. Richard Broholm, *Trustees of the Universe: Recovering the Whole Ministry of the People of God* (Shelburne Falls, Mass.: Seeing Things Whole, 2001), p. 3.

3. Kenneth Vernon (ed.), *A Strategy of Hope: Lay Ministry For Organizational Change* (Philadelphia: Metropolitan Associates of Philadelphia, 1972), p. 1.

4. Richard Broholm and John Hoffman, *Empowering Laity for Their Full Ministry* (Shelburne Falls, Mass.: Seeing Things Whole, 1979).

5. Broholm, *Trustees of the Universe*, p. 12.

6. Broholm, *Trustees of the Universe*, p. 12.

7. Broholm, *Trustees of the Universe*, p. 13.

8. Robert K. Greenleaf, "The Need for a Theology of Institutions," written in 1979 and republished in *Seeker and Servant: Reflections on Religious Leadership.* (San Francisco: Jossey-Bass, 1996), p. 192.

9. Robert K. Greenleaf, "Fable," written in 1983 and republished in *Seeker and Servant*, pp. 169–176.

10. This perspective had roots in Greenleaf's childhood upbringing. In his essay "Old Age: The Ultimate Test of the Spirit," he writes, "When I was about 13, I recall listening to a conversation with a committee from our church that had come to try and persuade father to raise his quite nominal contribution. Father listened patiently and then said, "No." He thought his contribution was about right. He was glad the church was there, but as an instrument for doing good in the world, he rated it well below both his labor union and his political party. The committee left in a huff." Published in *The Power of Servant-Leadership* (San Francisco: Berrett-Koehler, 1998), p. 265.

11. Robert K. Greenleaf, "Seminary as Servant," a collection of three essays written in 1980, 1981, and 1982, and republished as part of a volume titled *The Power of Servant-Leadership* (San Francisco: Berrett-Koehler, 1998), p. 170.

12. Greenleaf once observed that a promising starting point for the very large task of improving society through the renewal of a servant orientation with existing institutions would be to identify a *single seminary* genuinely prepared to rethink its training of clergy in order

to prepare church leadership capable of inspiring and supporting the men and women in their roles as regenerative forces within society's organizations. While at first glance this may seem a modest hope, the identification of a single seminary prepared to seriously embrace this challenge is no small matter. While it is not unusual for seminaries to offer intermittent programming (institutes and workshops) directed toward business leaders, these initiatives are largely limited to ancillary programs that do not shape or influence how the seminary approaches its more fundamental work of preparing church leadership. This kind of significant reorientation of a theological school's missional focus demands strong buy-in, capacity, and perseverance at multiple levels of the seminary including its trustees, administrative leadership, and a critical mass of key faculty. These factors came into alignment for a time at Andover Newton Theological School under the leadership of its president, George Peck, who was a passionate advocate for this vision. Following his untimely death in 1990, however, the seminary's focus on this emphasis waned. It may be that the necessary factors have come together once again in this moment at Luther Seminary.

13. Greenleaf, "The Need for a Theology of Institutions," p. 193.

14. These words are drawn from John Gardner's 1968 address at Cornell University, recalled in Vernon, A Strategy of Hope, p. 48.

15. Laura Nash and Scotty McLennan do a wonderful job of exploring this disconnect in opening sections of their book, Church on Sunday, Work on Monday (San Francisco: Jossey-Bass, 2001).

16. Walter Wink, Engaging the Powers (Minneapolis: Fortress Press, 1992), p. 66. In his own footnote, Wink credits this important insight to Hebrew Scripture scholar Gerhard von Rad.

17. Here we are particularly indebted to Russell Ackoff and Margaret Wheatley for helping us to come alive to the systemic nature of life in general and of organizations in particular.

18. Here again we are indebted for this insight to Walter Wink's Engaging the Powers, pp. 65–85.

19. For a fuller description of the theological roots of the Threefold Model, see Gabriel Fackre's essay, "Christ's Ministry and Ours,"

published as part of a collection entitled *The Laity in Ministry: The Whole People of God for the Whole World* (Valley Forge, Pa.: Judson Press, 1984), pp. 109–125.

20. For a fuller expression of this model, including the "shadow" expression of each of its dimensions, see David Specht and Dick Broholm, *Three-Fold Model of Organizational Life: Testimonies and Queries for Seeing Things Whole* (Shelburne Falls, Mass.: Seeing Things Whole, 2001).

21. Engineered Products is the fictitious name for a real company, one of several we have worked with during the past ten years in an action-research effort exploring the use of the threefold model of organizational life as a framework for supporting faithful organizational decision making and performance.

22. A description and facilitator's guide to this process for holding an organization in trust has been published as a monograph: Richard Broholm, Dale Davis, and David Specht, *A Theological Reflection Process for Illumining Organizational Faithfulness* (Shelburne Falls, Mass.: Seeing Things Whole, 1996).

23. Greenleaf, "The Need for a Theology of Institutions," p. 198.

Chapter Ten

1. R. K. Greenleaf, *The Servant as Leader* (Indianapolis: The Greenleaf Center, 1991), p. 18.

2. Greenleaf, *The Servant as Leader*, p. 19.

3. R. Fritz, *Path of Least Resistance*, revised ed. (New York: Fawcett Columbine, 1989).

Chapter Eleven

1. R. K. Greenleaf, *Servant Leadership*, 25th Anniversary ed. (Mahwah, N.J.: Paulist Press, 2002), p. 30.

2. P. G. Northouse, *Leadership: Theory and Practice*, 2nd ed. (Thousand Oaks, Calif.: Sage, 2001).

3. Greenleaf, *Servant Leadership*, p. 27.

4. J. W. Gardner, *On Leadership* (New York: Free Press, 1990).

5. B. M. Bass, *Leadership, Psychology, and Organizational Behavior* (New York: HarperCollins, 1960); J. M. Burns, *Leadership* (New York: HarperCollins, 1978); and R. Harrison, "Why Your Firm Needs Emotional Intelligence," *People Management* 3 (1997): 41.

6. P. M. Senge, *The Fifth Discipline: The Art and Practice of the Learning Organization* (New York: Doubleday, 1990).

7. D. Goleman, *Emotional Intelligence* (New York: Bantam, 1995); J. M. Kouzes and B. Z. Posner, *The Leadership Challenge: How to Get Extraordinary Things Done in Organizations* (San Francisco: Jossey-Bass, 1987); and R. A. Heifetz, *Leadership Without Easy Answers* (Cambridge, Mass.: Belmont Press, 1994).

8. Greenleaf, *Servant Leadership*.

9. M. K. Harris, "A Call for Transformational Leadership for Corrections." *Corrections Management Quarterly* 3 (1999): 24–31.

10. Greenleaf, *Servant Leadership*; L. C. Spears (ed.), *Insights on Leadership: Service, Stewardship, Spirit, and Servant-Leadership* (New York: Wiley, 1998); and D. M. Tutu, *No Future Without Forgiveness* (New York: Doubleday, 1997).

11. C. Taylor, *Sources of the Self: The Making of the Modern Identity* (Cambridge, Mass.: Harvard University Press, 1989).

12. Greenleaf, *Servant Leadership*, p. 15.

13. Greenleaf, *Servant Leadership*, p. 17.

14. H. G. Gadamer, *Truth and Method*, 2nd rev. ed.; trans. revised by J. Weinsheimer and D. G. Marshall (New York: Continuum, 1993); P. Freire, *Pedagogy of the Oppressed* (New York: Continuum, 1990).

15. Greenleaf, *Servant Leadership*, p. 21.

16. For excellent reviews of the will to forgive in individuals, marriages, and families, see M. E. McCullough, S. J. Sandage, and E. L. Worthington Jr., *To Forgive Is Human* (Downers Grove, Ill.: Inter-Varsity, 1997); and M. E. McCullough and E. L. Worthington, "Encouraging Clients to Forgive People Who Have Hurt Them: Review, Critique, and Research Prospectus," *Journal of Psychology and Theology* 33 (1994): 3–20.

17. R. S. Valle and S. Halling (eds.), *Existential Phenomenological Perspectives in Psychology: Exploring the Breadth of Human Experience* (New York: Plenum Press, 1989).

18. S. Ferch and M. Mitchell, "Intentional Forgiveness in Relational Leadership: A Technique for Enhancing Effective Leadership," *Journal of Leadership Studies* 4 (2001): 70–83.

19. M. L. King Jr., *A Testament of Hope* (San Francisco: HarperCollins, 1986).

20. N. R. Mandela, *Long Walk to Freedom* (New York: Little, Brown, 1994).

21. Harris, "A Call for Transformational Leadership for Corrections," p. 26.

22. Greenleaf, *Servant Leadership*, p. 320.

Chapter Twelve

1. For the latest on this book, see M. J. Wheatley, *Leadership and the New Science Revised: Discovering Order in a Chaotic World* (San Francisco: Berrett-Koehler, 1999).

2. *It's a Wonderful Life: Leading Through Service*, video, 22 minutes, available through The Greenleaf Center.

3. Margaret Wheatley, *Turning to One Another: Simple Conversations to Restore Hope to the Future* (San Francisco: Berrett-Koehler, 2002).

Recommended Reading

Autry, J. A. *Love and Profit*. New York: Avon Books, 1992.

Autry, J. A. *The Servant Leader*. Roseville, Calif.: Prima, 2001.

Bellah, R., and others. *Habits of the Heart*. Berkeley: University of California Press, 1985.

Bellah, R., and others. *The Good Society*. New York: Knopf, 1991.

Bennis, W. G. *On Becoming a Leader*. Cambridge, Mass.: Perseus, 1994.

Bennis, W., and Nanus, B. *Leaders: The Strategies for Taking Charge*. New York: HarperCollins, 1985.

Blanchard, K., and O'Connor, M. *Managing by Values*. San Francisco: Berrett-Koehler, 1997.

Bogle, J. C. *John Bogle on Investing: The First Fifty Years*. New York: McGraw-Hill, 2001.

Burns, J. *Leadership*. New York: HarperCollins, 1978.

Carver, J. *Boards That Make a Difference*. San Francisco: Jossey-Bass, 1997.

Carver, J. *John Carver on Board Leadership*. San Francisco: Jossey-Bass, 2002.

Covey, S. *Leadership Is a Choice*. New York: Free Press, 2004.

Crislip, D. D., and Larson, C. E. *Collaborative Leadership: How Citizens Can Make a Difference*. San Francisco: Jossey-Bass, 1994.

DePree, M. *Leadership Is an Art*. New York: Doubleday, 1989.

DePree, M. *Leadership Jazz*. New York: Dell, 1992.

DePree, M. *Leading Without Power*. San Francisco: Jossey-Bass, 1997.

Gardner, J. *Leadership: A Sampler of the Wisdom of John Gardner*. Minneapolis: University of Minnesota Press, 1981.

Greenleaf, R. K. "The Institution as Servant." Indianapolis: The Greenleaf Center, 1976.

Greenleaf, R. K. "The Leadership Crisis." Indianapolis: The Greenleaf Center, 1978.

Greenleaf, R. K. "The Servant as Religious Leader." Indianapolis: The Greenleaf Center, 1982.

Greenleaf, R. K. "Seminary as Servant." Indianapolis: The Greenleaf Center, 1983.

Greenleaf, R. K. "My Debt to E. B. White." Indianapolis: The Greenleaf Center, 1987.

Greenleaf, R. K. "Old Age: The Ultimate Test of Spirit." Indianapolis: The Greenleaf Center, 1987.

Greenleaf, R. K. *Teacher as Servant: A Parable*. Indianapolis: The Greenleaf Center, 1987.

Greenleaf, R. K. "Education and Maturity." Indianapolis: The Greenleaf Center, 1988.

Greenleaf, R. K. "Have You a Dream Deferred." Indianapolis: The Greenleaf Center, 1988.

Greenleaf, R. K. "Spirituality as Leadership." Indianapolis: The Greenleaf Center, 1988.

Greenleaf, R. K. "Trustees as Servants." Indianapolis: The Greenleaf Center, 1990.

Greenleaf, R. K. "Advices to Servants." Indianapolis: The Greenleaf Center, 1991.

Greenleaf, R. K. "The Servant as Leader." Indianapolis: The Greenleaf Center, 1991.

Greenleaf, R. K. *On Becoming a Servant Leader*. San Francisco: Jossey-Bass, 1996.

Greenleaf, R. K. *Seeker and Servant*. San Francisco: Jossey-Bass, 1996.

Greenleaf, R. K. *The Power of Servant Leadership*. San Francisco: Berrett-Koehler, 1998.

Greenleaf, R. K. *Servant Leadership*. (25th Anniversary ed.) Mahwah, N.J.: Paulist Press, 2002.

Greenleaf, R. K. *The Servant-Leader Within*. Mahwah, N.J.: Paulist Press, 2003.

Hesse, H. *The Journey to the East*. New York: Noonday Press, 1992.

Hock, D. *Birth of the Chaordic Age*. San Francisco: Berrett-Koehler, 1999.

Hunter, J. C. *The Servant: A Simple Story About the Essence of Leadership*. Rockland, Calif.: Prima, 1998.

Jaworski, J. *Synchronicity: The Inner Path of Leadership*. San Francisco: Berrett-Koehler, 1996.

Jones, M. *Creating an Imaginative Life*. Berkeley: Conari Press, 1995.

Kouzes, J., and Posner, B. *The Leadership Challenge: How to Get Extraordinary Things Done in Organizations*. San Francisco: Jossey-Bass, 1987.

McGee-Cooper, A., and Looper, G. *The Essentials of Servant-Leadership: Principles in Practice*. Waltham, Mass.: Pegasus Communications, 2001.

McGee-Cooper, A., Trammell, D., and Lau, B. *You Don't Have to Go Home from Work Exhausted!* New York: Bantam Books, 1992.

Moxley, R. S. *Leadership and Spirit.* San Francisco: Jossey-Bass, 1999.

Renesch, J. (ed.). *Leadership in a New Era.* San Francisco: New Leaders Press, 1994.

Spears, L. C. (ed.). *Reflections on Leadership: How Robert K. Greenleaf's Theory of Servant-Leadership Influenced Today's Top Management Thinkers.* New York: Wiley, 1995.

Spears, L. C. (ed.). *Insights on Leadership: Service, Stewardship, Spirit, and Servant-Leadership.* New York: Wiley, 1998.

Spears, L. C., and Lawrence, M. (eds.). *Focus on Leadership: Servant-Leadership for the Twenty-First Century.* New York: Wiley, 2002.

Turner, W. R., with Chappell, D. *The Learning of Love: A Journey Toward Servant Leadership.* Macon, Ga.: Smyth & Helwys, 2000.

Wheatley, M. J. *Leadership and the New Science Revised: Discovering Order in a Chaotic World.* San Francisco: Berrett-Koehler, 1999.

Wheatley, M. J. *Turning to One Another.* San Francisco: Berrett-Koehler, 2002.

Williams, L. E. *Servants of the People: The 1960s Legacy of African American Leadership.* New York: St. Martin's Press, 1996.

Young, D. S. *Servant Leadership for Church Renewal.* Scottdale, Pa.: Herald Press, 1999.

Zohar, D. *Rewiring the Corporate Brain.* San Francisco: Berrett-Koehler, 1997.

Index

Printed in the United States
202291BV00002B/373-396/A